Genders and Sexualities in History

Series Editors: **John H. Arnold, Joanna Bourke** and **Sean Brady**

Palgrave Macmillan's series *Genders and Sexualities in History* aims to accommodate and foster new approaches to historical research in the fields of genders and sexualities. The series promotes world-class scholarship that concentrates upon the interconnected themes of genders, sexualities, religions/religiosity, civil society, class formations, politics and war.

Historical studies of gender and sexuality have often been treated as disconnected fields, while in recent years historical analyses in these two areas have synthesised, creating new departures in historiography. By linking genders and sexualities with questions of religion, civil society, politics and the contexts of war and conflict, this series will reflect recent developments in scholarship, moving away from the previously dominant and narrow histories of science, scientific thought and legal processes. The result brings together scholarship from contemporary, modern, early modern, medieval, classical and non-Western history to provide a diachronic forum for scholarship that incorporates new approaches to genders and sexualities in history.

Men and Manliness on the Frontier is a groundbreaking study of the ways in which nascent frontier societies in Australia and Canada, shaped, challenged and were shaped by British men. In this original book, Robert Hogg provides a meticulously researched, incisive, and fascinating analysis of imperial frontiers, and the ways that experience of the frontiers tested masculine ideals to their limits. For some, the frontiers represented excitement, escape, liminality and personal transformation. For most, the frontiers and their hazards and privations were troubling, unsettled and frightening places. Hogg repositions our understanding of the significance of frontiers in the history of imperial masculinities, and challenges the mythology of frontier and manliness in the Australian and Canadian paradigms. In common with all volumes in the Genders and Sexualities in History series, *Men and Manliness on the Frontier: Queensland and British Columbia in the Mid-Nineteenth Century* presents a multi-faceted and meticulously researched scholarly study, and is a sophisticated contribution to our understanding of the past.

Titles include:

John H. Arnold and Sean Brady (*editors*)
WHAT IS MASCULINITY?
Historical Dynamics from Antiquity to the Contemporary World

Heike Bauer and Matthew Cook (*editors*)
QUEER 1950s
Rethinking Sexuality in the Postwar Years

Cordelia Beattie and Kirsten A Fenton (*editors*)
INTERSECTIONS OF GENDER, RELIGION AND ETHNICITY IN THE MIDDLE AGES

Chiara Beccalossi
FEMALE SEXUAL INVERSION
Same-Sex Desires in Italian and British Sexology, c. 1870–1920

Peter Cryle and Alison Moore
FRIGIDITY
An Intellectual History

Jennifer V. Evans
LIFE AMONG THE RUINS
Cityscape and Sexuality in Cold War Berlin

Kate Fisher and Sarah Toulalan (*editors*)
BODIES, SEX AND DESIRE FROM THE RENAISSANCE TO THE PRESENT

Christopher E. Forth and Elinor Accampo (*editors*)
CONFRONTING MODERNITY IN FIN-DE-SIÈCLE FRANCE
Bodies, Minds and Gender

Dagmar Herzog (*editor*)
BRUTALITY AND DESIRE
War and Sexuality in Europe's Twentieth Century

Robert Hogg
MEN AND MANLINESS ON THE FRONTIER
Queensland and British Columbia in the Mid-Nineteenth Century

Julia Laite
COMMON PROSTITUTES AND ORDINARY CITIZENS
Commercial Sex in London, 1885–1960

Andrea Mansker
SEX, HONOR AND CITIZENSHIP IN EARLY THIRD REPUBLIC FRANCE

Jessica Meyer
MEN OF WAR
Masculinity and the First World War in Britain

Jennifer D. Thibodeaux (*editor*)
NEGOTIATING CLERICAL IDENTITIES
Priests, Monks and Masculinity in the Middle Ages

Hester Vaizey
SURVIVING HITLER'S WAR
Family Life in Germany, 1939–48

Clayton J. Whisnant
MALE HOMOSEXUALITY IN WEST GERMANY
Between Persecution and Freedom, 1945–69

Forthcoming titles:

Matthew Cook
QUEER DOMESTICITIES
Homosexuality and Home Life in Twentieth-Century London

Rebecca Fraser
GENDER, RACE AND FAMILY IN NINETEENTH CENTURY AMERICA
From Northern Woman to Plantation Mistress

Melissa Hollander
SEX IN TWO CITIES
The Negotiation of Sexual Relationships in Early Modern England and Scotland

---

Genders and Sexualities in History Series
Series Standing Order 978–0–230–55185–5 Hardback
978–0–230–55186–2 Paperback
(*outside North America only*)

You can receive future titles in this series as they are published by placing a standing order. Please contact your bookseller or, in case of difficulty, write to us at the address below with your name and address, the title of the series and the ISBN quoted above.

Customer Services Department, Macmillan Distribution Ltd, Houndmills, Basingstoke, Hampshire RG21 6XS, England

Men and Manliness on the Frontier

Queensland and British Columbia in the Mid-Nineteenth Century

Robert Hogg
Lecturer in Australian Studies, University of Queensland, Australia

palgrave
macmillan

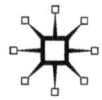

© Robert Hogg 2012

All rights reserved. No reproduction, copy or transmission of this publication may be made without written permission.

No portion of this publication may be reproduced, copied or transmitted save with written permission or in accordance with the provisions of the Copyright, Designs and Patents Act 1988, or under the terms of any licence permitting limited copying issued by the Copyright Licensing Agency, Saffron House, 6–10 Kirby Street, London EC1N 8TS.

Any person who does any unauthorized act in relation to this publication may be liable to criminal prosecution and civil claims for damages.

The author has asserted his right to be identified as the author of this work in accordance with the Copyright, Designs and Patents Act 1988.

First published 2012 by
PALGRAVE MACMILLAN

Palgrave Macmillan in the UK is an imprint of Macmillan Publishers Limited, registered in England, company number 785998, of Houndmills, Basingstoke, Hampshire RG21 6XS.

Palgrave Macmillan in the US is a division of St Martin's Press LLC, 175 Fifth Avenue, New York, NY 10010.

Palgrave Macmillan is the global academic imprint of the above companies and has companies and representatives throughout the world.

Palgrave® and Macmillan® are registered trademarks in the United States, the United Kingdom, Europe and other countries.

ISBN 978–0–230–25017–8

This book is printed on paper suitable for recycling and made from fully managed and sustained forest sources. Logging, pulping and manufacturing processes are expected to conform to the environmental regulations of the country of origin.

A catalogue record for this book is available from the British Library.

A catalog record for this book is available from the Library of Congress.

Contents

Acknowledgements	vi
List of Abbreviations	vii
Maps	viii
1 Masculinities and Frontiers	1
2 The Most Manly Class That Exists	23
3 The Sterling Qualities of the Saxon Race	54
4 Men without (White) Women	85
5 Blacks, Chinks and a Pig-Headed German	121
6 A Hand Prepared to be Red	152
7 A Wild Self-Dependence of Character	176
Notes	183
Bibliography	211
Index	228

Acknowledgements

In the course of writing I have benefited from the support of a large number of institutions and people. I would like to take the opportunity to thank them here.

At the University of Queensland, Australia, I wish to thank the staff of the Social Sciences and Humanities Library and the Fryer Memorial Library. At the School for History, Philosophy, Religion and Classics I would like to acknowledge the assistance of all the administrative staff, but in particular Serena Bagley, who has helped me through the entire process. I would also like to thank the staff at the John Oxley Library and the Queensland State Archives, without whose assistance this book would not have been possible.

In British Columbia, Canada, I wish to thank the staff of Rare Books and Special Collections at the University of British Columbia Library, in particular George Brandak and also Keith Bunnell, Reference and Collections Librarian. I also wish to thank the staff at the British Columbia Archives in Victoria.

My thesis (upon which this book is based) supervisors – Martin Crotty, David Carter and Kay Saunders – deserve special mention. Throughout my candidature they provided good advice and indispensable feedback on my work. They have also been generous patrons, taking me on, on a number of occasions, as a tutor or research assistant. Clive Moore has also been supportive in this regard. Additionally, I would like to thank Sarah Ferber, Geoff Ginn and Andrew Bonnell for their words of support throughout. I would also like to convey my special thanks to Leigh Dale, at whose suggestion I embarked upon this project.

A number of friends and colleagues have experienced the highs and lows of authorship with me. Thanks go especially to Heather Wolffram, Yorick Smaal, Andrea Humphreys, Catherine McTavish, Nikki Petzel and Craig Barrett. They provided advice, encouragement and fun.

The greatest thanks of all go to my beautiful wife Lynda, who has been my muse, coach and supporter throughout the life of this work. This book is dedicated to her.

Abbreviations

BCA	British Columbia Archives, Victoria, British Columbia, Canada
FL	Fryer Library, University of Queensland, Australia
JOL	John Oxley Library, Brisbane, Australia
mss	Manuscripts
QSA	Queensland State Archives, Australia
QV&P	Queensland Votes and Proceedings
UBCL	University of British Columbia Library, Vancouver, Canada

Maps

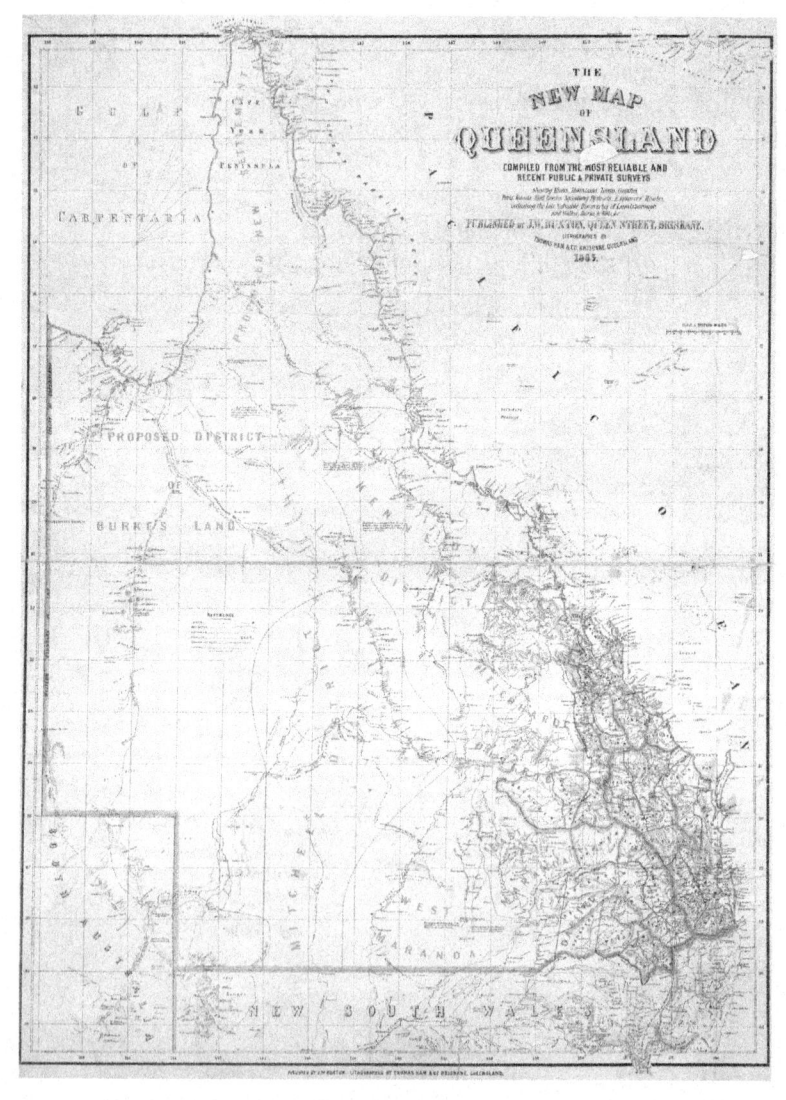

Map 1   Map of Queensland, 1863. John Oxley Library

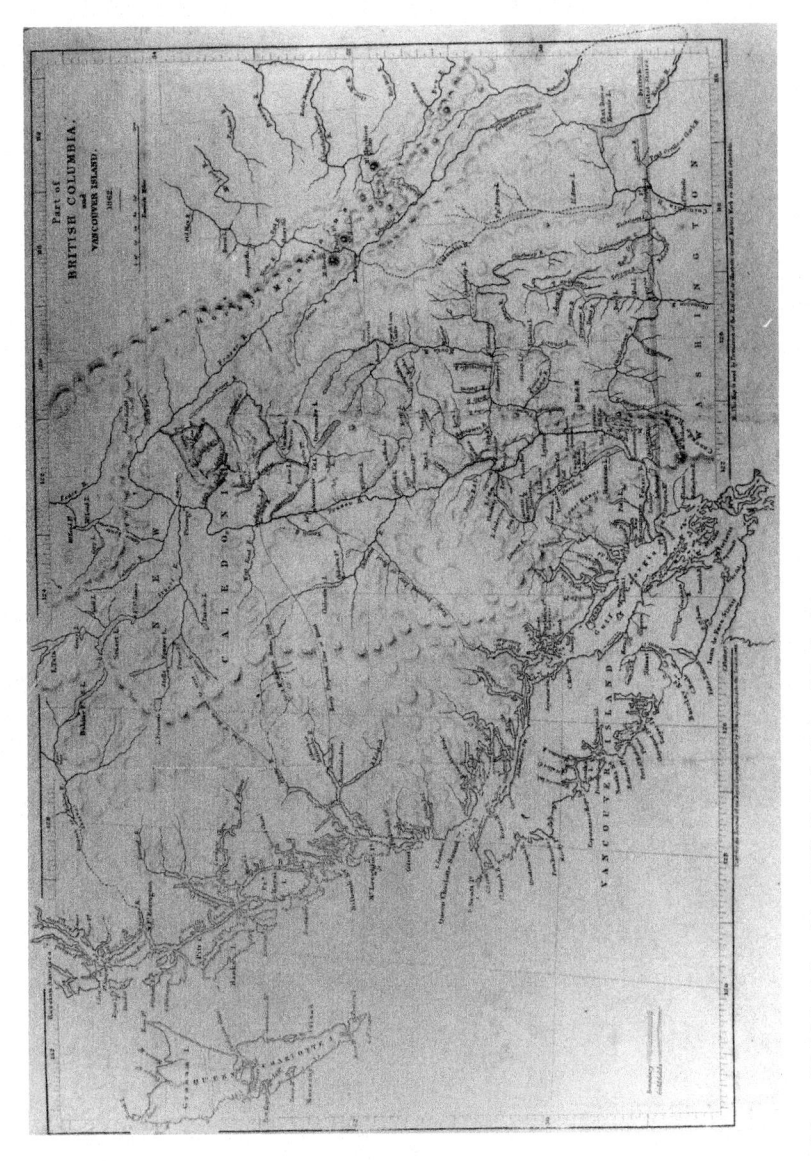

Map 2 Map of British Columbia, 1862. British Columbia Archives

1
Masculinities and Frontiers

> Say, I am a man; and you say it all.
>
> (Thomas Carlyle, 1829)

In 1867, Charles Kingsley, Rector of Eversley, author, Professor of History at Cambridge and stern advocate of what was derisively labelled 'Muscular Christianity', gave a sermon at Wimbledon to a largely military congregation. Taking as his text the Old Testament, Numbers, Chapter 24, Verse 9, 'He crouched, he lay down as a lion; and as a great lion. Who dare rouse him up?' he lectured the mostly male congregation on the virtues which made men and the nation great. The passage refers to the tribes of Israel which, according to Kingsley, through 'moral obedience' and loyalty to each other, saved themselves and 'their race', and made themselves 'men'. An important part of their survival was their physical training which had endowed them with 'hardihood, endurance, and self help'. However, this was insignificant compared to the moral training they had gained. Moral training had endowed them with 'the habits of obedience, self-restraint, self-sacrifice, mutual trust, and mutual help; the inspiration of common patriotism, of a common national destiny'.[1]

Kingsley proclaimed his confidence that through the soldiers' military training, they had taught themselves the lessons 'Israel had learnt in the wilderness', and that they would be better men for it.[2] There were also virtues which their military training ought to foster, and which were taught 'thank God', by 'the stern education of our public schools':

> For the moral discipline which goes to make a good soldier or a successful competitor on this ground, the self restraint, the obedience,

the diligence, the punctuality, the patience, the courtesy, the forbearance, the justice, the temperance, these virtues, needful for those who compete in the struggle which the idler and debauchee can take no share, all these go equally toward the making of a good man.[3]

In this sermon Kingsley encapsulated the mid-Victorian idea of manliness. Manliness was simultaneously a discourse, a code of behaviour and an aspirational standard. Founded on Christian principles, it valued manly vigour and self-control. Manliness encompassed the virtues of Christianity, honesty and integrity, and the practice of perseverance, temperance, diligence and self-restraint. If properly applied, these virtues would endow a man with 'character' and enable him to attain 'independence'. These standards of manliness were regarded as universal, applying to all walks of life, in all places in a world driven by competitive struggle. In mid-Victorian Britain, the code or ethos of 'manliness' was hegemonic, that is, it had wide and unquestioned acceptance as the 'true' or 'normal' way for men to be, although unevenly distributed through class and region.

In contrast, in 1858 adventurer and travel writer Kinahan Cornwallis had recorded his impression of British men, ones he had met on the frontier of British Columbia:

> We were a sunburnt, motley group, as camped together by the banks of the noisy river... There was something, I thought, of the hungry beast of prey in the eager, yearning flash of each others [sic] restless eyes, in which the fire of hardened desperation and unflinching physical bravery ever glowed, and which seemed to feed upon continual excitement. There was something embodying all the wildness of the savage and all the ghastliness of civilization in the hair-grown swarthy faces of the men.[4]

Would Kingsley have recognised Cornwallis's companions as manly Britons? More than likely he would have been shocked by what they had become, lacking many of the qualities he extolled at Wimbledon. Cornwallis's companions may well have been brave, hardy and strong, but would they have been courteous, temperate and self-restrained? One suspects not. Although he visited the West Indies for three months in 1869–1870, Kingsley had no experience of life on Britain's colonial frontier, no opportunity to assess how the attributes he recommended to his Wimbledon congregation were practised outside of Britain.

It would appear that among Cornwallis's companions, many of the manly virtues extolled by Kingsley had been lost in the transition between the metropole and the frontier. If they had been middle class, Cornwallis's companions would have been brought up to believe in and practice the manly virtues Kingsley preached. If they had been working class or from aristocratic backgrounds, they would have had similar, but perhaps not entirely identical, views on manliness. However, they seem to represent a different type of manliness: one perhaps anchored in metropolitan values, but which emphasised certain values and behaviours over others. Of course, Cornwallis's friends might not be a representative sample of frontier men. Not all men on the frontier would have been 'hungry beasts of prey'. But what sort of men were they? This book examines British men in frontier societies to determine how they practised the mid-Victorian idea of manliness. How did British men, remote from the environment in which they were raised, enact their manhood in new environments, namely, the frontiers of Queensland and British Columbia in the mid-nineteenth century?

The frontier was a place where masculine ideals were tested, and reworked. It was frightening, liminal, exciting and transformative. Men encountered challenges to their preconceived ideas of manhood, and responded to these challenges in a number of ways. Many were forced to surrender or change elements of their ideal, or found it almost impossible to fulfil their manly aspirations in the frontier environment. Some sought to replicate the social conditions of metropolitan Britain, in order to maintain their position at the top of the masculine and class hierarchy. The 'muscular' virtues came to the fore as the frontier provided a stage on which British men could 'perform' manliness, in particular by exercising courage, stoicism and perseverance, and developing 'a wild self-dependence of character'.[5] The frontier was imagined as a place which could be tamed and civilised by British men who possessed the manly virtues. It was a place of opportunity where the social and economic constraints of the metropole were absent.

However, for many men, the reality of the frontier was quite different. The frontier could be a more complicated, unsettling and troubling place than popular representations portrayed it. Many men struggled to adapt to the frontier environment – for them the pursuit of manliness was problematic. Though zealously performed by many, the manly ideal was not successfully practised by all. There are many stories Canadian and Australian frontier mythology neglects. By highlighting some of these stories and demonstrating the range of responses men had to the frontier, prominent frontier myths are challenged, resulting in a better sense of the reality of frontier life.

However, while many men did not live up to the manly ideal, it would be erroneous to simply conclude that they 'failed' to achieve a required standard of manhood. What an analysis of frontier men reveals, rather, are the contradictions inherent in the dominant construction of manhood. There was deep paradox in the Victorian ideal of manliness that made it impossible to achieve. The manly ideal was unstable and fluid, shifting in its emphases from the metropole to the frontier, from the early-nineteenth century to the latter part of that century. It encompassed or allowed for seemingly contradictory behaviours, structures and attitudes: Christian piety and the potential for violence; heterosexuality and the possibility of homoeroticism; family man and adventurer.

My aim is to reveal these contradictions and to illustrate the manifold ways that men experienced the frontier and manhood. Furthermore, I will examine how masculinity interacted with, and was defined by, other social variables such as race and class. Race, class and gender are mutually constitutive, and on mid-nineteenth-century British frontiers such as Queensland and British Columbia these social variables interacted and operated just as strongly as they did in the metropole to construct identities, relationships and status. British manliness had to be defended against alternatives, which were marginalised and excluded, but never fully suppressed.

In considering the experiences of individual men, differences as well as similarities emerge, the sum of which comprises masculine life on the frontier. Men on the frontier could be gold miners, explorers, pastoralists, priests or policemen. Indeed, the rubric 'pioneer' covers a multitude of occupational and social roles. I am interested in the variations in men's responses to the frontier as well as the commonalities. In the mid-nineteenth century, British Columbia and Queensland were frontier societies which gave British men the opportunity to enact 'manliness' under alien conditions, in a variety of roles and circumstances. An exploration of their experiences requires an understanding of masculinity, frontiers, race and class.

Key to this study is the idea that gender is not a passive characteristic – it cannot be understood as an essential, unvarying, biological attribute. Rather, gender is something one does: an act of creation. R.W. Connell uses the term 'configurations of practice' to denote that masculinity is performed or practised, manifested through the behaviour of men.[6] As Jeff Hearn puts it: 'Particular masculinities are not fixed formulae, but rather combinations of actions, part powerful, part arbitrary, performed in reaction and relation to complex material relations and emotional demands, and recognised by others as *signifying* that this is a man.'[7]

Judith Butler has also argued that gender is something one does or, in her words, is 'performative'. One becomes a man or woman through a 'stylized repetition of acts'.[8] For Butler, gender is a 'constructed identity, a performative accomplishment'. One's gendered self is structured by repeated acts, the purpose of which is to 'approximate' an ideal of gender identity. According to Butler, gender can never be fully internalised. The fact that occasionally one fails in this performance, that is, one is unable to continually successfully repeat certain acts, points to the contingent and non-essential nature of gender.[9]

While gender is something one does, what constitutes appropriate gender behaviour is the subject of pervasive discourses. In any age, a wide range of media convey and promote those behaviours and attitudes believed to apply to men and to women. In magazines, advice books, literature, schools, churches and social institutions of all kinds the lineaments of appropriate gender behaviour are circulated and recirculated, becoming dominant to the point of internalisation and naturalisation. When this occurs, it can be said that a particular view of gender is 'hegemonic'. Connell defines hegemonic masculinity as 'the configuration of gender practice which embodies the currently accepted answer to the problem of the legitimacy of patriarchy'.[10] As will be seen below, in mid-Victorian Britain, there was indeed a dominant model of manhood which operated to buttress the social, economic, legal and political position of men and to marginalise and subordinate women. It was this model of masculinity that British men took to the frontiers of Queensland and British Columbia.

Scholarly and popular interest in men and masculinity has been high. However, until the 1990s, the idea of masculinity was reasonably straightforward and it was only at the beginning of that decade that men and masculinity became 'more mysterious, more perplexing and more worrying'.[11] The result has been a burgeoning of scholarship on gender and masculinity occurring across a range of disciplines including psychology, sociology and history. Historians have heeded the arguments of John Tosh and sought to rectify a situation where the ubiquity of men as historical actors ensured a situation where they were the least understood sexual and gendered identities.[12] Consequently, British, Australian, Canadian, New Zealand and American historians have demonstrated that masculinity is an important and revealing historical construct.[13]

Canadian historian Adele Perry's *On the Edge of Empire: Gender, Race, and the Making of British Columbia* has particular relevance for this study, probing as it does the connections between race, gender and the making of colonial society. As Perry points out, British Columbia and other British colonies had much in common, and it is this commonality that this study seeks to exploit. Whereas Perry confines herself to British Columbia, this study includes Queensland, a colony that shared much with British Columbia both economically and socially. Perry's work explores how colonial authorities sought to tame an immoral and rough outpost of empire and transform it into a civilised and orderly domain of Victorian life. As Perry points out, investigating the place of gender in colonisation means exploring the significance of manhood as well as womanhood.[14] Here the focus is on a variety of British men, from the upper, middle and lower classes, and their particular experiences of frontier life. I examine the frontier lives of men to understand how they experienced and performed manliness. I also examine frontier conditions to determine how the environment in which these men placed themselves influenced their enactment of manliness.

When British men went to the frontier, what sort of place were they going to? The Turnerian thesis – that frontiers are tangible physical entities that advance across the landscape, a space where there is a 'rebirth' of society, a process which determines national character – dominated twentieth-century scholarship.[15] This idea of the frontier is one that has loomed large in Australian and Canadian historiography, as an influence on national identity and on the Australian male character. The frontier has provided Australia with its Genesis myth, the story of how a land was tamed, civilised and made productive by men, and this myth has had an enduring effect on Australian culture.[16]

As in Australia, the frontier as conceptualised by Turner has been a foundation of Canadian culture. Using Richard Slotkin's notion of 'frontier myth', Elizabeth Furniss explores how white identity in rural British Columbia is sustained by the idea of 'frontier'. According to Furniss, frontier was something 'out there' and 'empty' until the pioneers arrived from 'somewhere else, braved the unknown to eventually settle and put down roots in a new land and succeeded in creating a new life and a new society'.[17] This process was based on the values of individualism, self-sufficiency, freedom from external constraints, capped by rural common sense.[18] This was a process that 'affirms the unquestioned legitimacy and morality of the process of colonization'.[19]

Recently, frontiers have been reconceptualised, not as merely geographic spaces, but also as intellectual and psychological constructs, created by those who encounter them. They are hybrid spaces or 'zones of interpretation', where disparate elements combine and for which control is usually contested between indigenous people and settlers.[20] The frontier is a 'cultural membrane' or 'contact zone' where dissimilar cultures discover each other, resulting in ongoing relations which usually involve coercion, inequality and racial conflict.[21]

A further reconceptualisation has occurred in that frontiers are not necessarily sparsely populated bush or backwood locations. Penelope Edwards argues that, even more than remote districts, embryonic cities could be frontiers and sites of contestation between indigenous and invasive cultures.[22] Depending on where one is standing, the frontier may be imagined differently. If one is in London in 1850, one may imagine Victoria on Vancouver Island and Brisbane in Queensland as frontiers and regard them as very remote places indeed. However, if one is actually in Victoria or Brisbane the frontier may be imagined as far North Queensland or the Cariboo goldfields. This spatial relativity highlights the problem with defining frontiers solely by geography.

What Turner's thesis and more recent thinking retain in common is the idea that frontiers are places of transformation, where identities are made and remade, at both a social and an individual level. Frontiers are liminal zones, places of transitions and change. Those who live on the frontier occupy a zone which is simultaneously at the margins of the metropole and constitutes the initial stages of a new society. Colonial frontiers are both contingent upon the metropole and independent of it. They are contingent because the individuals who go to a frontier do so carrying with them the ideologies, values and knowledge of their original society which, in part, determines the type of society which emerges. At the same time frontiers are independent, because they are remote and experimental places where conditions lend themselves to social, cultural and personal change, and old institutions do not necessarily serve as well as they did in the metropole. Queensland and British Columbia are models of this dualism.

Engagement with a frontier was a two-way process. The outcome of a frontier experience may have been a transformation not only of the physical environment, but also of the people who went there and the original inhabitants. Put simply, frontiers were places where people could change. Frontiers were places where people did things they would not otherwise do, and lived in ways they would not normally have lived. As Ann Laura Stoler puts it, the frontier was 'transformative of cultural essence, social disposition, and personhood itself'.[23] On the frontier, men of the Old World with Old World ideas were relocated to a new environment. There were new landscapes, new challenges, new peoples and new imperatives to survive. Men were removed from the old sources of stability and security, and forced into contact with new peoples. Taking advantage of geographic and psychic distance they constructed new identities, and began and lost new careers.[24]

The frontier was not a gender-neutral space. Frontier narratives of possession and conquest commonly gendered the physical environment as female. Whether it was the explicitly sexualised African landscape of *King Solomon's Mines* or the 'virgin' plains of Queensland and western Canada described in the journals of explorers and pastoralists, frontier lands were feminine places and desirable possessions.[25] In these texts the frontier is metaphorically rendered feminine, becoming a feminine other against which frontier men are constructed as heroes. The frontier may also be a 'femme fatale' which entices men to their doom.[26]

The Queensland and British Columbia frontiers had much in common in the mid-nineteenth century. On 2 September 1864, Vancouver Island's *British Colonist* published an editorial headed 'Queensland and Vancouver Island'. The *Colonist* was 'amused' by Queensland's political problems and their similarity to Vancouver Island's a few years previously. Both colonial governments had spent money they did not have, misappropriated the money they did, run up debts and granted favours to friendly commercial interests and 'a thousand other things damaging to the best interests of the place'.[27] Nevertheless, Queensland had a few things going for it: immigration numbers were healthy, revenue was up and public works were numerous. Despite these advantages, Queensland, in the eyes of the *Colonist*, did not seem entirely attractive when compared to Vancouver Island. Brisbane lacked the 'energy' and 'general business habits' of Victoria. However, Victoria's schools, libraries and museums were a 'hundred years behind the town of Brisbane'.[28]

If the *Colonist* had been less concerned for Vancouver Island's status in the imperial hierarchy, it would have noticed that the two colonies had a great deal in common which outweighed the differences in public services: colonial origins, primary resources and similar population demographics. Both are located on the Pacific Rim, and the coastlines of both were charted by James Cook. Each had a period of initially limited settlement and exploitation followed by a larger influx of population in the mid-nineteenth century. Each had gold rushes. Settlers extracted resources to provide staples for export to the British market; wool, gold and sugar were the main products provided by Queensland, and timber, gold and salmon were the foremost in British Columbia. The climate of both colonies was attractive to Europeans, or, in the case of Queensland, at least not a deterrent.[29] Each had significant indigenous populations and both were integral parts of the British Empire governed by men sent out from the Colonial Office.

From the 1840s to the 1870s, both Queensland and British Columbia attracted large numbers of British male migrants. When Queensland was separated from New South Wales in 1859 it contained 23,520 predominantly British settlers and around 60,000 Aborigines and Torres Strait Islanders.[30] Over the next 12 years the immigrant population increased rapidly. In 1861 the general white population stood at 30,059, doubled in the next three years, and doubled again by 1871 to 120,104. Queensland had a more heterogeneous population than Australia's southern colonies, with significant numbers of Pacific Islanders, Chinese and other Asians.

In British Columbia in 1855 there were an estimated 774 colonists on Vancouver Island, two-thirds of whom were male. The Cariboo gold rush of 1862–1864 attracted large numbers of colonists. In 1863 there were 7,338 whites on Vancouver Island and the mainland combined, 95 percent of whom were male. This population was concentrated in a small number of towns such as Victoria, New Westminster and Nanaimo, although miners were scattered along the Fraser River and the Cariboo.[31] In 1870 the total white population was 8,576, two-thirds of whom were male, the decline of the gold rushes and a concerted effort to bring women to the colony accounting for the changed male-to-female ratio since 1863.[32] In 1871 the indigenous population was estimated at 45,000. As in Queensland, ethnic diversity was a feature.

Both places were British, socially transformative schemes that were 'localised, politicised, and partial, but also produced by larger historical forces and ways of understanding them'.[33] The white settlement of Queensland and British Columbia involved many individuals, each motivated by their own interests and objectives. Hence the histories of Queensland and British Columbia are simultaneously histories of empire and imperialism, and of the individuals, colonisers and colonised, who inhabited both colonies. If, as a secretary of the Hudson's Bay Company observed, the object of colonisation was to transfer to the new society what was best in the old, then such an endeavour was fraught with challenges as the bush and the backwoods defied imperial dreams and transformed them into an amalgam of the traditional metropolitan and unfamiliar local influences, resulting in new social forms.[34]

An examination of British manliness on the frontier requires an examination of how manliness was understood and practised in Britain itself. Masculinity as a central middle-class concern dates from the late-eighteenth and early-nineteenth centuries, with the emergence of those middle classes. The nature of the gender order which emerged during this period has been the subject of contestation and revision. The foremost interpretation of this period is Leonore Davidoff's and Catherine Hall's *Family Fortunes: Men and Women of the English Middle Class, 1780–1850*, in which they argued that the values of the rising middle class – companionate marriage, the affectional nuclear family, the precepts of evangelical Christianity and a strong ethic of wealth accumulation – resulted in a gender order which normalised and naturalised separate social, domestic and economic roles for men and women.[35] According to this formulation the concept of separate spheres for men and women – in which women were confined to the private domestic world and men were free to participate in work, commerce and politics – was a cultural idea that permeated work, family, religion, and social life. It underpinned a gender order in which most women were constrained to live in the private sphere, where science provided incontrovertible 'proof' of women's inferiority; where men of all classes had the freedom to circulate between private and public, exercising absolute control over their wives and children; and where middle- and upper-class men occupied all the leading positions in manufacture, commerce and politics.

While this formulation has been influential, it has been refined by more recent scholarship. In her account of gender and the British working class, Anna Clark has shown that middle-class values were not hegemonic.[36] Amanda Vickery has argued very strongly that the paradigm of separate spheres precedes the late-eighteenth century and that its relation to industrialisation and evangelical Christianity in this period was weak. She argues that what apparently occurred in the late Georgian era was little different to what occurred in previous centuries.[37]

Arguments about periodisation notwithstanding, the concept of separate spheres is an imperfect one, with many exceptions to the neat distinctions it suggests. John Tosh has shown that the home, far from being the preserve of women, was as integral to the establishment of masculine identity as it was to feminine identity.[38] Robert Shoemaker, in *Gender in English Society 1650–1850: The Emergence of Separate Spheres*, demonstrated that women had a substantial presence in religious affairs, politics and social and cultural life.[39] Perhaps the most useful conceptualisation is of a gender order containing broad parameters in which men and women were expected to operate. Thus while a man might be responsible for the disciplining of children in the home, particularly of older boys, he would perhaps not be expected to care for infants or do the laundry. While women might be active in public charities and certain political causes (e.g. the abolition of slavery), they could not be ordained in the Church of England or sit in Parliament.

If men and women have always operated in separate, but overlapping, spheres, the late-eighteenth to mid-nineteenth centuries saw a flourishing of ideological tracts about the place of men and women in society. William Cowper, Hannah More, Sarah Stickney Ellis and others were prolific in setting forth what they regarded as the proper roles of men and women.[40] Their works emphasised sexual difference and gave prominence to the home as the place where women could find fulfilment. Hence, while perhaps not a new idea, the concept of separate spheres was given a fresh impetus in the late-eighteenth and early-nineteenth centuries.

British society was certainly patriarchal, both in the literal sense of 'father-rule' – men were expected to rule their households – and in the wider sense that men had considerably more power than women, and used that power through law, custom, politics, science and economics to maintain a position of superiority over women. Marriage and the establishment of a household was an important aspect of gaining recognition as a fully independent male adult. Furthermore, a man was expected to wield authority in his home. The Reverend William Secker counselled husbands to love and respect their spouses, but emphasised: 'The wife may be sovereign in her husband's absence, but she must be subject in her husband's presence.'[41] In the seventeenth century, very definite parallels had been drawn between a man's ability to rule over his wife and dependents and his fitness as a citizen to take part in public affairs. The family was viewed as a microcosm of the state: the absence or failure of masculine rule in the family would lead to the instability of the state. By the nineteenth century the patriarchal theory of political authority had been superseded by contract theory – but male dominance continued to hold sway in the family, and men continued to dominate in the public sphere.[42]

Discourses of evangelical Christianity, industrial capitalism and medical science conspired to keep women subordinate to men. The precepts of evangelical Christianity held that woman's place was in the home, not in the public world of commerce and politics. God had ordained that man should be the head of a household and that women, children and servants should obey him. The dissenting churches played a strong role in keeping working-class men in conformity with this domestic ideal. They pressured men to be responsible, sober and protective husbands, who shunned the hard drinking of their fellow workmen. The moral discipline of the dissenting churches strengthened patriarchal authority within working-class and plebeian culture. The elders and deacons of these churches were all men. Women were expected to be submissive to patriarchal authority, although sometimes they could safely express theological dissent.[43] Like their middle-class counterparts, working-class women were expected to devote themselves to domestic life, although economic imperatives could dictate otherwise.

Industrial capitalism exacerbated the inferior economic position of women compared to men. One of the most significant ways it did so was in the spatial separation of work from home. Whereas for many centuries women and children had worked alongside men in providing for household wants and commodity production (albeit often in distinct roles), the rise of factory production meant that many commodities once produced on a small scale were mass produced, mostly by men. If they were employed in factories, women invariably received lower wages than men. For working-class women workplaces could be demanding and hostile. Combined with a conservative labour movement which sought to exclude women from trades, industrial capitalism entrenched the role of the male as the chief breadwinner and economically impoverished women.

The subordination of women was justified on scientific grounds. Writers of all descriptions were insistent that there were fundamental differences between male and female sexuality, and these were due to observable biological distinctions. The sexes were different in every possible physical and moral dimension.[44] Models of human sexuality that had been based on the notion that men and women were of the one sex, but that women were merely an inferior sexual version of men, were replaced by ideas based on new ways of understanding human biology. While ostensibly value neutral, these ideas were utilised to define women entirely in relation to their bodies and their sexual capacity in terms of reproduction. Medical literature began to stereotype women as medically unique but inferior beings, whose femininity determined their health. This representation of biological sexuality and the conceptualisation of sexual difference based upon it underpinned monogamous marriage, a sexual division of labour and an economic relationship between men and women.[45]

As part of this patriarchal gender order the middle classes formulated an ideal of manhood which, in a number of ways, they attempted to impose upon other classes. This manly ideal was disseminated and promulgated throughout British society via didactic texts, schools and popular literature. This man's world operated according to normative codes of masculinity which defined what it was to be manly. These codes were not immutable, and over the course of the nineteenth century were modified and influenced by prevailing religious, educational and imperial ideologies. From the late-eighteenth to the late-nineteenth century, conceptions of masculinity evolved through a number of iterations and under a number of influences and the idea of 'manliness' became a significant concept.

The term 'manly' was an adjective that could be applied to encapsulate a wide range of attributes, virtues and behaviours. 'Character' was of paramount importance to Victorians. This was a somewhat intangible concept, embracing a number of virtues, each important in its own right. Combined, these virtues made the man, and the man who possessed 'character' was held in esteem by peers, superiors and inferiors alike. Despite some differences among historians, as to what 'character' entailed, there is a fair degree of consensus regarding the essential virtues. Character could entail self-restraint, perseverance, strenuous effort and courage in the face of adversity.[46] Alternatively, it could include realism, self-control, temperance, thrift and hard work.[47] It was a manifestation of the qualities needed to cope with life.

Self-help advocate Samuel Smiles placed character at the apex of manly virtue:

> The crown and glory of life is Character. It is the noblest possession of a man, constituting a rank in itself, and an estate in the general goodwill; dignifying every station, and exalting every position in society... It carries with it an influence which always tells; for it is the result of proved honour, rectitude, and consistency – qualities which, perhaps more than any other, command the general confidence and respect of manhood.[48]

It would seem that for Smiles, a doctor and journalist turned didactic writer, to possess 'character' was to be the perfect man. Character was noble, exalted and glorious. Character was a political necessity for a moral, well-governed society. In Smiles's *Self-Help* 'manly' and 'manliness' are key epithets. Hard work, perseverance, self-reliance, and energetic action were the attributes essential to the acquisition of a 'truly noble and manly character'.

Qualities such as self-control, perseverance, courage and energy became the mark of independent manhood, defining the new middle-class order. As the middle class redefined work as something virtuous, manliness involved the capacity to work for oneself, to get ahead on one's own merits, to gain 'independence' rather than live off an inheritance.[49] According to the arbiters of manliness, the most important goal for men was independence, and this was an aspiration they consistently promoted throughout the nineteenth century.[50] Independence meant supporting oneself, relying neither on charity nor on inherited wealth. 'To wish to live on the labour of another is,' wrote William Cobbett in 1829, 'to contemplate a *fraud.*'[51] Happiness ought to be a young man's object and it was only to be achieved through independence. The earlier the virtues of independence were learned the better. For another self-appointed arbiter of manliness in the 1870s there was 'no surer sign of an unmanly and cowardly spirit than a vague desire for help – a wish to depend, to lean upon, somebody, and enjoy the fruits of the industry of others'.[52]

The discourse of manliness was pervasive. The manly virtues were promoted in a range of media and institutions during the first half of the nineteenth century and beyond. Literature, advice books, sermons, magazines and public schools promulgated a consistent discourse of manliness. It would have been difficult for the literate person not to have absorbed at least some aspects of the manly ideal. The term 'manly' was an adjective that could be widely applied to describe what was desirable in any sphere and it was a quality only the qualified were equipped to define.

In the early- to mid-nineteenth century young men who were unsure about how they would make the transition from youth to manhood could avail themselves of a plethora of advice books and self-help manuals, brimming with information and admonition regarding the true nature of manliness. Aimed at the lower-middle and middle classes, books by Samuel Taylor Coleridge, William Cobbett, Samuel Smiles and many others offered counsel on manners and morals, habits desirable and undesirable, dress, social duties and privileges, religion, sex, wealth and poverty, exhorting men to embrace hard work and perseverance, and warning of the 'readiness with which young men imbibe bad habits'.[53] There was no art, science, commerce or industry – no field of human endeavour – to which the manly virtues could not be applied with profit to both the individual and society.

There was a basic assumption in these texts that manliness was not innate, but was the product of a set of attitudes and behaviours that could only be acquired with conscientious effort and self-monitoring. Thus the belief that certain men, namely, 'gentlemen', innately possessed manly attributes, coexisted uneasily with the belief that other men had to cultivate these same qualities. The theme of self-governance is implicit in these didactic texts – young men needed to exercise control over 'unmanly' thoughts and deeds. Every male was a potential social subversive. It was only through constant attention to behaviour and self-reflection that a desirable state of manliness could be maintained.

The advice books also conveyed warnings of sexual misadventure. True manhood would not be achieved via sexual adventure but by self-control through commitment to religion. The author of *Letters to Young People Single and Married* predicted dire consequences arising from impure thought:

> Young man! You who are so modest in the presence of women – so polite and amiable; you who are invited into families where there are pure and virtuous girls; you who go to church, and seem to be such a pattern young man; you who very possibly neither smoke, nor chew, nor snuff, nor swear, nor drink – you have one habit ten times worse than all these put together – a habit that makes you a whited sepulchre, fair without, but within full of dead men's bones and all uncleaness. You have a habit of impure thought, that poisons the very springs of life.[54]

Sobriety was another key theme of those who had wisdom to impart. The author of *Advice to Young Men*, journalist and political radical William Cobbett, not only regarded drunkenness and gluttony as 'nasty and beastly', but believed that even indulgences 'far short of this gross and really nasty drunkenness' were 'destructive to human happiness'.[55] Similarly, in Cobbett's opinion, taking a drink occasionally would make a young man either a 'demon or a dolt'. A young man who 'forms the habit of drinking, or places himself in danger of forming the habit, is usually so weak that it is not worth while to save him'.[56]

In the first half of the nineteenth century the dominant idea of manliness was that encapsulated in the phrase employed by David Newsome – 'godliness and good learning' – which held that education and religion were fundamentally allied.[57] This was a philosophy that was at least implicitly masculine. In this version of manliness young men should enjoy the outdoor life in typically non-competitive physical pursuits such as hiking. Such young men would also be well read, imbibing the classics at school and pursuing higher education at Oxford or

Cambridge, where they would acquire the habits of hard work and the virtues of honesty and piety.

In the second half of the nineteenth-century earnestness, selflessness and piety became somewhat less important in defining who was manly. Christian faith was still important but was now allied with virtues that were less intellectual and more physical. More emphasis was placed on athleticism, stoicism, moral courage, hardiness and endurance to comprise a manly code which became known as 'muscular Christianity'. Headmasters emphasised the formation of character as the principal objective of schooling. The headmaster of Uppingham, Edward Thring, believed that 'the whole efforts of a school ought to be directed to making boys manly, earnest and true'.[58] The methods of the public schools, particularly their disciplinary arrangements, were considered to be conducive to the formation of real men:

> The advantages of this arrangement could hardly be obtained in any other manner. They consist not only in the physical qualities they develop; nor in the production of that special form of courage... which consists in readiness to brave obvious and immediate danger... but in a knowledge of the world and of human nature, altogether invaluable to society at large, and singularly conducive to the complete formation of the manly character.[59]

The greater emphasis on physical virtues led to the cult of athleticism – the encouragement of sport as character building and the promotion of the sportsman as the ideal masculine type.[60]

Promoters of manliness such as Charles Kingsley and Thomas Hughes presented Christianity as a muscular doctrine, and Christ was represented in masculine terms.[61] This physical code of manliness was promulgated not only in schools, but in literature as well. Kingsley's *Yeast*, *Alton Locke* and *Westward Ho!*, and Hughes's *Tom Brown's Schooldays*, extolled the 'great importance and value of animal spirits, physical strength, and a hearty enjoyment of all the pursuits and accomplishments which are connected with them'.[62] There was no incompatibility between physical and spiritual pursuits. The *Saturday Review*, reviewing Kingsley's *Two Years Ago* in 1857, felt that

> there is no satisfactory reason why a man should not come home from a good run with the brush in one pocket, and a prayer book in another. Therefore, let Mr Kingsley encourage us all to pursue the path that leads to so blessed a possibility. He does but set before us

the picture of that which, if we reflect, we must all pronounce to be a rare but admirable combination.[63]

If the metropole did not provide adequate opportunity for independence and the exercise of the manly virtues, distant territories did. A new iteration of the ideal of manliness came to the fore in the late-nineteenth century as Britain ramped up the expansion of its empire. In these colonies, settlers sought to replicate the structures and institutions of Britain they thought were desirable while at the same time rejecting the structures and hierarchies they deemed undesirable. Many men travelled to the colonial frontier to renew themselves. There, in an environment where the usual social forces were weakened or absent, the ethos of manliness faced new challenges.

Terry Eagleton has argued that in the nineteenth century, as reading increasingly became a mass pursuit, literature became an increasingly important tool for the production and dissemination of dominant ideologies.[64] A plethora of adventure stories published throughout the nineteenth century such as *Midshipman Easy* (C.F. Marryat, 1834), *The Young Fur Traders* (R.M. Ballantyne, 1858) and *King Solomon's Mines* (Rider Haggard, 1885), fiction aimed at boys and young men, reinforced muscular constructions of masculinity.[65] The popularity of these books indicates that the stories they offered and the ideals they promoted were widely accepted and absorbed – or at least enjoyed.[66]

The instrumentality of Victorian adventure literature in sustaining codes of masculinity suggests that the metropole was shaped by colonial encounters just as much as the colonies were shaped by the metropole.[67] Indeed, Richard Phillips argues that in the 'geography of adventure', British masculinity was not transplanted but created.[68] Literary representations of imperial maleness, not confined to adventure literature but found in a range of texts including parliamentary debates and government reports, were part of a wider public conversation on the moral and physical well-being of boys.[69]

The middle-class ethos of manliness was problematic for working-class men. If the gentleman was the embodiment of the manly virtues, how then could working-class men be manly? This notion of masculinity, combined with the ability of middle-class men to act in the public sphere and maintain their wives at home, was not available to working-class men. The doctrine of separate spheres was difficult to apply among the working class as most working men could not earn sufficient wages to support women and children in the home. Working-class women had to work in factories, laundries and the homes of the wealthy *and* take full responsibility for cooking, cleaning and child-rearing. During the 1830s middle-class men were politically enfranchised, while working-class men remained excluded from that part of the public domain.[70]

Instead of the gentlemanly virtues, property and political rights, manliness for working men was denoted by 'property in skill', fraternal bonds, hard drinking, physical prowess and collective organisation. Working-class masculinity did embrace a notion of independence similar to that held by the middle class. For working-class men, independence was tied to citizenship and political rights, and 'property in skill'. Independence meant being free to sell one's labour, so one could support oneself and one's family without depending on charity. It also entailed the freedom to associate and to regulate one's trade. Independence was conditional on maintaining working conditions and the status of one's employment.[71]

As Chartism became the vehicle of working-class politics, the conservative doctrine of the separate spheres was gradually adopted by the working class. Initially egalitarian, Chartists increasingly defined their struggle for the vote as a struggle for manhood, using highly gendered language which excluded women. The turn towards domesticity and the separate spheres was in large part to rebut claims that working people were immoral and undeserving of both family and political rights. The opponents of wider suffrage denied working men the vote by claiming they were not good husbands and fathers. Chartist men manipulated the doctrine of separate spheres, claiming that domesticity was a right all should enjoy. Domesticity was a means of simultaneously defending working-class families and appealing to women without threatening men.[72]

The ideals of manliness were not limited to individual men. Manliness was the stuff of which nations were built. For Samuel Smiles, the spirit of self-help (a form of self-governance), and the acquisition of the manly virtues, was the 'true source of national vigour and strength'.[73] Nations would decay through individual idleness, selfishness and vice. Through the individual industry, energy and uprightness of men a nation would progress.[74] Possession of the appropriate masculine attributes made a man fit to rule – his family, his nation, its colonies and their inhabitants. If the nation failed to provide opportunity for men to exercise their prowess, the British Empire provided the ideal challenge to men who wanted to hone their masculine virtues and put their ideals of manliness and virility to the test.

While masculinity and frontier are the foci of this study, race constitutes a third influential variable in the response of men to the frontier, and the performance of their masculinity. Race, like gender, is a cultural construction which has worked to naturalise difference and power relationships, to depict them as immutable categories when in fact race is historically contingent and variable.[75] Mrinalini Sinha has argued that the construction of the ideal of colonial masculinity 'demonstrates that masculinity has as much to do with racial, class, religious and national differences as with sex difference'.[76]

The European occupation of Queensland and British Columbia confronted and overwhelmed indigenous populations. While the pattern of interaction between Europeans and the indigenous people differed – Queensland Aborigines neither formed mercantile relationships with Europeans nor intermarried to any significant extent, and the indigenous people of British Columbia were not subject to the same level of raw violence suffered by Queensland Aborigines – neither Queensland nor British Columbia were racially harmonious places. Of north Queensland in particular it has been said that race is an 'inescapable theme'.[77] The rest of Queensland was scarcely any different. In British Columbia race was central to the social dynamics of frontier life, a prominent variable in law, commerce and sexuality, permeating all social relations.[78]

Race intersected with masculinity and British men constructed non-white, non-British masculinities as inferior and 'uncivilised', thereby defending and affirming their own version of masculinity. White colonists depicted indigenous and other non-white masculinities as the antithesis of their own ideal, and in doing so defended and affirmed the dominant British version of manliness. Frontier Queensland and British Columbia were violent places and the ethos of manliness had within it the potential for violence. When combined with racial differences, this potential became manifest. On the colonial frontier manly attributes such as courage, strength and rationality could be distorted and could become manifestations of subjugation and violence.

My approach in this study is historical and biographical. Sources include unpublished manuscripts, autobiographical writings, diaries, letters and published accounts of travel and exploration. The diaries, memoirs and letters of British men on the Queensland and British Columbia frontiers tell similar stories of adventure, physical hardship, hard work, risk, remoteness, fraternity, loneliness, alcoholism, perseverance and endurance. They are written by the scions of aristocracy, middle-class adventurers and ministers of religion. On the frontier these men became pastoralists, shepherds, gold miners and labourers. The stories of shopkeepers, bakers and men of no particular occupation in search of one provide a window onto the experiences of the lower middle and working classes. Regardless of their background, these men dug for gold, washed sheep, crossed rivers and mountain ranges, herded cattle and shot deer. In Queensland they pushed the indigenous people off their land in order to graze sheep and cattle. In British Columbia the indigenous population was diminished by smallpox and dispossessed through legal trickery. There were few women in these men's stories – certainly few white women – and non-white women feature only incidentally. These men write about the land, its exploitation and other men.

It is important to understand that while their accounts were undoubtedly written with integrity and the intention of historical accuracy, these narratives are acts of self-representation. They are autobiographical writings, a genre described by Paul Delany as a 'performance' staged by the author for the benefit of his or her audience.[79] Through this performance, the authors are revealing themselves to others. Their letters, journals and memoirs contain their 'displayed self', the self they want others to know.[80] In accounts of their frontier experiences, men could 'accentuate the positive', so to speak, by portraying themselves as manly, by depicting themselves as conquerors of the wilderness, as hardy and self-reliant pioneers who could overcome any obstacle, physical or psychological. At the same time, they may be seeking to protect (or suppress) elements of their character. The point is that these texts are not detached accounts of events and experiences; each is a 'determinate work of self-portraiture'.[81]

Nevertheless, they are still revealing of the way masculinity was performed on the frontier, and of the way men felt it should be. In the words of Paul de Man, 'the autobiographical project may itself produce and determine the life'.[82] At the same time these journals and diaries are documents of lived experiences and reveal the vicissitudes of frontier life. Furthermore, their stories laid the foundation of the frontier myths of Canada and Australia – the myth of the independent, freedom-loving Canadian pioneer described by Furniss, and of the men who worked the land and tamed the environment in Hirst's pioneering legend.

The reader of these memoirs is soon struck by their similarities. One could swap the titles or authors of texts such as W.S.S. Tyrwhit's *A New Chum in the Queensland Bush* with A.W. Stirling's *A Ride in the Never Never* or Charles Eden's *My Wife and I in Queensland* (in which his wife is barely mentioned), and one would scarcely know the difference.[83] Similarly, British Columbian narratives such as the journal of W.B. Cheadle, the reminiscences of Reginald Pidcock or the diary of Henry Guillod tell such similar stories that a sense of *déjà vu* on the part of the reader is inescapable.[84] Similarities are also apparent when one compares accounts from British Columbia with those from Queensland. Robert Harkness' evocative letters from the Cariboo to his wife in eastern Canada convey the same sense of loneliness and isolation as R. Henderson's barely literate diary of his year in western Queensland.[85] These similarities suggest a common masculine experience, and essential similarities in Queensland and British Columbian frontier life. A sense of adventure and opportunity is common, as is physical hardship and risk. These similarities also indicate the pervasiveness and ubiquity of the mid-Victorian masculine ethos. The letters, diaries and memoirs of men who lived on the frontier are taken as its principal evidence and the 'lived experiences' of frontier men and events of which they were a part are revealed. By placing 'manliness' at the centre of their experiences and demonstrating the complexities of men's responses to the frontier, we enrich our understanding of frontier men and frontier life.

The manner in which men expressed their frontier experiences was shaped by ideological, social and economic forces. Their view of the frontier was coloured by ideas and assumptions based on their personal histories and experiences. Many of them would be changed by their frontier experience as the frontier modified the views and assumptions they brought to it. However, no one could entirely escape the cultural beliefs taken to the frontier, and these beliefs influenced how men perceived and recorded their experiences. Therefore, to the extent that such preconceptions influenced perceptions, the reminiscences, letters, and diaries considered here are to be regarded as constructions of historical actuality, written with an intention of veracity, but inescapably shaped by the authors' background and predilections and, in the case of some, commercial and potential readership considerations. While somewhat wary of the nomenclature, I draw from post-colonial literature the recognition that race, gender and imperialism are fundamentally important to the social experience of both white imperialists and non-white subjects of imperial ventures. Following the 'linguistic turn', which argues that the narrative forms in which men recorded their impressions shaped their records, I recognise the discursive nature of sources and the historically constructed nature of social relations. Throughout the text, where the words 'Aborigine' or 'Aboriginal' are used, I am referring to the indigenous peoples of Australia. Although Queensland did not become a self-governing colony under that name until 1859, when discussing events prior to that time the name Queensland is used for the sake of simplicity. Similarly, the name 'Canada' is used to refer to the eastern parts of British North America prior to confederation in 1867.

On the Queensland and British Columbia frontiers 'manliness' was an important ideal but a problematic practice. There were ample opportunities for men to enact their 'manliness'. Many men responded to frontier challenges with courage, fortitude and strength. The frontier offered the enterprising man the chance to gain his independence and the harsh physical conditions called for stoicism, perseverance and self-reliance. These characteristics were affirmed and recycled to the metropole in the form of journals, memoirs, letters and fiction, which were consumed by friends, family and the general public, and which fed the discourse of manliness. British manliness could not be taken for granted, and British men responded to challenges to their ideal with various strategies aimed at defending and maintaining this ideal against alternatives. However, not all men responded to the frontier in the same fashion. Some responded to the isolation and loneliness with despair and some resorted to alcohol to relieve that despair. On the frontier self-restraint, sobriety and sexual propriety often fell by the wayside. In many ways the discourse of British manliness refused to admit the realities of frontier life.

2
The Most Manly Class That Exists

> I don't know that there can be a much happier life than that of a squatter, if the man be fairly prosperous, and have natural attributes for country occupations. He should be able to ride and shoot – and to sit in a buggy all day without inconvenience. He should be social – for he must entertain often and be entertained by other squatters; but he must be indifferent to society, for he will live away from towns and be often alone with his family. He must be able to command men, and must do so in a frank and easy fashion – not arrogating to himself any great superiority, but with full power to let those around him know that he is master. He must prefer plenty to luxury, and be content to have things around him a little rough. He must be able to brave troubles – for a squatter has many troubles. If a man have these gifts, and be young and energetic when he begins the work, he will not have chosen badly in becoming a squatter.
>
> (Anthony Trollope, *Australia*)

Throughout the nineteenth century, young men of genteel background and public school education left Britain to seek wealth and opportunity in the colonies, including Queensland and British Columbia. Although differing somewhat from the qualities desirable in a gentleman at home, the social skills, mastery and energy of Trollope's idealised squatter can be encapsulated in the word 'gentleman'. In mid-nineteenth century British Columbia and Queensland 'emigrant gentlemen', the scions of the aristocracy and ambitious middle-class men, formed a frontier elite. They were pulled to British Columbia by gold and adventure, and to Queensland by the lure of land, and pushed from Britain by the constraints of patrimony and the lack of opportunity. Many young men of the upper and middle classes discovered that the emerging professions were overcrowded. These and younger sons who would not inherit any significant portion of their families' wealth had to look elsewhere for a livelihood and the best outlets available (considering their class and status) were the colonies.

George Carrington found that despite a degree from Oxford he was not really qualified for anything much, and emigration seemed the only option for the independently minded gentleman:

> When I left Oxford... the only chance of employment which I saw before me for some time to come, was that of being an usher or undermaster in a school. This was a course which my soul abhorred; the restraint and dependent position seemed too ghastly... I thus, knowing nothing about colonial life, and very little about any other, with no idea of any kind of work, and with about as much fitness for living in a colony as for living on the moon, turned my thoughts to emigration. I believe I had a floating notion of making my fortune in a general way, without very much exertion.[1]

Like George Carrington, Patrick Leslie could not bear the thought of being dependent upon others, to the extent that despite failing once as a pastoralist he set out for a second attempt:

> I really cannot believe that I ever thought of setting down in Scotland upon some £100 pr an [sic] factor to anyone but I was perfectly bedevilled and my mind upset in every way and I cannot now be too thankful that I had sufficient sense left to prompt me to come here again. I wish nothing more than to go on quietly here and work out an independence and my brothers will without doubt do as well as men could wish here.[2]

These passages highlight the importance of 'independence' in achieving manly status. Both Carrington and Leslie yearned for independence. For Carrington the thought of working for someone else was abhorrent and 'ghastly'; for Leslie it was almost inconceivable.

In Britain the hegemonic masculine ideal rested on a shaky base. The country experienced frequent economic uncertainty in the early decades of the nineteenth century. In a society where masculine identity had become dependent on a man's independence, industrial capitalism and the activities of the free market often brought anxiety and vulnerability.[3] This vulnerability was hidden, and underlined, by the hegemonic discourse of character and independence.[4] In the early- to mid-nineteenth century when opportunities for men with small amounts of capital were few, the colonial frontier offered opportunity and adventure and a chance to put the manly virtues into practice. Charles Eden explained in the introduction to *My Wife and I in Queensland* that 'every profession and calling in England being already overcrowded, and those unfortunate beings, younger sons, continuing to be born, there can be no doubt that these and other portionless individuals must direct their attention to the only outlet left open, viz. our Colonies'.[5] Thus driven by the imperatives of patrimony, lack of opportunity and the manly ideal of independence, gentlemen headed for Queensland, British Columbia and other British colonies. In Queensland, the younger sons of the landed gentry took up wool growing and occupied positions of social and political influence. In British Columbia, the officers of the Hudson's Bay Company, colonial administrators and settlers of middle-class and upper-class backgrounds dominated economic, social and political life, and set about transferring British social customs to the new society. Although not necessarily born to the appellation 'gentleman', the officers of the Hudson's Bay Company and the Northwest Company comprised a gentlemanly caste within the fur trade.

Originally used to describe men of aristocratic lineage, in the early-nineteenth century the term 'gentleman' became applicable to men of the middle class, particularly those engaged in the professions, such as law and medicine, which were undergoing a process of gentrification.[6] As the nineteenth century progressed, the sons of the mercantile middle class joined the ranks of gentlemen. They were educated in English public schools, not necessarily Eton or Harrow, but at least in one of the scores of schools of lesser pedigree that modelled themselves on the 'Great Schools', established to educate the sons of middle-class merchants. The Clarendon Commission, examining the state of education in six of the 'Great Schools', found that

> it is not easy to estimate the degree in which the English people are indebted to these schools for the qualities on which they pique themselves the most – for their capacity to govern others and control themselves, their aptitude for combining freedom with order, their

public spirit, their vigour and manliness of character, their strong but not slavish respect for public opinion, their love of healthy sports and exercise...they have had perhaps the largest share in moulding the character of the English gentleman.[7]

In these schools boys imbibed the doctrines of manliness and gentlemanly behaviour, and acquired a disposition to serve and to rule. Self-governance was critical to the acquisition of character and the ability to govern oneself was linked to the ability to govern others. The capacity for self-governance that the schools instilled qualified young men to occupy positions of political, economic and social leadership in Britain and its colonies.

The nineteenth-century gentleman had his antecedents in the code of chivalry adopted by medieval knights. In the nineteenth century this ideal was reborn. It was embraced by political movements, promoted by youth organisations, taught in schools and dramatised in literature. In everyday social life, the chivalric ideals were embodied in the image of the gentleman. A gentleman was upright, brave, honourable, benevolent and loyal to Queen and country. He was a natural leader, fearless in war, in the hunt and on the sporting field. As tough as he could be when circumstances demanded, he could be equally gentle when required. Above all these attributes, he was respectful and courteous to women of all classes.[8]

Apart from embodying and practising these virtues, a gentleman led his life in a certain manner. Traditionally proper gentlemen did not associate themselves with labour. Unpaid pursuits – classical study, voluntary service as a magistrate – conferred prestige by the very token that they were unpaid.[9] The concepts of public service and duty were closely bound to the gentlemanly ideal. Gentlemen were expected to lead. As the manly ethos emerged and took hold, this tradition began to break down. If a man of genteel background had to work, the Church, the military and the emerging professions of law and medicine were regarded as suitable. Over time, commerce became an acceptable field of employment. By practising the gentlemanly virtues, a man demonstrated that he deserved a position in the military or professions. Nevertheless, the gentlemanly ideal attached a great importance to leisure, a point emphasised by Rupert Wilkinson: 'The gentleman's premium on leisure was closely bound up with the amateur tradition, so faithfully perpetuated by the public schools.'[10]

On the frontiers of Queensland and British Columbia, British gentlemen formed a masculine 'caste'. That is, they shared a similar background, education and outlook which bound them in a loose social formation, to protect which they went to great lengths. On both frontiers, expatriate gentlemen sought to maintain and police their status via a configuration of practices through which they 'performed' as gentlemen. These practices included social monitoring, patronage and the practice of the muscular virtues, which combined to establish and defend a position of masculine dominance among frontier men. Through these practices frontier gentlemen sought to recreate and maintain the social and gender boundaries of the metropole. In Queensland, the masculine ideal was embodied in gentleman squatters who, as a caste, formed a masculine elite, as well as a political and social elite.[11] In British Columbia, the same hegemonic ideals were practised by transplanted gentlemen. However, the gentlemanly caste was more diverse in British Columbia than in Queensland, and included fur traders, naval officers and men 'on spec'.

By the mid-nineteenth century then, significant numbers of men of similar genteel background, upbringing and education emigrated to Queensland and British Columbia. There are two aspects to the concept of 'class'. Firstly, there is the relatively objective element of socio-economic status, that is, one's wealth and family 'breeding'. Secondly, there is a more subjective element, an awareness that one's social status is shared by others, and that one has interests in common with these others. A more complex perspective includes the variables of power and prestige. These elements are usually closely connected, and wealth can of course confer both. While gentlemen were usually wealthy and possessed varying degrees of power and prestige, it is the consciousness that one had of being a gentleman that on the frontier was most significant, and where the concept of 'caste' is more useful. Caste refers to the social character a person derives from their profession or vocation, or from that of his or her family. This social character is independent of the caste member's individual personality. A caste is not a formal organisation, and its members may not necessarily constitute an active group. The term refers to a set of traits which form an important characterisation of an important number of people.[12] Caste is a particularly appropriate descriptor for Queensland's and British Columbia's frontier gentlemen. On the frontier, wealth was not a necessary condition for membership of the gentlemanly caste, although it certainly helped. More important was one's family background and a consciousness of a shared social character. Frontier gentlemen subscribed to the 'configuration of practice' which made a gentleman, and exhibited common 'tendencies' in thought and deed.

In Queensland emigrant gentlemen found that wool growing offered opportunity for wealth and independence. Since it became economically dominant in the early-nineteenth century, pastoralism has been seen as one of the foundations of Australian culture. Pastoralism's economic, social and mythic status has been proclaimed and affirmed in both romantic and popular representations and in more candid and realistic accounts of squatters and pastoral life.[13] Most of these works, to varying degrees, delve into squatters' backgrounds, and reveal that many had strong gentlemanly credentials. Stephen Roberts notes that 'the striking feature about the first squatters was how many of them were men of good birth, education and capital'.[14] In New South Wales Governor Gipps believed that 'among the Squatters of New South Wales are the wealthiest of the Land, occupying with the permission of Government thousands and tens of thousands of acres; Young men of good family and connexions in England. Officers of the Army and Navy, Graduates of Oxford and Cambridge are also in no small number amongst them.'[15] W. Stamer's *The Gentleman Emigrant: His Daily Life, Sports and Pastimes in Canada, Australia, and the United States*, published in 1872, was part travel guide, part emigration pamphlet and a cautionary self-help manual for would-be settlers. Stamer describes squatting as 'undoubtedly one of the most profitable pursuits open to the gentleman immigrant'.[16]

The gentlemen of British Columbia were a more occupationally diverse group than those of Queensland. Unlike pastoralism in Queensland, no one industry or occupation operated as a magnet for unemployable younger sons who had been given a few thousand pounds with which to make their own way in life. Nevertheless, British Columbia and other parts of Canada had attractions which appealed to the British gentleman's sense of adventure and aspirations. William Stamer knew what sort of men the Canadian frontier needed. The only men likely to succeed on the frontier were those with capital or, lacking such, who were possessed of 'iron thews and sinews'.[17] 'Sinewless [sic] mill operatives, effeminate clerks, and shopmen', he wrote, need not bother emigrating.[18] The intemperate, imprudent and lazy could stay at home. The cultivation of the soil was the proper activity for the gentleman emigrant and this required sobriety, industry and manly vigour. In Stamer's view Canada was one of the best locations for the gentleman of limited means, especially if he was married. If a gentleman was prudent, frugal and hardworking, he would at least make a comfortable living, if not accumulate great wealth. He would not be entirely dependent on the proceeds of his farm for his daily bread; and he would live well, if not sumptuously. His wife would have her piano, her flower-garden and her poultry-yard.[19] Thus the domestic order of the metropole would be reproduced in the colonies, together with male status as a landowner and breadwinner.

Patrick Dunae in *Gentlemen Emigrants* describes the manner in which English gentlemen, with contacts and some capital, and a buoyant confidence bestowed by their education and breeding, settled in Canada and 'imported, implanted, and nurtured a great many of the institutions, traditions and rituals associated with Britain'.[20] Dunae, while noting that gentleman emigrants came from a patriarchal society, does not interrogate the nature of this form of masculinity. For most of these gentlemen emigration meant wild sport and high adventure in the Canadian West. It meant wide open spaces and a life free of the crowds and social constraints of Britain. They would subdue the wilderness and, perhaps, a few Indians. They could exercise their grit, pluck and other manly virtues. Many went into 'ranching' on the prairies, an occupation conducive to the gentlemanly life. As pioneers in the Canadian West, they did not have to compete with an entrenched social elite, and could set the tone for others to follow.[21] On the Pacific coast, British Columbia was seen to hold particular advantages: 'There is no portion of the world's surface which possesses greater natural advantages, or a field more suited for the employment of the energies, industry and capital for the British Colonist...than...British Columbia.'[22]

In Queensland, numerous contemporary observers recorded their impressions of squatters and their lives, and revealed the prevalence of gentlemanly ideals on the Queensland frontier. The letters of Rachel Henning, for example, reveal that on the frontier of Northwest Queensland gentlemanly manners and habits were observed. She describes a typical Sunday scene: 'Biddulph arrayed in white trousers, white coat and regatta shirt (nobody ever sits in the parlour without a coat) is lazily reading in an armchair.'[23] Further on she mentions: 'On the whole, we are very well off having such a gentlemanly set of men in the house, for some of the sons of the bush are very rough; but I do not think Biddulph would ever stand living with anyone who had vulgar manners and habits.'[24] In Henning's view manliness included knowing how to dress and how to behave in polite company.

W.S.S. Tyrwhitt's *A New Chum in the Queensland Bush* is an account of 'the every-day life of a Colonist in the Bush'.[25] This includes a description of people according to their occupation and social status and 'squatters of course head the list'.[26] According to Tyrwhitt squatters are the 'natural aristocracy of the country', a position which they hold due to their superiority in enterprise, brains and hard work.[27] The squatter is 'monarch of all he surveys, and his will is law... they are almost to a man keen, far-sighted, hardworking men of the world. They are perhaps the most manly class that exists.'[28] In the bush it takes one to know one and squatters will freely give their hospitality to a stranger provided he gives his name 'and has the manner of a gentleman'.[29] It was not always possible to tell a gentleman by appearance. The outward signs of 'gentlemanness', how one was dressed and groomed, for example, were often missing:

> The men in the bush all dressed alike, in moleskin trousers and Crimean or dark twill cotton shirts, with the sleeves rolled up above the elbows. Some kept themselves clean and others did not, but it was not the men of the highest class who were the cleanest, by any means; the working man who had always been used to doing things for himself was often cleaner and tidier in his appearance and habits than the Duke's son who had been used to nurses and valets to look after him. Very few men had coats of any sort. No one minded what a man wore or how he looked if he was a good fellow.[30]

In some ways, a lack of concern about one's appearance might indicate a lack of caste consciousness. However, in a society where everyone often dressed alike, other factors became important. Speech, manner and connections were of increased significance in delineating one's caste. This is where the public school education equipped gentlemen with the manners and habits that distinguished them from non-gentlemen.

Being educated, frontier gentlemen were literate, and recorded their experiences in letters, diaries and memoirs. Collectively, these narratives reveal how the gentlemanly caste was maintained, and how 'gentlemanness' was performed, on the colonial frontier. The narratives of four gentlemen – Patrick Leslie, Oscar de Satgé, Arthur Bushby and Edmund Hope Verney – are representative of the many accounts of frontier life penned by gentlemen. They provide ample evidence not only of the existence of a gentlemanly caste on both frontiers, and the importance placed on the possession of the gentlemanly virtues, thousands of miles away from the society in which they were conceived, but also of the desire to be perceived as respectable by those who remained in Britain. As Ann Laura Stoler has observed, Europeans in the colonies were 'so often viewed disparagingly from the metropole as *parvenus*, cultural incompetents, morally suspect, and indeed "fictive" Europeans, somehow distinct from the real thing'.[31]

Although by birth and breeding these men were gentleman, the colonial frontier seems to have brought to the surface a significant degree of concern surrounding their status. The social fluidity of the frontier and the lack of established networks meant that social position had to be re-negotiated or re-asserted. There is a self-conscious tinge to their assertions of respectable behaviour and dutiful deeds. This is suggested by the large amount of attention at least three of these gentlemen give to their own behaviour or the behaviour of others. Perhaps the firmness with which they held their gentlemanly ideals, and then wrote about it, was a means of arresting their concerns. These 'autobiographies' of Leslie, De Satgé, Bushby and Verney show how each man occupied his place in the caste, maintained this position and policed caste boundaries. Devoted to the archetypal masculine pursuits of exploration, conquest and settlement, these men collectively embodied that combination of character and muscularity which constituted the gentlemanly ideal and saw the frontier as a place where these virtues could be practised and fostered.

The three Leslie brothers, Patrick, George and Walter, of whom Patrick was the eldest, sons of the Tenth Laird of Warthill, Aberdeenshire, are inextricably part of the history of squatting in Queensland and typify the gentlemanly ethos which pervaded the squatting ranks. Prior to leaving Britain their father wrote letters to each son, setting out what he saw as the potential dangers that awaited a gentleman in the colonies, and imparting stern advice on how to avoid them. His advice to Patrick is typical:

> I sit down to recall to your recollection some of the instructions which you have received during your early years and to add a few words of advice which may prove useful to you when beyond the reach of parental councils.[32]

After pointing out that 'you are going...into a new world...where you will find the general standard of morality and religion at a very low ebb', Patrick's father proceeded to counsel his son to guide him through the impending moral morass and equip him for a prosperous life. The first injunction concerned religion:

> Never, never my Dear Boy forget or neglect the precepts of your God. He will never withhold all his powerful assistance in forwarding your progress in the paths of virtue, nor his Almighty protection in all the dangers to which you may be exposed.[33]

The second concerned character:

> The strictest honor and integrity, accompanied by a rigid adherence to the truth and straightforwardness in all your thoughts, words and actions, are not only of primary importance but of indispensable obligation... and can only be attained by accustoming yourself to habitual reflection, and to a cool and attentive application of your reasoning faculties.[34]

The Laird had some advice regarding the people Patrick was likely to meet:

> The propriety of your own conduct and manners as a Gentleman can alone secure to you their future attentions and regard. Cautious circumspection will be necessary in your general intercourse.[35]
>
> Be particular and select in the choice of your companions, and still more so if possible in establishing friendships.[36]

The Laird clearly nursed a number of anxieties about the place to which his son was going. In William Leslie's mind, the Australian frontier was a place of insecurity and moral danger. There were traps for novices. One of these was alcohol and Patrick was admonished to pursue a course of moderation:

> Never allow yourself to acquire a strong taste for liquors when living alone, and in company, half a bottle of wine is fully sufficient for all the legitimate purposes of conviviality. On festive occasions you should always retire at as early an hour as propriety will permit, and invariably when symptoms of boisterous mirth or inebriety appear.

The frontier also possessed sexual pitfalls. The maintenance of proper relations between the sexes was of utmost importance, and the consequences of laxity in this regard could be disastrous:

> Illicit intercourse betwixt the sexes is a vice of the most debasing nature, and of the most pernicious tendency. However little of it may be thought of nowadays, no one can read the Bible without finding it denounced as a sin of the first magnitude in the sight of God, and the perverted minds and shattered constitutions of the generality of youth bear ample testimony to its horrible effects.

Financial propriety was as important as sexual propriety and what the Bible was to the latter, bookkeeping was to the former:

> Inconsiderate expenditure is also a rock on which many a promising youth has made a shipwreck of his future fortunes. Continuing the practice of keeping a regular and exact account of your receipts and disbursements, will, at all times, place in your view the proper limits to which your liberality and economy ought to be restrained.

He should not waste time when he should be working at making himself an independent man:

> In a young man, too, being much in company is attended with a most unprofitable waste of time which ought to be devoted to useful pursuits, besides not infrequently substituting thoughtless and dissipated habits for those of active exertion, and disease and misery for health and independence.

William Leslie wrote similar letters to his two younger sons, Walter and George, when they joined their elder brother in Australia. Presumably he imparted similar written advice to his eldest son William, who perpetuated Leslie family values in Hong Kong.

William Senior was not going to let his sons build their contributions to the Empire on shaky moral foundations. In his imagination the frontier was an uncivilised environment, a dangerous place where young gentlemen, free from the constraints of metropolitan society, would face many temptations and destructive influences. Men like Patrick would be tested and would need all the virtues British society wanted in its men on the frontier. William Leslie's letters espouse most of the values the early Victorians saw as desirable in a male: character, independence, Christianity, sobriety, sexual propriety, self-reliance and a strong work ethic. These would protect and advance a young man as he made his way in a new society.

Patrick Leslie arrived in Sydney in March 1835 to manage a cattle station owned by his uncle, Walter Davidson. Davidson was one of the founders of pastoralism in Australia – he had been a partner of John Macarthur in the breeding of merinos and this connection was to be instrumental in the lives of the Leslie brothers. According to Patrick, Davidson's property, Colleroi, had not been well managed by his Australian partner, Jones.[37] By his own account Patrick worked hard to improve it, making decisions and incurring expenses which eventually severely strained relations with his uncle and which led to protracted legal proceedings.[38] In the meantime Patrick's younger brothers, George and Walter, arrived to join the 'New South Wales venture', as it was known within the Leslie family. The brothers were financed by their father, each possessing £1,000 in capital.

In 1839 Patrick met explorer Allan Cunningham and heard of the grazing prospects on the Darling Downs. In 1840 Patrick and Walter set out with two convict servants to see the region for themselves. They established a camp at a place called Falconer's Plains and Patrick, and a convict lifer called Murphy, pressed on to the Downs, and saw its pastoral potential. George had remained behind in the south to assemble the men, stock and equipment needed to start their own enterprise. At the end of their 600-mile trek they set up a head station at Toolburra, and established other stations as they explored further.[39]

Patrick Leslie has been described by Stephen Roberts as 'the very type of squatting pioneer'. Absolutely fearless and something of a rough jewel, he was active and energetic, 'hale fellow well met' and 'the prince of bushmen'.[40] Fearless, active and energetic he may well have been, but beneath the egalitarian bushman suggested by Roberts dwelt a gentleman who was well aware of his social position and who carefully assessed everyone he came in contact with as to their suitability for friendship and business. Patrick Leslie was a man acutely aware of his membership of the gentlemanly caste, who undertook extensive monitoring of himself and others in order to protect this status.

In giving Patrick Leslie parting advice his father had cautioned that his behaviour had to be beyond reproach and that he should be careful who he associated with. Patrick Leslie was well aware of the importance of being a gentleman and of mixing with other gentlemen, and he heeded his father's advice from the outset. His letters, mostly to his parents, over the next ten or so years, relate his progress on the colonial frontier, both economically and socially. When not detailing the price of land or wool, Leslie is accounting for his behaviour and assessing the behaviour of others. On arriving in Sydney, Patrick Leslie wrote to his parents of his travelling companion, Donaldson: 'My friend Donaldson has been of the greatest assistance to me ever since I left England, in every way. He is a most gentlemanly fellow and quite different from what I thought on first sight.'[41] Not everyone deserved this accolade, but it would have been ungentlemanly to let on: 'Nothing is more unpleasant,' wrote Patrick of an Irishman, Captain MacDonnell, who had also been on board, 'than to sit and hear a man telling stories at a dinner table, which from their nature it was impossible to believe, and still you must almost seem to swallow them as gospel, as no gentleman would appear to disbelieve what another says, whatever he may do in his own breast.'[42]

Patrick was confident that on board ship his behaviour and that of his friend Donaldson was above reproach – that they had behaved as gentlemen: 'I am happy to say that both Donaldson and I landed from the *Emma Eugenia* satisfied that no one on board would point his finger at us and say that we have never done an ungentlemanly thing all the time we were on the vessel.'[43] In Sydney, he had clear intentions of mixing only with his caste; he was not going to risk his status by associating with other members of society: 'There may be great temptations in Sydney to vice as there are in all towns but from what Mr. Jones tells me and from the little I have seen myself – I am happy to say that there is plenty of society of first class people for any man without the least need of associating with any other sort.'[44]

Patrick's class consciousness is at the fore when he apprises his parents on the 'state of society in New South Wales'.[45] He carefully monitored who was 'in' and who was 'out' of society. There were clearly well-defined grades of people and accepted ways of 'getting into' the right circle. New South Wales society was

> excellent and the first people here are so very particular that you cannot get into their circle without first rate introductions and can only keep in it by first rate conduct. The first error in a man's conduct here (which would be scarcely noticed at home) would send him out of the first immediately, which is most proper in a country where there are so many different grades.[46]

The 'first people' were clearly protective of their primacy, and had rules designed to maintain their position and ensure the continuance of their caste.

In Patrick's opinion, not everyone who belonged to the gentry had what it took to be a gentleman. No matter how likeable a man, lack of refinement and social know-how could not be hidden. Friend Ernest Dalrymple received condemnation and pity for his failure to perform as a gentleman:

> It is shameful to send a man out in the world with such an education and his own knowledge of it makes him very shy and backward. Everyone (when they know him) likes him very much but Erny has not the remotest idea of the common usages of society and

is frightened at the sight of a Lady. How or where he could have been tutored since he ought to have been in society I can't tell but he certainly is free enough of any outward appearance of a high caste man.[47]

Patrick's opinions of his fellows are not merely the precipitate musings of a callow youth. Age and experience does not alter his gentlemanly predispositions. After ten years in the colonies he is still assessing his fellow settlers: 'The Hays seem very nice young fellows and will I think make capital settlers – R. Farquharson came up to Brisbane by the last steamer...he is not the same style of man that the Hays are by any means.'[48]

If a fellow met with his approval, Patrick would look out for him, to ensure the new arrival avoids the social pitfalls that await:

> You may assure Lord Strathallan that I have the greatest pleasure in paying Fairholme every attention. He is very young and a fine lad as I have seen for long and his blood is exceptional which is a great thing. I took a great fancy to him as well from his nice gentleman like letters and appearance...as Mr. Kinghorn who was to have Fairholme with him at some of his stations is (tho I have no doubt an honest man), not at all in that society of which a man of Fairholme's birth should be associated as Kinghorn is in very different society.[49]

Patrick Leslie wanted to ensure that Fairholme joined the right caste. Fairholme wrote like a gentleman, looked like a gentleman and most importantly had a gentleman's 'blood'. He would have been a very valuable acquisition to the colonial gentleman caste, and could not be lost to a lesser caste. Leslie's monitoring of self and others indicates that he was extremely self-conscious about his behaviour and demeanour and the behaviour and demeanour of other men. He had firm ideas of what was and what was not gentlemanly behaviour. He took it upon himself to ensure the survival of the gentlemanly caste on the colonial frontier, by policing who qualified for membership and who did not. Donaldson, the Hays and Fairholme clearly qualified. Farquharson and Dalrymple appear to be borderline cases, and Kingholm was certainly not of the gentlemanly caste.

Despite his endeavours to ensure that gentlemanly standards were maintained, there was one aspect of the gentlemanly ideal at least which did not survive on the Queensland frontier – the gentleman's aversion to physical labour. The life of the typical squatter was not one of gentlemanly leisure. While the most important asset they brought to the Queensland frontier was their capital, they were also required to be practical men. In their new environment the threat posed to one's gentlemanly status by performing physical work was low. As Charles Eden advised his readers: 'No one loses caste by performing bodily labour, indeed it is just the reverse; and the more a man can do for himself the better he will get on.'[50] Men accumulated their skills quickly, and once they were on the job necessity dictated that they acquired a wide variety of skills.[51]

Patrick Leslie had a leisurely initiation into the physical demands of squatting. In the five years between arriving in Australia and taking up land on the Darling Downs, Patrick acquired his practical skills on properties owned by the Macarthurs, his uncle's Colleroi property and his own farm, Dunheved. As a guest of the Macarthurs at Camden he commenced his squatting career, not by crutching sheep or building fences, but in a distinctly gentlemanly mode: 'We start after breakfast, on horseback, ride over some part of the farm and visit different flocks of sheep till half past 1 or 2 o'clock then return to the house, have lunch, change our horses for fresh ones, and ride till dinner.'[52] In due course, however, he acquired the requisite knowledge and skills, learning about shearing and sorting wool on James Macarthur's Murrumbidgee property and becoming a horse breaker on Colleroi. On his farm Dunheved near Penrith he grew small crops and ran a dairy.[53]

In his letters to his parents, Patrick Leslie is clearly trying to reassure them that he has 'performed' as a gentleman, that he has practised the 'cautious circumspection' recommended by his father and maintained his position in the gentlemanly caste. He has done his bit to ensure the continuation of the caste and its masculine values by recruiting others who conform to its gentlemanly standards. Indeed, the letters themselves constitute a gentlemanly performance as their language and erudition is that of a gentleman.

Oscar De Satgé's gentlemanly credentials commence with the fact that he was the second son of Ernest Valentine, first vicomte de Satgé de St. Jean and his wife Caroline, daughter of the high sheriff of Brecon. While his family's lineage could be traced to antiquity, his father was exiled from France for his involvement in a royalist plot.[54] De Satgé was educated at Rugby from 1849 until 1852 and at 17 he and his brother Ernest set sail for Melbourne aboard the *Essex*. In his memoir *Pages from the Journal of a Queensland Squatter*, De Satgé states: 'My brother and I, yielding to the *res angusta domi* of a considerable household, determined to try our fortunes in Australia.'[55] In other words, his family being large and of narrow means, the two of them were compelled to make their own way in the world.

After working as a clerk for the Gold Commissioner in Victoria (he had a letter of introduction to Governor Latrobe), De Satgé moved to Queensland in the mid-1850s to gain experience in the pastoral industry. In 1861, in partnership with George Sandeman he stocked and developed Gordon Downs and Wolfgang stations in the Peak Downs District of Central Queensland, near present-day Clermont. In 1872 he bought a run at Aramac in Western Queensland in partnership with James Milson. De Satgé's memoir describes his life firstly as a worker in the pastoral industry, and subsequently as a manager and owner of a number of large runs. His first encounter with the bush was on horseback through Cunningham's Gap to the Darling Downs town of Warwick. On meeting his brother in Warwick they rode to his Mangoola station. En route they camped, the first time he had slept in the bush. He attributed his enjoyment of it to being 'young, strong and fresh'.[56]

The men Oscar De Satgé met in Queensland (and it appears from his journal that he met only men) were invariably 'gentlemen'. His memoir clearly reveals the existence of a gentlemanly caste, which exercised political and social power. The members of this caste not only possessed the manners and habits of gentlemen, but were also well endowed with the muscular virtues. On the whole, De Satgé thought the squatters of the Darling Downs 'were a fine set of men; generally men of education and mostly of refinement, who had brought to that favoured portion of Queensland the habits and ways of gentlemen'.[57] That they were of this ilk was of great political importance for 'if the Darling Downs did for many years... rule Queensland to somewhat selfish ends, this early legislative power might certainly have fallen into far less scrupulous and more dangerous hands'.[58] Caste members included Arthur Hodgson of Eton Vale, Hope and Ramsay of Rosalie Plains, Deuchar of Glengalan, Kent and Weinholt of Maryvale, Fassifern and Jondaryn, Issac of Gowrie and the Bells of Jimbour. These men 'left little to be desired in the way of reputation for industry, courage, honesty of purpose, and absolute good faith; their word being their bond, their agreements seldom written, their servants well used, their animals cared for, and their homesteads open to the most ungrudging hospitality'.[59] In De Satgé's view these men shared certain personal traits, came from similar backgrounds and had common political interests. He clearly saw them as members of a caste of gentlemen.

De Satgé believed that the 'younger school' would do well to remember these men and emulate them, struggle as they did, trusting in providence and fair seasons, and to the wheel of 'Colonial history'. He reminded them that they had civic duties, and should not allow any 'socialistic or other combination to do them out of their legislative rights, as gentleman squatters kept their tenure of the land to the advantage of all classes'.[60] To De Satgé the individualism, sense of duty and *noblesse oblige*, of gentlemen squatters, which he took for granted, were evidence of their caste and class superiority. In 1869 De Satgé himself recognised the obligations of a gentleman to serve and lead, standing for the parliamentary seat of Clermont and Copperfield in order to afford 'security to the pastoral interest'.[61]

Not only did these men possess the virtues exclusive to gentlemen, they also practised to the highest order the muscular virtues. The owner of Waverly, Macartney, was 'full of physical vigour' and could 'ride a hundred miles and over in one day, and that on the same horse'.[62] Henry Gregory 'was as tough as whalebone, and used to ride from Gwambagyne to Burandowan, a two days ride...with one pocket full of oatmeal and the other of sugar, and no other provision, disdaining, in that semi-tropical climate, blanket and ration bags'.[63] Sydney Beavan Davis was a good neighbour at Capella and 'a quondam hard rider of the Cotwold and V.W.H. packs'.[64] Cheeseborough Macdonald, the owner of Logan Downs, was 'gallant'.[65] William Kilgour of Surbiton was 'keen, hardy and resolute'.[66]

Like Patrick Leslie, De Satgé had to overcome any aversion to physical labour he might have held, and the reader of his journal is left in no doubt that he too practised the muscular virtues. At his brother's property, Mangoola, he acquired the skills of a stockman: mustering and branding calves, breaking in horses, lambing and sheep washing, working from daylight to dark.[67] He led cattle and sheep firstly to Ipswich and then on a longer journey to Victoria. He came back from the 'Never Never' (the country around the Dawson River), 'a good deal wiser and more self-reliant'.[68] He was very much a mix of tough stockman and polished gentleman. He was equally capable of droving sheep and cattle and building yards and sheds as he was of fraternising with the colonial elite at the Brisbane Club or the Melbourne Cup.

The publication by De Satgé of his journal, in which he praises his peers and flourishes his own manly attributes, was itself an act which perpetuated the colonial gentlemanly caste. De Satgé's performance as a gentleman and the performances of other gentlemen were recorded in his journal for others to read. Like Leslie's letters, De Satgé's memoirs demonstrate his education and erudition – and perhaps his sense of history. It would no doubt have been gauche to boast openly about one's virtues. In De Satgé's book there is no sense of the extempore that one might expect from a daily journal. *Pages from the Journal of a Queensland Squatter* is a well-considered production, with little spontaneity and none of the immediacy of a daily journal. It is more like a moral fable with a didactic purpose, which is to promote the worthiness of the gentleman caste. It is the promotion of sectional interest disguised as memoir.

In British Columbia too, British gentlemen worked hard at maintaining their status. Edmund Hope Verney was commander of the gunboat HMS *Grappler* on Vancouver Island from 1862 to 1865. He was the eldest son of Sir Henry Verney MP, second baronet of Claydon estate. He spent a short time at Harrow before joining the Royal Navy in 1851 when he was 12 years old. Verney was given command of the *Grappler* when he was 24, after establishing a good reputation during the Crimean War and in India at the time of the 'mutiny'. Prior to assuming command of the *Grappler* he served on the HMS *Calliope* and HMS *Havannah* in South America and Australia and on the HMS *Arethena* in the Mediterranean.[69] Hudson's Bay Company Doctor John Helmcken described the officers stationed on Vancouver Island as 'generally well off and connected with the landed gentry...they behaved themselves like what they were – gentlemen'.[70] While on Vancouver Island Verney wrote regularly to his father, sending him letters in dated instalments, very much like a journal. His letters encompassed a broad range of topics. Most frequently he wrote about naval affairs, but also about many aspects of colonial life. He wrote about colonial politics and his fellow colonists, about the landscape and the wildlife, and about his private pursuits such as fishing, riding and gardening.

Like De Satgé and the Leslies in Queensland, Verney in British Columbia was very concerned about the state of colonial society and the type of men who inhabited it. Scattered throughout the letters are character assessments of his fellow naval officers, colonial administrators and settlers. Verney's judgements of others reveal much about himself, as his own values are expressed in his assessments of his fellow colonists. He is also very concerned to give accounts of his own actions, displaying a strong sense of personal responsibility and duty. Right behaviour in all situations, the correct performance of gentlemanly conduct, either personal or professional, is of the utmost importance. Verney's concern for the 'tone of the colony' is expressed in his contrasting views of the Anglican Bishop, Hill, and Governor Douglas:

> If the Bishop would go to England and fetch out a good wife, and if you would send us out a good Governor with a good wife I believe the whole tone of the colony would be immensely raised: nobody seems to respect any-body else, but people aim at establishing the most odious fraternity: I hear a grocer address a lieutenant R.N. by his unadorned surname, with every familiarity.[71]
>
> Considering his great disadvantages governor Douglas is a wonderful man, but he has no pretension to be a high-minded, superior gentleman; he is very pompous and ridiculous, and always cruizes [sic] about in uniform, with a bombardier [sic] of Engineers lashed onto a cavalry sword following in his wake: this solemn procession of two may be seen parading Victoria every evening.[72]

Governor Douglas could not be trusted to know with whom he should mix. Verney had observed the Governor talking to a man who was living in adultery with an Australian woman who 'should not be admitted to decent society'. Verney felt that while such loose social mores may well have been acceptable in the days of the Hudson's Bay Company, now 'it shocks refined people, and turns the balance the wrong way, with those who are not very decided'.[73] He was clearly keen to maintain the social distinctions of Britain on the colonial frontier. Moreover, in Verney's view, 'refined people' needed to set an example for the social waverers. 'Those who were not very decided' could not be trusted to act appropriately.

Men lower down the social rank than the Bishop and the Governor, those ostensibly of the same rank as Verney, were assessed for their family pedigree and character, and not all could be accepted at face value:

> One man was introduced to me, bearing the honoury title of captain, in virtue of having once served in a Turkish regiment; he stated himself to be a relation to Lord Galway, and said he had come out because his father-in-law said he had no energy, and now having proved his energy, would I lend him, or stand surety for him for £60, to go home again, or failing that, would I introduce him to the Governor and ask him to lend it? He went on board the Bacchante, and amused the mess by handing round his marriage lines to prove his identity: he

may be seen any-day swaggering down Government street, with a generally horse-y appearance, and a little cavalry forage cap stuck on one side of his head. I believe he is going to the diggings after all, so his father-in-law will be delighted with his energy: I think he may very likely turn out to be a groom out of place: he certainly is out of place here.[74]

Others come from well-recognised stock, and demonstrate the right qualities:

Sitting alongside me at the moment is a young man of the name of Everard, a great-nephew of Lord Berners: I have often heard you speak with great admiration of Lord Berners, so I thought you would like me to be civil to his great-nephew... he seems a very sensible sort of young man, really worth something. He is the sort of immigrant who is wanted in this colony: not to go about telling people who are their relations in England, but to settle down manfully to whatever work they can get.[75]

Verney, like Patrick Leslie, assumed responsibility for assessing gentlemen new to the colonial frontier, and ensuring that the right type was welcomed into the colonial gentleman's caste. Connections were important, but alone they were not enough. A new colonist had to approach the task of colonisation with a manly attitude. In other cases, appearances and pedigree could be deceptive, and some performances were fraudulent:

Dundas... told me that Hastings had gone off to Callao: I dare say you will remember that you gave him a letter of introduction to me, and at the same time wrote to me about him... he dined on board with me one day; he never presented your letter as he said he had lost it: he has now swindled several people, Dundas amongst the number, and gone off leaving a number of unpaid debts... I thought Hastings was a safe character both because he brought a letter from you and because Dundas thought well of him and asked me to be civil to him: his manners were certainly engaging and gentlemanlike.[76]

On the other hand, the status of gentleman gives the holder a great deal of latitude in Verney's mind. The commander of the British Fleet at Esquimalt, Admiral Denman, leaves a lot to be desired in terms of administrative competence and management: 'However, he is a gentleman, and that covers a multitude of sins.'[77] Verney's concern with the behaviour of others is an extension of his own self-reflection and concern about 'right' behaviour. In his view the behaviour of some people puts them outside of 'decent society'. Verney identified with a group of people which included the Bishop, Dundas and even Admiral Denman, who he considered shared the behaviours and attitudes of gentlemen. They belonged to the gentlemanly caste of Victoria.

Verney's letters reveal that he was principally concerned with two aspects of life: right conduct on his own part and advancement in his career. The most enduring topic of the correspondence was Verney's prospects for promotion, an issue which constantly exercised his mind. Early in his posting to Vancouver Island he told his father that he liked his new appointment very much; indeed, 'it is the best a lieutenant can hold'.[78] A month after expressing his satisfaction, he was pondering the likelihood of promotion, which would have meant leaving Vancouver Island, expecting to hear of it early in the new year of 1863. The new year came and went and by April, with no word pending, he was considering renting a permanent residence. In August that year he asserted that he had ceased worrying about promotion, content to be 'philosophical' about attending to his daily duties.

The year 1864 brought fresh hope and he began lobbying the Governor to intercede with the Admiralty on his behalf. Presumably this was to no avail as several months later he asked his father to wield his influence. The opportunity for service on the royal yacht at the end of which promotion 'is sure' passed Verney by and he considered requesting a personal recommendation from his admiral. This failed to yield a result and in the middle of 1865 Verney finished his tour of duty on Vancouver Island and departed at the same rank with which he arrived.[79] After 14 years in the Royal Navy, he was still a lieutenant.

While a desire for promotion is a natural part of military service, Verney's emotions in this regard varied from apparent nonchalance to anxiety, as he alternately professed to be entirely happy in his position as commander of the *Grappler* and implored his father to lobby the Admiralty on his behalf. It is clear that Verney had expectations, and that he led his life in a deliberate manner which he believed would bring him personal and professional success: 'Promotion is about achievement, making one's mark in the world.'[80] Promotion for Verney was not merely an occupational reward, but would have been the capstone of his gentlemanly life. Despite professional disappointment Verney felt that he 'must just go steadily on with my duty and trust'. He is sure that 'the man who acts from a sense of duty must always stand higher than he who acts on impulse'.[81]

Verney was committed to the gentlemanly ideal of voluntary service, in the form of a position on the female immigration committee and as honorary administrator of lighthouses. Voluntary service was a way he could make a mark:

> I am going the road to distinction by working at the lighthouse, to bring them up to high order and efficiency, and on the committee of immigration I will try to be of use, and under the patronage and with the advice of the dear bishop, I may leave a worthy footstep behind me.[82]

He also appears to have adopted Smiles's maxims regarding the necessity of self-reflection. He thought the climate of Vancouver Island conducive to 'higher enjoyments and worthier aspirations':

> I can see one or two decided improvements in myself lately: I am getting into the habit of regular private morning and evening prayer which has always hitherto been fitful and irregular, I am regulating my accounts, and writing a small scrap of daily journal.[83]

It seems that conditions on the frontier, in Verney's case at least, encouraged the virtues of self-discipline, prudence and diligence. Verney would have been an exemplary case study for Samuel Smiles's *Self Help*.

Compared to his Queensland counterparts, Verney avoided physical labour and placed a premium on leisure, though he did not take his advantages entirely for granted:

> I can really not be too thankful for having got this appointment: it seems quite strange to me to rise in the morning and feel that I have not a care or anxiety: full leisure of mind and body to read, or to do a little nautical astronomy: so much to do that I can never reproach myself with being idle, so little to do that I am free to choose my own employments.[84]

As Verney did not perform physical labour there is perhaps a difference in this respect between him, and Leslie and De Satgé. Unlike these men, Verney seems not to have considered himself a settler, and it was not necessary for him to perform physical labour to establish himself as an independent man. He already had a respectable manly occupation.

Nevertheless, Verney practised manliness by hunting and horse riding, setting off on a solo tour of British Columbia on horseback. However, in his outdoor recreational pursuits he kept physical exertion to a minimum: when he went duck shooting he took two of his crew along to paddle the canoe.[85]

The emphasis on conduct in Verney's letters, like Patrick Leslie's to his parents, is to reassure his father that he is performing as a gentleman. While comfortable and assured of their status in Britain, in an environment where society was less settled and more fluid, Verney and Leslie were concerned about their status. In giving accounts of their behaviour they were also reassuring themselves. Through surveillance of self and others, and the careful exercise of patronage, they sought to recreate and perpetuate the gentlemanly caste of the metropole, and to separate the frauds from the genuine article.

If Edmund Hope Verney went to British Columbia with a sense of purpose and duty borne of military service, and if Patrick Leslie and Oscar De Satgé went to Queensland to establish their manly independence, Arthur Thomas Bushby's ambitions were less well defined. Despite being the son of a London merchant and owner of West Indian estates, Bushby was not attracted to the business world. Nor did his training in voice, piano, violin and Italian equip him with skills in demand on the British Columbia frontier. Nevertheless, Bushby found his niche in the nascent society, largely due to his status as a gentleman and his ability to court and befriend the influential, including the Governor Sir James Douglas, who eventually accepted him as a son-in-law. Dorothy Blakely Smith has edited Bushby's journals and describes him as a 'sensitive, intelligent, generous-hearted, and sometimes rather naïve young man who had come from the very centre of British civilisation'.[86] According to Smith the journals not only record the impact of the frontier on such a young man but are also 'a frank and immediate comment on men and affairs in early British Columbia'.[87] An alternative interpretation is that the journals provide an insight into the operations of the gentlemanly caste in early British Columbian society, where one's connections and social skills could overcome practical deficiencies. Although Vancouver Island's gentlemanly caste differed from Leslie's and De Satgé's milieu, the existence of a group of gentlemen acting as a caste is evident from Bushby's journal.

No description of Arthur Bushby is more apt than the appellation 'decent chap'. He is thoroughly likeable, relaxed in the company of women and men, fond of a lark and ready to take part in whatever the colonial frontier has to offer. His life in British Columbia perfectly illustrates the maxim that who you know is more important than what you know. While he lacked commercial or practical skills, Bushby's social skills and musical proclivities propelled him to the centre of colonial society. He made connections that would prove both fruitful and enduring on his voyage to British Columbia: 'Met a great many British Columbians Mrs & Col Moody an excellent person – The clergyman Mr. Crickmer & his wife – a civil engineer Mr. Cochrane & his wife – Bedford and Burnaby on board also a young fellow, named Elwyn – going out on speck.'[88]

Bushby's first day on Vancouver Island – which happened to be Christmas Day – set the tone for the rest of the year: 'On getting to the Hotel Xmas day – we determined to have a good dinner so some 12 of us sat down to [sic] at 5/6 a head – 12 bottles of ale what a treat & we enjoyed ourselves with a vengeance. After we adjourned to a large drinking saloon & regaled ourselves with hot whiskey punch.'[89] Bushby found life on Vancouver Island very convivial, spending a great deal of time socialising and drinking and he immersed himself in Victoria's drinking culture. He made the acquaintance of the officers of the Royal Navy stationed at Esquimalt, and his visits were occasions for imbibing beer and sherry. Bushby frequently enjoyed the Navy's hospitality and was often given a hammock to bunk in after a convivial evening aboard one of its vessels. A trip to Langley with Colonel Moody commenced with 'wine and spirits ad lib'.[90] The gentlemanly pursuit of leisure, noted by Rupert Wilkinson, was taken very seriously in mid-nineteenth-century Victoria, though perhaps not in the way the gentlemanly creed implied. Bushby's journal entry for Wednesday, 9 February 1859, reveals the flavour of his social life:

> On Wednesday some 12 of us dined with Lennard – went to the Phil afterwards – & Franklin after that. Dropped into Begbie's at 11 o'clock & then took a walk with him came back in time for a champagne breakfast with Major Foster and some 8 others at the French Hotel – mooned abt with the fellows – had some more champagne & cigars – then started for Esquimalt with Begbie Crease Bob and Lennard to see him off p steamer – but as she did not sail until 12 o'clock Friday morng – Skinner (who was with us) insisted upon our turning off at his house – dined us there – gave us all a shakedown.[91]

Finding an occupation and earning an income was less of a priority. Bushby notes in his journal after Christmas: 'We find it very dull here &

[sic] nothing to do so we must sit idle until a good time comes.'[92] What was a priority was meeting the local elite. In these first few days in Victoria Bushby became friends with James Begbie, at that time the colony's only judge, the Reverend Edward Cridge, barrister Henry Pellew Crease and Chartres Brew, who was to become Chief Inspector of Police, gold commissioner and stipendiary magistrate. These friendships were to become valuable.

The friendship with Moody, Burnaby and Cochrane yielded Bushby's first business opportunity – a steam sawmill at Langley on the British Columbian mainland. Cochrane was to be the engineer, Burnaby the 'Victoria man and capitalist', and Bushby the manager.[93] While the venture ultimately came to nothing, it would seem that Bushby's membership of the gentlemanly caste was enough to secure his involvement, as he had no business qualifications. While he was finding his feet in the new colony, Bushby received other offers of employment from his new friends. The Reverend Crickmer offered him free board and lodging at his rectory, and lessons in Latin, Greek and theology, in return for help with the choir and the service, with a view to becoming an ordained minister. Bushby found the offer attractive, but as the sawmill venture was on the cards at the time, declined the invitation.[94] Henry Crease was able to provide employment copying law papers, and this gave Bushby something to do in between social engagements, which were numerous.

The most fruitful associations in the long run were with the Governor, James Douglas, and Judge James Begbie. On arriving in Victoria Bushby put his letters of introduction to Governor Douglas to immediate effect, which resulted in an invitation to dinner that same evening. Bushby seems to have enjoyed himself, describing the Governor as a 'jolly brick'.[95] Bushby was to spend a considerable amount of time at Government House, receiving his second invitation only a week after the first. On his first visit he noticed how pretty the Governor's daughter Agnes was and after his second visit wrote in his journal: 'They say she looks with no savage eye on me & [sic] true she is a stunning girl black eyes and hair & larky like the devil half a mind to go in for her.'[96] Go in for her he did, enjoying regular and frequent dinners, musical evenings and excursions with the Douglas family, eventually marrying Agnes in 1862.

The friendship with Begbie and the Governor eventually bore fruit when Begbie persuaded Douglas to appoint Bushby as his private secretary on £250 a year.[97] A few months later he had been appointed clerk of the court assize, clerk registrar and 'clerk of the arraigns &c'. Such multiple endowments surprised Bushby himself: 'As I had never been in a court of justice before the thing seemed strange indeed to me.'[98] As strange as the role was Bushby took to it with gusto:

> I had to open the proceedings by reading the proclamation of silence O Yes O Yes O Yes which I did at the top of my lungs... It was most strange work however I got through alright & once I heard my voice at the other end of the room I bawled away like fun.[99]

One advantage of being a decent chap was that one could count on the other chaps in time of need. In February 1859 Bushby and Burnaby received a summons for indecent and riotous conduct after a complaint by their landlord, after he had been disturbed by their late night singing, including a rendition of *God Save the Queen*. The gentleman caste of Victoria put on a performance in full regalia. In court the whole bar appeared for the defendants and naval officers attended in full dress uniform in support of Bushby and Burnaby. This display of caste unity caused the court to dismiss the case with costs.[100]

After he was married, Bushby's devotion to leisure diminished. His professional life developed, and he held a number of important government posts. He was Acting Post-Master General in 1866, Registrar-General until 1870 and was made Post-Master General in 1870. He was also a member of the legislative assembly from 1868 to 1870. As his professional life developed, so did his sense of public duty. Bushby had arranged the first concert of the Victoria Philharmonic Society in 1859.[101] In 1862 he became founding honorary secretary of the Royal Columbian Hospital, and in 1868 he became secretary of the Board of the New Westminster Public Library. He was involved with education in the colony as a member of the Board of School Trustees for New Westminster and was active in the New Westminster Rifle Corps.[102]

Bushby did not perform physical labour to earn a living, but when the opportunity presented itself, took to the outdoor life with enthusiasm:

> What a glorious sight the downright wood log hut, a fire place big enough to roast an ox &such a fire logs too big for me to lift we had a regular pic-nic lunch. Then Crease & myself jumped into a regular canoe & paddled away some 3 m. up a creek to shoot ducks – got wet through after a regular exploring excursion, had a jolly supper and shook down our blankets in the corner of the hut... next morning – Sunday – rambled about after [sic] descended and washed in the river – cold, but a capital bath.[103]

When this adventure took place Bushby was on a circuit with Judge Begbie. It was his first experience of outdoor life. While he enjoyed roughing it Bushby did not forsake his gentlemanly pleasures: 'Olgivie knocked me up a bed on the floor of his room in the H B Co's store – what a nice fellow he is such a fine fellow – we had our cigar in bed before going to sleep and a cup of hot coffee and a cigar before getting up.'[104]

The fact that Bushby benefited from his membership of the gentlemanly caste does not belie Smith's assessment that he was 'sensitive, intelligent, and generous-hearted'. Nor is there necessarily anything improper or unreasonable in the manner in which Bushby lived or the benefits he received from having the right friends. His life in British Columbia does, however, illustrate how a gentleman could 'get on' merely by virtue of his social status. Bushby does not appear to have been motivated by a sense of duty as was Edmund Hope Verney. His conduct may not have been above reproach when set by the standards of Patrick Leslie. Nevertheless, he was unquestionably a member of the gentlemanly caste of Victoria. He was a 'decent chap', and this virtue was as highly regarded in British Columbia as it was in Queensland.

Not all gentlemen had successful frontier experiences. Some found that the frontier did not respect class or caste distinctions. Despite one's efforts to maintain status, the frontier could bring a man down to the lower echelons of society. 'University Man' George Carrington found that his education was no advantage and that the frontier could be arduous for a gentleman who had no experience of physical labour. On the frontier, Carrington was for the first time confronted with the reality of having to earn a living. He started out with optimism and hope. Not being qualified for anything in particular, Oxford-educated Carrington spent his first weeks in North Queensland receiving one rejection after another as he sought employment in the towns. He got to know the working class:

> I had seen little, if anything, of the working man, and had no expectation that I should ever be driven to associate with them. Now I was brought suddenly to their level, and I was astonished to find what an intelligent and companionable set of men they were...they are far above the ordinary level. There is a total absence of that crawling deference to those who happen to have money in pockets and good clothes on their back.... the working men of Queensland are far superior, both in their mental and physical capacity to the same class in England.[105]

While Carrington's class consciousness could probably be taken for granted, phrases like 'driven to associate with them' and 'brought suddenly to their level' indicate that he was not expecting that the frontier could dilute, if not extinguish, distinctions between men. After exhausting all the possibilities of work in an office or behind a counter, he was forced to go to work on a road gang. He described his first day of physical labour:

> Now came the tug of war: I began chipping the granite with the crowbar and shovelling it out; but, alas, there were very few chips to shovel, and my hands began to blister, and my back to feel half broken, added to this the sun began to get hot, and I was streaming with perspiration. When the sun had reached the meridian, I felt as if I should never get to the bottom of my hole... the harder I worked the less results I seemed to produce... and I greeted the setting sun at last with a great sigh of relief. I was so tired and stiff that I could scarcely walk back to camp, and I had nothing to scarcely show for the last five hours work but blisters. The next morning we went out as before, and I resumed my toil; but I found it no better. So about 11 o'clock in the morning I threw down my tools in the hole, and fairly ran away.[106]

Carrington's ineptitude with the crowbar and shovel led him to feel 'a sense of disgrace and degradation'.[107] While superior in education and upbringing, he was vastly inferior when it came to physical work. Without connections, what counted amongst his class at home was of no value on the colonial frontier. Like many others in the bush, Carrington was forced to adopt a transient life. He wandered through the Queensland bush and towns, taking whatever work came to hand. He spent a considerable time as a shepherd, an occupation that he found to his liking, though the loneliness of the job could be unnerving. He worked on a surveyor's gang, stripped bark, was a blacksmith's mate, made candles and dug for gold.

Carrington summed up his colonial experiences:

> I have related as best I could, such incidents, in a very ordinary colonial experience, as would best illustrate the probable career of an educated man cast adrift in a colony, without many friends or practical knowledge; I say in a colony, because I should imagine that the result would be much the same as in any. The men who are wanted in the colonies are such as can work, and have been used to work.

An educated man will find, that his education, so far from being an advantage to him, will only expose him to the ridicule of those whose arms are stronger than his own, and whose frames are more enduring.[108]

Gentlemanly attributes did not necessarily transfer seamlessly to the frontier. The frontier could be a great leveller and those who held pretensions could be cut down to size.

While on the one hand William Stamer lauded gentlemen and the qualities they took to the frontier, on the other he observed that Australia was full of gentlemen who had squandered their capital, and had fallen off the social ladder: 'On one station we visited the storekeeper was a baronet's eldest son, the ration carrier an ex-lieutenant of dragoons, and the tailer of a quiet mob a young gentleman who had served in the navy, whilst the squatter, the master of all three, was an individual who could barely sign his own name, and whose manners were on a par with his education.'[109] Stressing the importance of capital for the would-be pastoralist, Stamer argued that £1,000 was woefully insufficient, £5,000 adequate and more was better.

In her memoirs of bush life Charlotte May Wright points out that not all gentlemen of the bush were particularly manly or at the head of the social list. She observed that the bush was full of 'broken down swells', young Englishmen who had been sent out to Australia because they were an embarrassment at home; younger sons without an inheritance and disgraced army men, ostensibly gentlemen, but who failed to live up to the gentlemanly ideal, either in Britain or in Queensland.[110] According to Wright upper-class men were particularly vulnerable to the hardships of the bush and resort to liquor was a common coping mechanism: such men had not been raised to work and were incapable of pulling their weight on a sheep station. They drank whenever they got the chance and eventually hit rock bottom. Wright wrote:

> There were very few people of the working class in the bush at the time, but numbers of what were called 'broken down swells', Englishmen who had been sent out to Australia to get rid of them; younger sons, cashiered army men etc. They had a dreadful life, and it was no wonder they drank whenever they got a chance, and sank lower and lower.[111]

> There were many waifs and strays who had almost lost their identity...They were 'on the spree' whenever they had any money,

though they always intended to go somewhere right away, to Brisbane, Sydney or even England, when they saved up enough, but the nearest pub on the road was generally the end of their journey and after a week or two of drinking they would crawl back, wrecks in mind and body... After wandering along the tracks in the heat they would go completely insane, and throw off all their clothes. Many men must have died in the bush, and never been heard of again.[112]

Implied in Wright's account are certain beliefs about class and gender. If the men Wright observed had been working class, their fate would have probably elicited little comment. Working-class men were supposed to be hard drinkers, less disciplined, less in control, and it would be unsurprising that some of them would be ruined by alcohol. Upper-class men, on the other hand, should have been able to exercise self-discipline and control. However, due to alcohol Wright's 'broken down swells' 'sank lower and lower' morally, physically, socially and psychologically. They 'lost their identity' as men, becoming 'waifs and strays', in other words, helpless children. Like the shepherds referred to by Carrington above, the insanity of these men rendered them unmanly, demonstrating that manliness was not a construct impervious to the physical and cultural environment in which it was performed.

The memoirs and letters of Patrick Leslie, Oscar De Satgé, Edmund Hope Verney and Arthur Bushby read like compendiums of the gentlemanly virtues. Many British gentlemen successfully transplanted themselves to the frontier, securing superior positions in frontier society, and the gentlemen of the Queensland and British Columbia frontiers constituted an identifiable caste holding common values and traits. The frontier gentleman possessed courage, honesty and good faith. He mixed mostly with members of his own caste. In order to maintain and defend his caste the gentleman regularly examined his own conduct to ensure that it was above reproach, and carefully monitored the behaviour of other caste members. On their own account the frontier gentlemen possessed refinement and social know-how. They did his duty. Apart from these moral virtues, many frontier gentlemen displayed a range of physical virtues which set them apart from lesser men. They showed industry and courage, and were physically strong.

The gentlemanly aversion to physical labour did not last long on the colonial frontier. Frontier life often necessitated a willingness to roll up one's sleeves and get stuck into the digging, fence building, shearing and chopping. Leslie, Verney, De Satgé and Bushby all, to varying degrees, found challenge and satisfaction in the rugged outdoor life.

Even George Carrington, after his initial profitless experience, became accustomed to working with his hands rather than his mind. The colonial frontier provided physical challenges to men whose life prior to emigration had been relatively sedentary and meeting them required the vigorous performance of the muscular attributes.

Despite the success of Leslie et al., not all gentlemen were able to maintain their position. One's status and upbringing as a gentleman might go a long way, but it did not guarantee frontier success. As George Carrington found, education and refinement was not necessarily esteemed and indeed could be a hindrance. Under frontier conditions many men found that maintaining gentlemanly behaviour and status was impossible. So why did some men succeed in doing so while others could not?

Firstly, the capricious circumstances of frontier life meant that some gentlemen, such as George Carrington, were destined to fail as frontiersmen. Secondly, one of the differences between Leslie and his brother gentlemen on the one hand and Carrington and Charlotte May Wright's 'broken down swells' on the other is that the former had money and connections – the positive backing of family and friends. With such support they found it relatively easy to establish themselves and maintain their status. Other emigrant gentlemen were not so fortunate. Wright mentions that many gentlemen had been sent to Australia because they were an embarrassment in England. Unable to perform as gentlemen at home, they were 'cast adrift' to manage by themselves in the colonies. When they were failing, there was no one to help them. Evidently, membership of the gentlemanly caste did not guarantee unlimited support.

Finally, the gentlemanly ideal was constituted by standards that were almost impossible to achieve. No one man was able to perform as a gentleman the entire time. Arthur Bushby was often inebriated and did not possess the sense of duty of Edmund Hope Verney. Oscar De Satgé could scarcely count humility amongst his virtues. Patrick Leslie and Verney displayed considerable self-consciousness about their performances as gentlemen, and monitored themselves constantly. Being upright, brave and honourable was a full-time occupation in itself. That others were less able to practise the self-governance required is hardly surprising.

3
The Sterling Qualities of the Saxon Race

> There is a savage heroism in all this, which the pampered conservative may denounce, but which, nevertheless, all must admire. It is such men as these that are now populating the new colony on the banks of the Frazer [sic] River; they have strength, courage, enterprise.
>
> (Kinahan Cornwallis, *The New Eldorado or British Columbia*)

Men of all classes, raised in an urban environment or in the cultivated English countryside, showed a remarkable degree of adaptability on the colonial frontier. British upper- and middle-class men had little, if anything, in the way of skills, knowledge or experience which would equip them for life on the frontiers of British Columbia or Queensland. These men were not used to trekking overland on foot, paddling through rapids or camping out under the stars. They had not experienced the bitter winters of Hudson's Bay and the Rocky Mountains nor the scalding summers of Northwest Queensland. They were not shearers, they had not dug for gold, they had not driven cattle overland, they had not ridden or walked for three days to get from point A to B. Yet these were the occupations on offer on the colonial frontier.

In Britain, as the middle class expanded and industrial capitalism demanded human resources, and the doctrine of the separate spheres took hold, men of this emergent class invested a great deal in doing productive work and earning an income sufficient to maintain a family and a home. However, one of the reasons upper- and middle-class men went to the frontier was precisely because of the lack of suitable occupations at home. Britain was modernising and domesticity and modernity were seen as feminising influences. How then were men to express manliness?

The frontiers of the British Empire provided the answer. A man was more likely to find an outlet for the performance of manly attributes on the frontier, than in Britain itself. Men of the lower classes were also attracted to the colonial frontier and its opportunities. John Tod, son of a clerk in the cotton printing industry, heard the siren's call: 'A murmuring voice, if not direct, beckoning, seemed to hold me to a mission in the wilds.'[1]

The colonial frontier offered a stage on which British men of all classes were able to perform the muscular virtues. Driven by the idea that 'a man must act', and seduced by the 'murmuring voices' of the frontier, men strove to establish their independence, to achieve full adult manhood. On the frontier they could exercise the courage, self-reliance and physical prowess there was little opportunity to practise at home. Moreover, in doing so they could achieve the manly independence they desired. Thousands of miles away from family and friends, most men had to rely on their own wits. This was both an attraction of the frontier and a necessity it imposed. Many found gratification in the vigorous and often severe outdoor life the frontier imposed on them, and took pride in their physical achievements.

Although frontier life was tough, men were able to learn, apply, demonstrate and profit from a range of skills, talents and opportunities that they were unable to at home. They could construct their manly personas in a contest with nature and the frontier. In the narratives of frontier men, on the open plains or in the mountains and forests, a man was defined by his actions. Going from the metropole to the frontier was a rite of passage leading to manliness. On the frontier manliness could be constructed, naturalised and normalised. In the hard work the frontier demanded, men found an opportunity to construct an alternative to the relatively predictable and comfortable life of metropolitan Britain, an alternative life of uncertainty which would require the full application of the muscular virtues. In this way the manly ethos was a driver on the frontier, influencing actions and determining responses to frontier conditions.

According to Edward Said, immigration and settlement was motivated not only by conquest and profit, or by personal necessity, but also by a commitment to imperialism which allowed Europeans to accept the idea that distant territories and their inhabitants should be settled and exploited. Settlement and exploitation was a long-term obligation to rule subordinate, inferior people. In this view, the enterprise of empire depended on having the idea of empire, by having an authoritative cultural predisposition to rule.[2] Said finds evidence of this predisposition in Europe's cultural productions. He identifies a 'consistency of concern' in English literature that establishes England as a centre of power and connects it to distant lands seen as desirable but inferior.[3] Sir Thomas Mitchell's *Journal of an Expedition into the Interior of Australia* suggests not only a predisposition to rule, but a belief that divine providence dictated that Britons had earned the right to rule:

> Curiosity alone may attract us into the mysterious recesses of regions still unknown; but a still deeper interest attaches to those regions, now that the rapid increase of the most industrious and, may we add the most deserving people on earth, suggests that the land there has been reserved by the Almighty for their use.[4]

Prominent among the cultural productions of the English-speaking world in the first half of the nineteenth century was the myth of the frontiersman. America was the fabled frontier of the nineteenth-century English-speaking world and James Fenimore Cooper's Leatherstocking novels defined frontier adventure.[5] By the middle of the nineteenth century, fiction writers and artists found in the frontier a seemingly inexhaustible supply of raw material for adventure and romance. The adventure stories of C.F. Marryat, R.M Ballantyne and Rider Haggard demonstrate that throughout the nineteenth century fiction aimed at boys and young men not only reinforced hegemonic constructions of masculinity but also continuously re-inscribed the frontier as a masculine space where boys could become men.[6] Martin Green has argued that 'the adventure tales that formed the light reading of Englishmen for two hundred years and more after Robinson Crusoe, were, in fact, the energising myths of English imperialism'. They were, collectively, 'the story England told itself when it went to sleep at night; and, in the form of its dreams, they charged England's will with the energy to go out into the world and explore, conquer and rule'.[7] The memoirs examined in this chapter are 'real-life' adventure stories, supporting Richard Phillips's view, cited in Chapter 1, that metropolitan masculinities were created in the colonies.

The frontier was often depicted as an alternative to a metropolitan society that had become degraded, corrupt and feminised. On the frontier, provided he possessed the virtues and put in the necessary hard work, a man could transform himself and the environment he found there. Adventurer and travel writer Kinahan Cornwallis believed that

British Columbia was the New Eldorado, where a man could escape the vice and effeminacy of England:

> *This can be done through* the enterprise which propels a man into a strange and distant country, there to combat with the rude hand of nature, and build up to himself a habitation, become a founder of new nation, the basis of whose social structure may rest upon more independent ground than does the tinsel fabric of his mother country. Such a career, gilded with wealth and attended by all the excitement and pleasures of dazzling promise, is open to any and every son of enterprise, who, discontented with his present lot and endowed with physical energy, may go forth to the New Eldorado of the North Pacific.[8]

In contrast to the shallow, 'tinsel' world of the metropole, the frontier was seen as an authentic, unadulterated environment, which gave men freedom to fulfil their potential, where manly enterprise would result, not only in material wealth, but in a degree of independence unattainable in Britain.

According to Cornwallis, the British Columbian frontier could be an idyllic paradise, inviting men to seek their fortunes in a golden land: 'The lurid sun shot out its rays of fire in dazzling brightness, and hope-inspiring effulgence far and wide, over the river and the grassland, lighting up the mountains in beauty of many shades, and displaying the mighty foliage of the forest in gilded loveliness.'[9] If the would-be frontiersman found this a bit too good to be true, other writers offered more sober but still extremely favourable impressions:

> Yet even where the weather is least propitious, British Columbia proves as salubrious as in those districts where she is blest with summer skies; sustained by the buoyant mountain air, the miner goes unscathed through countless hardships, brings a keen appetite to his beans and bacon, and rarely indeed suffers from rheumatism.[10]

Sir Thomas Mitchell's descriptions of inland Australia could hardly be more encouraging to the would-be pastoralist:

> Unencumbered by too much wood, it yet possessed enough for all purposes; its soil was exuberant, and its climate temperate; it was bounded on three sides by the ocean; and it was traversed by mighty

rivers, and watered by streams innumerable. Of this Eden I was the first European to explore its mountains and streams – to behold its scenery.[11]

Poet Thomas Campbell sought to inspire men with flattering classical allusions:

> As in a cradled Hercules, we trace
> The lines of empire on thine infant face.
> What nations in thy wide horizon's span
> Shall team on tracts untrodden yet by man![12]

Literature, poetry and exploration narratives imparted a consistent, if sometimes grandiose, message to the impecunious younger son or middle-class male who found the professions overcrowded: on the colonial frontier there was adventure and opportunity, the potential for independence and lands waiting and desiring civilisation.

Men's desire to carve out an independent life in the colonies was allied with an unshakeable self-belief. If doubts were harboured they were rarely expressed. Kinahan Cornwallis felt 'ready to plunge wherever the hand of fate beckoned, and, being reckless of consequences, wherever destiny determined'.[13] When the Hudson's Bay Company recruiter expressed concern at John Tod's youth, Tod replied, 'Never mind, sir. I will try to do my duty.'[14]

Fur trader Tod was, like most of his profession, a Scot, born in Dunbartonshire in 1794.[15] His first job upon leaving school was as a clerk in a cotton-yard warehouse in Glasgow. Dismissed for refusing to do two jobs for the one-pay packet, he returned home and remained unemployed for several months. On an uncle's advice he signed up with the Hudson's Bay Company for four years at £20 a year and in June 1813 embarked for Hudson's Bay. He was to spend nearly 40 years 'in service', starting as an apprentice clerk and rising to the rank of chief trader. His placement in the ranks of the clerks meant that he was in the class of 'gentleman' and was eligible for commissions in the higher grades.[16] After retirement Tod gave a series of interviews to Gilbert Malcolm Sproat, editor of the Victoria *Daily Times*, and G.H. Wilson-Brown, a journalist. Although Tod died in 1882, the interviews were not published until 1905 in the *Daily Times* as a series of articles in the form of a memoir titled 'Career of a Scotch Boy Who Became Hon. John Tod'. Tod's family life was unconventional even by fur trade standards. He was formally married twice and had two other wives *à la façon du pays* (in the custom of the country), fathering nine children in the process. Perhaps this unconventionality provided a reason for the delay in publication.

Many officers of the Hudson's Bay Company formed relationships with Indian women and such relationships were a normal part of life in the fur trade. None of these relationships had the benefit of being formally sanctioned by clergy, and they usually produced mixed-blood children whose parentage and legal position would almost certainly be subjected to great scrutiny if family matters were ever disputed in a British court.[17] By the mid-nineteenth century Victorians were deeply committed to the home and domesticity and to rigorous standards of home life. The family became the centre of middle-class Victorian life and, Catherine Hall argues, 'the fulcrum of a complex set of social values which comprised middle-class respectability'.[18] At the core of the domestic ideal stood 'patriarchal yet companionate' marriage – the warm and affective relationship between a man and a woman.

While Victorian Britons were committed to marriage, the home and family, Tod's marriages to native women would have been considered well and truly outside the pale. And while the belief that siring children was an important part of masculine performance, nine mixed-blood children would probably have been considered excessive. Nevertheless, what is clear from Tod's experience is that the absence of women of one's own race was not an impediment to sexual and domestic satisfaction. On the contrary, on the frontier white men could enter into relationships with non-white women freely, and free from the obligations that similar relationships entailed in Britain. The fact that he had two native wives did not prevent Tod from marrying European women (his first European wife died after a long mental illness).

Tod served in some of the Hudson's Bay Company's most remote posts – he spent nine unrelieved years at the solitary post at McLeod's Lake where he almost forgot how to speak English.[19] He endured all the hardships that the fur trade entailed: long, hazardous journeys by canoe and overland, monotonous food (often nothing but salmon for months on end), near starvation, extreme cold and often hostile Indians. How could a man spend 40 years in such an environment and find satisfaction? In the long run, the financial rewards were very attractive. The Hudson's Bay Company had a profit-sharing scheme in which the shareholders and the 'wintering partners', as the traders were known, shared the returns; 60 percent to the shareholders and 40 percent to the traders, the latter amount being further divided according to whether one was a chief trader or a chief factor (manager). As a chief trader, Tod earned £600 per year, with no expenses. But the financial rewards were incidental to the challenges of the wilderness, which offered the opportunity to enact the full panoply of manly virtues, and which Tod felt were their own reward:

> The pitting of your wit against the savage, the retreat from conventions, the outdoor life, the possibleness [sic] of adventure, even the danger in it all, together with the gratified instinct of the hunter and the naturalist, with, of course, the prospect of acquiring a modest competency in middle-life – these perhaps, in some degree, account for the satisfaction expressed.[20]

When conventional life failed to excite John Tod, he was attracted to the frontier by the challenge of conquering a dangerous opponent. The frontier offered Tod what the metropole did not. The metropole was conventional, civilised and risk free. It offered fewer challenges against which a man could pit himself and perform the role that was expected. Tod embraced the romantic view that remote territories were wild and therefore should be tamed. For him, risk and danger were reward enough, a 'modest competency' a bit of a bonus. Although he does not refer to it, the life of a fur trader would have afforded Tod a greater degree of independence than he would have had as clerk in a warehouse.

Fifty years after John Tod signed on with the Hudson's Bay Company, British Columbia was still attracting men seeking risk and danger. In the 1860s the allure was not furs, but gold. In 1862, several groups of men from eastern Canada decided to pit themselves against the frontier by crossing the Canadian prairie and travelling through the Rocky Mountains. Their object was to reach the Cariboo district where gold had been discovered in the summer of 1861. Collectively these groups were known as the 'Overlanders'. They travelled on foot, using horses and oxen to pull carts loaded with supplies. Several accounts by men who undertook this journey have been published. The leader of one party, Thomas McMicking, published his account of the journey in the *British Columbian* newspaper in December 1862. In 1981 his journal was published as *Overland from Canada to British Columbia*. The reminiscences of A.L. Fortune, a member of another party of Overlanders, were published in instalments by the *Kamloops Sentinel* in 1936.[21] At one level, the accounts of McMicking and Fortune illustrate the satisfaction and the sense of achievement, even joy, felt by the Overlanders, as they negotiated the hazards of a cross-country trek. At another, they demonstrate how the frontier was constructed as simultaneously a place of danger and risk, and a place of beauty and opportunity. Most importantly, the frontier provided a stage on which the Overlanders could perform manliness, taking advantages of opportunities not available in eastern Canada.

The lure of gold provided the stimulus for this masculine enterprise. Rumours of gold finds in British Columbia had begun to filter into Hudson's Bay Company posts as early as 1852. By 1856, the Hudson's Bay Company was documenting specific discoveries and was providing the Indigenous people with tools to collect the precious metal. By the end of 1857 Governor Douglas realised the futility of keeping out prospectors any longer and proclaimed British Crown authority over all gold deposits. All miners were required to obtain a licence and there were restrictions on the size of the claim a single miner could make. By 1858 miners from California had begun converging on the colony, clogging vessels from San Francisco and turning Victoria on Vancouver Island into a tent city. From there they crossed the Georgia Strait to the mainland and journeyed up the Fraser River to the goldfields. It is estimated that over 30,000 men and women passed through British Columbia in 1858.[22] During 1860, prospectors started pushing eastward to the spurs of the Rocky Mountains surrounding Quesnal and Cariboo Lakes. The earth proved to be unusually rich and by the summer of 1861 the area boasted a number of thriving towns which possessed all the facilities the miners deemed necessary, such as barber shops, whiskey shops and gambling halls.

Prospects on the goldfields were boosted by journalists such as Donald Fraser who contributed to *The Times*. Scampering north from San Francisco he wrote dozens of stories describing the gold rush, each story becoming more exciting as the rush unfolded.[23] These stories attracted adventurers from all over the world, including men from eastern Canada. Fortune records that there were nine parties of Overlanders. They included men from Montreal, Toronto, St. Catherine near Niagara and Huntington County in Ontario.[24]

Alexander Fortune was born in Huntington, Quebec, in 1830 to Scottish parents. In 1862 he married Bathia Ross, and established himself as a merchant in St. Anticet. It was only four months later that he joined the Overlanders. Fortune was separated from Bathia for 12 years before she joined him in British Columbia. He had been advised to live more in the open on account of ill-health; hence he joined one of the overland parties known as the Acton Party.[25] Thomas McMicking was born in Stamford Township, Upper Canada, in 1829, on a farm established by his grandfather who had left the United States after the

Revolutionary War. He married Laura Chubbuck in 1854, working on his father's farm. He tried teaching at Queenston and in 1861 he went into business there. However, the business did not do well, but he stuck at it until he decided to go to the Cariboo.[26] Most of the Overlanders were from farming families and some were immigrants from Ireland, Scotland and England. Some had worked as clerks or schoolteachers or had professional training.[27]

It would seem that in 1862, at the ages of 32 and 33, respectively, neither Fortune nor McMicking considered themselves established in any calling or profession. As discussed in an earlier chapter, in the mid-nineteenth century the attainment of a suitable occupation and the achievement of 'independence' was a crucial part of full adult manhood. Not finding any satisfaction at home, and lured by the beguiling reports of gold discoveries in British Columbia, Fortune and McMicking sought their independence on the frontier. Fortune wrote: 'We thought we might be among the lucky ones who could go to the Cariboo gold fields and be back in a few short years with a competency to live among our friends and have comfortable homes for the time of sickness and old age. Why not succeed as well as others?'[28] Why did they choose the overland route to the goldfields as opposed to one of the alternatives? Instead of an arduous overland trek, they could have sailed to British Columbia via Cape Horn and San Francisco. Alternatively, they could have sailed to Panama, trained or trekked across the isthmus, and sailed on to British Columbia via San Francisco. Going via the Cape of Good Hope was the most expensive and time-consuming way to travel. By the time they arrived at the Cariboo the gold rush could have been over. Travelling via Panama carried the additional risk of contracting malaria. Trekking overland was the quickest and cheapest means of travel.

There is a further possible explanation for choosing this route. Nineteenth-century overlanding and exploration has been described by Catherine Hall as a 'quintessentially male activity'. She describes exploration as 'the ultimate expression of frontier masculinity', the extension in the European mind of man's conquest over 'virgin territory'.[29] The Overlanders were quintessential pioneers, who saw themselves as opening up the prairie country for others to follow. In fulfilment of Edward Said's thesis, McMicking and Fortune felt they had an imperial mission, and expressed the masculine nature of pioneering:

> We often thought of the future of this extensive wonderful country – pictured a time when railways and farming developed, when stock

raising and dairying industry and homes of comfort would excel those of more southern climes. Soil, land, fertile hill and dale, all inviting the home seeker to settle down with his bride and enjoy the blessings and luxury of earth and heaven in this great Lone Land.[30]

Fortune's frontier was one to which the idealised domesticity and patriarchy of Britain and eastern Canada could be successfully transplanted. The frontier was inviting domestication. Men would build railways – that quintessential nineteenth-century symbol of progress – and transform the 'Lone Land' into 'home', where women could assume the roles of homemaker and nurturer, and men could work and provide for their families. This theme of settlement and domesticity echoes adventure literature. Consider this passage from R.M. Ballantyne's *The Coral Island*: 'Then we'll build a charming villa, and plant a lovely garden round it, stuck all full of the most splendiferous tropical flowers, and we'll farm the land, plant, sow, reap, eat, sleep and be merry.'[31]

Similarly, Thomas McMicking looked back on the journey and saw it as an opportunity to populate and develop 'waste' land: 'Why, then, should the overcrowded cities of Europe still continue to be overburdened with a redundant population, while upwards of *two hundred thousand square miles* of such land, with such a desirable climate, are lying waste and uncultivated and inviting occupation?'[32] McMicking thought that the territory the Overlanders had traversed would become 'the very heart and centre of the great British American Empire that will unite in one grand confederation the present widely separated provinces'.[33] McMicking and Fortune constructed the frontier as a land of opportunity. It was a place of transformation and they would be the 'transformers'.

McMicking's and Fortune's narratives are very much in the mould of the classic tale of action and adventure. Men set out on a quest, and there are many risks and dangers: hostile Indians, wolves, thirst, a shortage of food. Each account is set against a backdrop of wilderness that is sometimes idyllic and sometimes threatening. The Overlanders are real-life heroes performing daring deeds and displaying endurance and self-sacrifice. Each crisis provided an opportunity to enact the manly virtues – perseverance, courage and resourcefulness save the day. Fortune relates:

James Kelse of Acton, in his efforts to urge the cattle to leave the land and swim the river, stepped into deep water and sank to the bottom at once. He was given up as lost, when a good friend, George Reid, stripped off his clothes, plunged into the river, and dove after our drowning comrade. He came up like a hero with the helpless body of Kelso. We found a spark of life and kindled that into a flame and after long labor got him to breathe and show signs of restoration.[34]

A number of scholars have argued that the desire of men to be manly and conquer the wilderness is reflected in the way the physical environment is depicted in their narratives. Kay Schaffer has described the changing conceptualisations of the Australian frontier. Variously described as a scientific paradise by late-eighteenth-century explorers such as Cook, as a 'howling hell' in the convict era, a luxuriant Eden by the overland explorers and as harsh, raw and cruel by Henry Lawson, imaginings of the Australian frontier have not been stable.[35] In the stories of frontier men, the frontier is either a paradise waiting to be settled or a wild place of danger. In Fortune's eyes it is both simultaneously. His story conveys the varying ways in which men regarded the physical environment. The frontier presented simultaneous alternative visions:

> The slope was facing the south-southwest; it was a large pasture field where the early grass would invite the hungry sheep in the spring. Oh for the pen of a ready writer! My powers fail me. I am lost in wonder! No pen picture is equal to satisfy or do the least justice to describe the wonderful amphitheatre before us as we rested for a while on that high ground.[36]

From the same vantage point the frontier possessed awe-inspiring beauty and dignity:

> As we looked northwest, we viewed the great Jasper Mountain with its high crest lost in the clouds and eternal snows, showing a great majestic slope starting from the melting snows near the crest and mostly covered with grasses and flowers except where the streams of water formed gulches not too deep to form chasms, but easy water courses nearly straight down the side of the mountain; each gulch decorated with ornamental trees and foliage.[37]

Yet it was forbidding, dangerous and unyielding:

> To the south, mountains of harder rock standing boldly – a forbidding barrier to the foot of man, while to the southwest neighbouring steep

and bluff rocks without room for trees and grass. On our left and southeast were rough and jagged slopes mostly covered with timber scrubby and gnarled. Again near the foot of the mountain we were resting on, was a wild mountain stream (Rocky River) roaring like a cataract and grinding the rocks and pebbles into sand.[38]

Each conceptualisation provided a stage on which masculinity could be performed. In the first extract the frontier is a benign, inviting place where men can enact their resourcefulness, turning it into a bucolic paradise. In the second, the frontier is a veritable Garden of Eden which seems to invite men of character to enact their most noble aspirations. In the third extract Fortune's forbidding frontier poses dangers which could only be overcome by men with strength and courage.

McMicking's tale similarly contains lyrical descriptions of nature. He writes of the 'vast and lovely plains', and the 'immense trackless prairie'.[39] The rugged Rockies evoked feelings that were almost transcendental: 'We were somewhat surprised to find the weather in the valleys of this elevated region so mild and warm, surrounded as they were on every side with immense heaps of perpetual snow, while some of the vast glaciers extended far down beyond them. There was a clearness, a lightness and salubrity about the atmosphere that was really delightful.'[40] But the admiration of unspoilt nature was accompanied by thoughts of a greater purpose: 'The mind was intuitively invited to contemplation, and to enquire whether these sounds might be recognized as the footfalls of advancing civilisation, or to wonder...whether eternal silence and solitude were again to succeed.'[41] As beautiful and serene as the wilderness might be, to McMicking's mind it was a blank space on which strong and courageous men could build a new world.

The source of this strength and courage was, in part at least, Christianity, a fundamental tenet of the texts of mid-Victorian manliness, and integral to the Overlanders' mission. Christianity provided common ground when differences emerged and energised them for what lay ahead:

> But tomorrow would be the Sabbath, and no wonder that its approach should be regarded with pleasurable anticipations, as furnishing an opportunity for restoring the exhausted energies of both man and beast, for smoothing down the asperities of our natures, and, by allowing us time for reflection, for regaining a just

appreciation of our duties toward one another; and the vigor with which our journey would be prosecuted, and the cordiality and good-feeling that characterized our intercourse after our accustomed rest on the first day of the week, are sufficient evidence to us that the law of the Sabbath is phisical [sic], as well as moral obligation, and that its precepts cannot be violated with impunity.[42]

Christian faith was a fundamental aspect of the Overlanders' worldview. Leonore Davidoff and Catherine Hall have argued that for many middle-class men in the first half of the nineteenth century, estranged from the world of wealth and power, one's piety, rather than material wealth and possessions, became the principal criteria of social status. Demonstrations of faith through involvement with their church, public works and business practices provided a basis for claims to political influence and power. A man who could be a trustee for God and a steward for the fiscal affairs of his church could be relied upon to undertake other positions of public responsibility with probity. If they could not gain access to political power by virtue of birth and wealth, middle-class men found other means to push their way into public affairs. They joined benevolent societies and institutions devoted to the advancement of education, science and culture.[43] The Overlanders' was a practical faith. They regarded their actions as part of God's work. Their mission was facilitated by religious observance, and their belief was at the core of their endeavours. Indeed, both Fortune and McMicking were devout Presbyterians who had studied for the ministry at Knox College in Toronto. McMicking was subsequently ordained, but Fortune failed to complete his studies due to his ill health.[44] He and McMicking display an earnestness, selflessness, integrity and erudition redolent of Britain's emerging middle classes in the late-eighteenth and early-nineteenth centuries. Religion also armed them with the practical qualities needed to come to terms with the tragedies that occurred on the frontier:

> Thus six of those who left their homes with us, whose hopes for the future were as bright, whose expectations were as boundless and whose prospects for a long life were as promising and brilliant as our own, are now numbered with the dead. The Supreme Disposer of all events, in the exercise of His inscrutable wisdom, has disappointed their earthly hopes; and I trust that those of us who were exposed to the same accidents, and who still survive the same or like dangers, will not fail to acknowledge His goodness in the preservation of our

lives, and to recognise His providential care over us through all the vicissitudes of life.[45]

The frontier tested faiths as well as physiques. McMicking and Fortune's Christianity helped arm them with the manly virtues of courage, stoicism and fortitude they needed to survive the deprivations and challenges of the frontier.

On 11 September after months on the trail, the Overlanders arrived at the mouth of the Quesnell River. McMicking could record that they were all 'heartily glad' that they had reached the end of their journey. However,

> it was only after we had been allowed a little time for reflection, and had an opportunity to take a retrospective view of all the way which we came, to consider the innumerable perils to which we had been continually exposed, through all the vicissitudes of our journey, during a period of nearly five months, and to talk of our numerous hairbreadth escapes, that we could fully realize or comprehend the magnitude of our achievement.[46]

What made their negotiation of the 'innumerable perils' an 'achievement'? They had not yet discovered gold (the ostensible purpose of their quest), or established homes with their brides as Fortune foresaw. What they had achieved at the end of their journey, at least to their own satisfaction, was their manliness, and with the publication of their stories, public recognition of their manly status. Their desire was to possess and conquer the western Canadian landscape and their means of doing this was to journey across it and survive its hazards. Their achievement became the fact that they had survived the dangers of the frontier. The Canadian west was the testing ground for their manhood. The hazards of the frontier could have emasculated them by exposing their lack of manliness. In conquering these hazards they overcame their fears and proved that they were manly.[47]

Neither McMicking nor Fortune were successful prospectors, but they were ultimately successful in establishing themselves as prominent men in their communities, as middle-class men had done in Britain. McMicking turned his hand to civic affairs and in 1864 he became town clerk for New Westminster. In April 1866 he was appointed its deputy Sheriff. He was active member of St. Andrew's Presbyterian Church and a member of the voluntary fire brigade and a lieutenant in the local home guard.[48] Alexander Fortune ultimately established a ranch on the

Spallumcheen River near the present town of Enderby in the Okanagan Valley of British Columbia. Fortune helped establish a Presbyterian Church, and he ran the first Sunday school there.[49] Gold did not provide them with their 'competency', but it seems that the frontier did provide them with the opportunity for manly independence and achievement in more conventional ways.

On the Queensland frontier men could find similar challenges that would test their muscular attributes to the full. When he was not much older than John Tod, Ernest Henry migrated to Queensland when a military career was closed to him. Born into the landed gentry, Henry was the grandson of James Henry, a Jamaican sugar planter and member of the Legislative Council there, and Susan Hall, the daughter of another planter. His father was their eldest son James, and his mother was Mary Francis Norris, fourth daughter of John Norris of Hughenden Manor, Buckinghamshire. Henry first visited Australia in 1853 as a junior officer on Australian Royal Mail Service Company's *S.S. Victoria*. Upon the outbreak of the Crimean War he attended the Royal Military College at Sandhurst and was gazetted as an Ensign in the 72nd Highlanders. Invalided out of war service at 19, he resigned his commission and emigrated to Queensland, taking up Baroondah Station on the Dawson River. He was a member of George Dalrymple's party which explored the areas of the Bowen and Burdekin Rivers, and in 1859 he took up Mt. Connell Station on the Burdekin.[50]

Ernest Henry was a frontiersman who was no stranger to the physical demands of the wilderness. In fact, he thrived on the physical challenges posed by squatting. In his personal narrative, *An Account by Ernest Henry of an Exploring Trip Resulting in the Taking up of Hughenden Station*, he depicts himself as the most muscular of men. His short narrative is quite an adventure tale, replete with risk and danger, 'untamed' wilderness, savage natives and personal heroics. By his own account Henry emerges as a tough individualist, who knew how to exercise leadership and authority. He assumed mastery over men and the land, and stamped himself as a man who could undertake physical feats others would not even contemplate.

Leaving Mt. McConnell in late November to search for grazing land, Henry records that the outward trip was uneventful. Most of the country his party passed through was in Henry's view 'indifferent and worthless', and it was not until they had travelled 200 miles that 'the valley of the Flinders broke into view' and they could see 'stretches of open downs in the distance, which experience told us was first class pasturage'.[51] Henry described this view of the land that became Hughenden Station as

> a lovely valley of undulating downs, studded here and there with groups and belts of graceful myall trees, whose shadows were thrown far over the green herbage by the rising sun. The grass had evidently been burnt off a few weeks previously, but now clothed the rising and falling ground with the very richest pasture, trackless and undisturbed by a single hoof. A small creek, whose winding course is indicated by the trees that grow on either bank, trends northward through the centre of the valley, which later, to the south, narrows picturesquely amongst the hills; on the west it is bounded by another low range, only a few miles distant; while to the north, it widens out and joins the extensive valley of the river, along whose course open downs stretch far away, unbroken, save by narrow bits of timber.[52]

> Never again will it wear its virgin loveliness. Ages hence, when the world becomes more densely populated and men shall prize what is beautiful more than what is profitable, it may be adorned by art; gardens and crops may replace its natural herbage, irrigated from artesian wells, but no eye will ever again behold it in its wild, silent solitary beauty, as we saw it that early morning, bathed in the light of the rising sun.[53]

With his gaze and these words Henry appropriated the (seemingly uninhabited) land.

Descriptions of landscape such as Henry's are a conventional feature of adventure and travel writing.[54] Travellers often find the countryside continually 'opening' before them, as if it was dormant, needing European eyes to command it into existence by recognising the 'harmonious arrangement of its constituent parts'.[55] The frontier as 'virgin land', as feminine, is a common trope. According to Anne McClintock the myth of the virgin land is the myth of the empty land, involving both a gender and a racial dispossession.[56] She coins the phrase 'anachronistic space' to describe the displacement of Indigenous people who are not supposed to be present, but who are supposed to exist in a permanently anterior time, a position which allows colonisers to claim original possession.[57] The frontier as a luxuriant Eden, as Henry saw it, allowed men to turn the wilderness into a productive estate.

In Henry's mind the land required the affirming presence of Western agriculture. He took for granted that the land and its resources belonged to those who could best exploit it. The Aboriginal people were rendered invisible, though it was quite likely that they who, through regular burning, maintained the land in the condition had made it such an attractive pastoral proposition. While he envisaged an Arcadian time 'when... men shall prize what is beautiful more than what is profitable', that vision turns out to be of European cultivated farmland, which has erased everything that is natural, including its original inhabitants.

Having 'discovered' this prime pastoral country, Henry had to make it his own by being the first to stock it. Upon returning to Mt. McConnell he found two parties there who had heard about his expedition and who each planned to get there ahead of him with their cattle. Henry took a week to round up 800 cattle of his own and with supplies for 12 months and an unspecified number of men set off to overtake the other parties – a feat he achieved in ten days.

The journey to set up Hughenden Station was three months of 'incessant toil and many hardships'.[58] They had to cross the flooded Flinders River. Incessant rain made the ground boggy and impossible for the horses and drays to travel. The party was often up all night in the rain, either watching cattle or attempting to stem flooding waters from washing away their campsites. Later, it took two days without water to get the cattle across a stretch of desert country. These trials provided Henry with numerous opportunities to rise to the physical challenges by displaying strength and courage. He swam flooded rivers that inferior men could not.[59] He displayed coolness in danger:

> I was lying across the doorway of the tent reading, having my shirt open... when my attention was attracted by something trying to work its way under my right shoulder, and, guessing what it was, without moving, turned my eyes down, and saw a large brown, venomous snake. Just then it started to come over me, and it was an anxious moment till his head was well past my chin and I knew he had missed going into my shirt. So soon as he was clear of me I jumped up and slew him. To keep quiet under such circumstance is the only safe thing to do.[60]

After giving instructions to his manager about the establishment of the station, Henry had to return to Mt. McConnell before making his way to Rockhampton to be a witness in a court case. With his Aboriginal guide Dick, Henry began the trek back to Mt. McConnell, during which he accomplished the 'greatest feat he ever performed'.[61] The going was tough, but it was after they reached Natal Downs, the outermost station at that time, that the real adventure began. On the day they reached

Natal Downs, Henry and Dick had travelled 30 miles. There they met a man who was anxious to travel south and who proposed to accompany them, but who could not swim. Knowing that the Suttor River which they had to cross would be flooded, Henry attempted to dissuade the man, but he would not be put off. Hoping to make him change his mind, Henry boasted that he would not stop until he reached Mt. McConnell, a distance of 90 miles. Such a grand boast met with derision from the hands at Natal Downs, but the ridicule made Henry all the more determined to succeed.

The three departed Natal Downs in the afternoon and at sundown Henry left them to camp while he continued alone. He rode on until 1:30 in the morning by which time his horse was exhausted, and Henry continued on foot. Just before daylight he came across an Aboriginal camp which he evaded by taking off his boots and detouring off the road through the bush. After 12 hours of walking he reached the Suttor River which indeed was flooded and 200 yards wide from bank to bank. Despite having walked for 12 hours Henry, though he claimed he was not weary, fell into a 'momentary sleep'. Feeling this was a sign of weakness, he tried to resist but again and again sleep overtook him. Henry is almost apologetic to the reader for this inexplicable frailty: 'Again and again I tried to rouse myself to eat with the same result. It seemed to me the most extraordinary thing, for my body and limbs were not weary.'[62] Eventually, with stern resolution, he secured his valuables on his head, took off his boots and plunged into the flooded river. A third of the way across he encountered trouble:

> The swollen and foaming stream, the while, was fast carrying me down with it, and I began to feel very like drowning. Noticing, however, down the river, a tree standing out in the water considerably further than the rest, I strained every nerve so as to make sufficient headway to enable me to catch hold of it ere the current, which was swift and strong, should carry me past. It was a desperate struggle, but my arms closed round the trunk just in the nick of time, and as I did so, the current swung me round, stretching me out to full length, but I clung on till breath was regained, which had been exhausted the sooner from the pressure of the strap under my chin, which held the parcel on my head. I then climbed onto the first limb, tightened my belt, and, after five minutes rest, jumped in again and reached the opposite bank without distress.[63]

His trials were not to end there. Now without boots and with ten miles remaining, he left the stony road for the paddocks only to discover that they had recently been burnt off and the stumps of the grass stuck up like wires. Not only did his feet suffer with every step, but he was attacked by swarms of mosquitoes and sand flies. Henry travelled non-stop for 36 hours, 50 or 60 miles on foot, the last 10 miles without boots.

Henry's narrative is not the story of a modest man. He appears to be constantly measuring his manliness against other men: the Yorkshireman who failed to swim across the flooded Flinders; the other settlers whom he beat to Hughenden; the men of Natal Downs who did not believe he could travel non-stop to Mt. McConnell; his Aboriginal companion. By his own reckoning Henry is the superior male, willing to work harder, travel further and take more risks than other men. Perhaps he was trying to make up for being invalided out of the army. It is not entirely clear who he was trying to impress, no clue as to who his reader might be. He mentions an event that 'you have read the particulars of in one of my old letters', but neither the 'you' nor the event in this statement is identified.[64] There is no reason to think it was intended for a wide reading public, but it was intended to be read by someone. There is no reason to doubt that the events Henry relates happened. But he was not writing an objective account of 'what happened'; he was writing about performing the muscular virtues on the frontier, of the perceived necessity to out-perform other men, to maintain one's position at the top of the masculine hierarchy. Henry's was a performance that was clearly meant to impress.

Except for the last part of his journey, Henry was not alone in his exploration. He was the leader of what must have been a large party – one man cannot drive 800 cattle 200 miles on his own. As Henry had to leave the party to go to Rockhampton, Hughenden Station was actually established by his manager and his employees. Yet in Henry's account other men are almost invisible except as rivals he must outdo. Henry depicts himself as a rugged individual who achieved all that he did on his own, without relying on others. He is the strong, independent male, carving out his own place in the wilderness.

Impressive masculine performances were appreciated by the British public, but they took place in the imagination as often as in actuality. Celebrated by the Royal Geographical Society, authors of *The Northwest Passage by Land*, which ran to eight editions between 1865 and 1901, Viscount Milton and his friend Doctor Walter Butler Cheadle, in the mid-nineteenth century earned a reputation as intrepid gentlemen adventurers.[65] With no frontier experience they undertook a journey overland from Fort Garry (near present-day Winnipeg) to Fort Edmonton and across the Rockies to Kamloops in British Columbia, armed only with an unwavering faith in their courage, vigour and perseverance to overcome the hazards of the wilderness. *Northwest Passage* depicts the British gentleman as a conquering, trailblazing hero, who can easily make the transition from the metropole to the frontier. However, a comparison of the published account with Cheadle's daily journal, unpublished (until 1931), reveals that their frontier prowess existed as much in their imaginations as in reality.

William Wentworth-Fitzwilliam, Viscount Milton, was the son and heir apparent of William Thomas Spencer-Fitzwilliam, Sixth Earl Fitzwilliam, and Francis Douglas Harriet. Educated at Eton and Trinity College, Cambridge, he was a gentleman with an appetite for travel. He made his first trip to British North America in 1860, visiting the Red River Settlement in western Canada, before returning to England to give a number of lectures to scientific and literary groups.[66] This experience sharpened his taste for adventure and in 1862 he arrived in Quebec with Dr. W. B. Cheadle, with the aim of exploring the country between the Red River Settlement and the Rocky Mountains and thereby finding a route through the Rockies to the Cariboo goldfields. Walter Cheadle was the son of Reverend James Cheadle and Eliza Butler. Like Milton he studied at Cambridge, but the two did not meet there. After receiving his B.A. Cheadle began his medical studies at Cambridge and completed them at St. George's Hospital, London, in 1861. He met Milton the following year.[67]

Their adventure started in Montreal and from there Milton and Cheadle travelled to Fort Garry via Toronto, Chicago and St. Paul. They spent the winter of 1862–1863 northwest of Fort Carlton, where they hunted and trapped. They engaged a Métis guide, and together with his wife and son, and an Irishman called O'Beirne, set off again in the spring, crossing the Rockies via Edmonton, Jasper and Yellowhead Pass. Being inexperienced, under-equipped and unskilled, the exigencies of survival diverted them from the original purpose of their trip – to find a short, direct route to the Cariboo. Instead, they followed the North Thompson River to Kamloops in British Columbia. Their journey was fraught with danger and difficulties, many of their own making. Nevertheless, they reached Kamloops on 29 August 1863, and proceeded to the Cariboo and then on to Victoria.

The pair published several accounts of their journey which were very popular, including *The North-West Passage by Land*. While the published accounts bear both names as authors, a reading of Cheadle's daily journal makes it abundantly clear that he was the principal author of subsequent versions. The journal and *The North-West Passage by Land* record the trials and tribulations of their expedition, and show how two men, born to the genteel life, exalted in their frontier experience. A comparison of the two also reveals what was hidden from the reading public. There are significant differences between *The North-West Passage by Land* and Cheadle's daily journal. The latter is a relatively frank account of the difficulties they faced, their shortcomings and mistakes. The published account, on the other hand, leaves out much of the detail of Cheadle's journal. It is a circuitous account of their adventures and praises the Canadian west and its prospects for settlement and development.

Milton and Cheadle undoubtedly possessed Said's 'cultural predisposition to rule'. Their optimistic preface states:

> One of the principal objects they [the authors] have had in view has been to draw attention to the vast importance of establishing a highway from the Atlantic to the Pacific through the British possessions... another advantage... would be the opening out and colonisation of the magnificent regions of the Red River and Saskatchewan, where 65,000 square miles of a country of unsurpassed fertility, and abounding in mineral wealth, lies isolated from the world, neglected, almost unknown, although destined, at no distant period perhaps, to become one of the most valuable possessions of the British Crown.[68]

In *The North-West Passage by Land* both Milton and Cheadle appear as joint leaders of the expedition, manfully and skilfully leading it across flooded rivers, precipitous mountain paths and miasmic swamps, and Cheadle's journal, to the extent that it is an immediate account, confirms that the trek was rugged and often dangerous:

> Our experience was as bad or worse than yesterday. Water overflowing everywhere, & one marsh the horses only just helped swimming [*sic*]; all the bags got well soaked, but we found no place to stop. We crossed Moose river by fording; stream strong and deep in some places, but our man found a good passage, the water however streaming over our horse shoulders as we faced the stream.[69]

The journal also records that they had time for the gentlemanly pursuit of leisure:

> Fine bright morning with nice breeze; reach Lake St. Ann's about noon, & dined there, getting fresh fish. In the afternoon Milton & I went over to Mr. Fraser's to drink milk & have a lesson in fly-making. We made several large flies on gimp hooks with worsted & coloured silk for bodies and speckled duck's feathers for wings.[70]

The North-West Passage omits the afternoon's leisure – perhaps drinking milk was thought to be inimical to the image of manly adventurers.

From the journal it is quite clear that Cheadle was for all intents and purposes the leader of the expedition. While both the journal and the published account are opportunities for self-display, the journal has a degree of verisimilitude regarding Cheadle's role. What he lacked in knowledge and skill he made up for with a certain amount of initiative, common sense and a willingness to listen to those who knew better. Milton, however, was less at home in the wilderness, less willing to adapt to its demands, less able to meet its physical challenges.

The journal indicates that Milton had a very leisurely approach to the journey, often stopping to pan for gold, which he never found, or to catch fish, which eluded him. He did not like getting out of bed too early. For Milton, the journey was more like a holiday excursion than a journey of discovery and exploration. One day, after yet another late start (which was not unusual due to Milton's sleeping-in), they came to the Athabasca River and found it flooded from heavy rain in the previous 24 hours and impassable. Had they been two days earlier they could have crossed. Milton's casual approach to the trip exasperated Cheadle: 'Will Milton ever learn the value of time?'[71] However, there were many days when the wilderness made leisure redundant:

> After dinner we had an awful experience of muskegs, overflowing streams, marshes, &c., & did not reach Moose lake as we had hoped, being compelled to camp the night in a muskeg. The worst and hardest work, as well as the longest day we ever had, track frequently under water, & the little rivers we had to cross up to the horse's bellies.[72]

On 23 June 1863 the party lost its way. It camped for the night but their horses trampled on some embers of the fire and spread them into nearby trees, setting the forest alight. Milton and Cheadle sprang manfully into action:

> I seized an axe & cut down the nearest trees. But then the little black horse getting burnt a little, got frightened & rolled in the fire & I had to seize a great pole & beat him about the head before he would get out again. Whilst this was going on, the fire had again got head, & I set to work with the axe, & shouted at the rest to bring water, & Milton's activity & presence of mind in helping me to some at once saved us, and we got the fire under by sundry pansful.[73]

In this episode, Milton was to the fore. Although Cheadle was giving the orders, in a dangerous and unexpected situation he acted with courage and calmness, in the manner expected of a man.

But there were limits to Milton's strength and perseverance. When the going got tough Milton could easily lose the presence of mind he demonstrated on the night of the fire. During several days of driving the horses across difficult terrain Milton was frequently left behind. The path was often obstructed by fallen trees, making it all but impassable. The party had to lead the horses over, beating them with sticks, the horses often becoming stuck with their loads. Milton lost his temper several times, abusing Cheadle and the guides. Milton and Cheadle quarrelled furiously. Cheadle's view was that Milton had 'neither the patience, activity or constant attention necessary to drive horses in the woods...he was always in tremendous difficulties & calling out for the rest to stop'.[74] Elsewhere Cheadle states that 'Milton's laziness is a great drawback'.[75] Milton's inactivity, his complaining and bad temper are not mentioned in the published account.

Nor is Milton's illness. He is prone to frequent, unpredictable 'symptoms' which Cheadle is able to ameliorate, but not cure. At Lake St. Ann on 8 June, Cheadle recorded: 'Here Milton had a very severe symptom, followed by two more not quite so strong after our return to camp. He happily got through them all.'[76] On 2 July Cheadle's journal notes: 'I had intended starting at daybreak...but during the night Milton had two symptoms, & I could not go...after getting up, Milton had another symptom but got through.'[77] Milton's illness is not specified, but the apparent unpredictability and brief but severe nature of his 'symptoms' suggest he may have been epileptic. The absence of this information from the published account suggests that Milton's illness was regarded as a weakness, to be concealed lest he be considered unmanly.

In *The North-West Passage by Land*, Milton and Cheadle are the embodiment of frontier manliness. The frontier was a stage on which they could invent and reinvent themselves as men. They were the vanguard of colonisation, conquering virgin territory. In the public story the pair relished frontier life, demonstrating the courage, perseverance and leadership of the British gentleman. In Cheadle's journal a different picture emerges. They were gentlemen adventurers, but not the confident, able-bodied frontier men of *The North-West Passage*. Their amateurish approach to the journey endangered their lives and the lives of others in the party. They displayed endurance, but it was stubborn rather than heroic. They may have displayed courage and occasional resourcefulness, but only in situations created by their own ineptitude. They may have persevered, but only because there was no other way out. If it had not been for their Métis guide they probably would have died.

Milton was neither physically nor temperamentally suited to frontier life. He lacked perseverance, and, while not shirking work entirely, preferred to sleep in or fish, leaving Cheadle and the Métis guide to make the decisions and take the risks. He was manifestly 'unmanly'. Although by birth he was entitled to the appellation 'gentleman', he displayed few of the attributes which, in the middle of the nineteenth century, a gentleman was supposed to possess. He lacked leadership and the publication of *The North-west Passage by Land*, with its misleading account of their adventures, demonstrated a lack of integrity. Obviously, Milton saw no need to adapt his genteel habits to the exigencies of the frontier. His behaviour suggests that his idea of manliness was rooted in aristocratic ideals of sport and the pursuit of leisure. He seemed oblivious to the fact that that he was in a different environment to that in which he had acquired his idea of manhood. Perhaps as a member of the landed aristocracy, as a member of Britain's ruling elite (he was a member of the House of Commons from 1865 to 1872, and was anyway entitled to sit in the House of Lords), he could take his manhood for granted. He did not have to establish his social position or independence by the accumulation of wealth through commerce or manufacturing. He was the heir apparent of William Thomas Spencer Wentworth-Fitzwilliam, the sixth Earl Fitzwilliam, and therefore he did not have to worry about a profession. Unlike many British men of his class Milton did not go to the frontier to seek opportunities for advancement. He was an adventurer seeking interesting diversions, and while he had Cheadle to look after him, he did not have to put in much effort.

The North-West Passage by Land helped to popularise the image of the frontier, firstly, as a place of adventure and danger, and, secondly, as a site where the British gentleman could exercise his virtues and abilities, for the ultimate good of the Empire. On such a hazardous journey, it may be that mere survival is an achievement. Milton's whingeing notwithstanding and even though they had only just survived, stubborn self-belief and determination got them through. The discrepancies between the published account and Cheadle's journal are sins of omission rather than commission. There is nothing to suggest that the events described did not happen. A comparative reading, however, reveals that Milton and Cheadle used the frontier as a place to construct their manliness, to supposedly enact the attendant virtues, and that *The North-West Passage by Land* was a public announcement of their manliness.

While Milton and Cheadle were stumbling across Canada, optimism and self-confidence drove 23-year-old Londoner and chemist Harry Guillod and his 17-year-old brother George to join hundreds of other prospective miners making their way to the Cariboo goldfields. Harry wrote a daily account of his time in British Columbia on scraps of paper which he later compiled into a journal, which he sent to his mother as a long letter. On reaching Victoria the brothers and their friend Philip Johnston bought a decrepit horse, and caught the steamer to the mainland and from New Westminster caught another to Douglas. From there they began the trek to Cariboo. The journey, like all overland trips in British Columbia, was arduous to say the least. Mosquitoes, mud, rain, steep mountain passes and a poor diet combined to make the trip physically and mentally draining and Guillod and George both became ill: 'George had a violent attack of Diarrhoea. My face gathered and was very much swollen, so I had to tie it up in a pair of drawers which, with a red handkerchief and my mosquito netting surmounted with a Scotch cap, made me look a bit of a fright.'[78] Despite the difficulties, Guillod maintains a cheerful and optimistic outlook. He has an artist's eye for scenery and some of his descriptions of the journey make their trek sound like a pleasant, albeit strenuous, country excursion:

> The road up thus far had been through deep valleys with snow capped mountains towering above the trees in the distance; every mile or two we came to a swift running stream of deliciously cold water from the mountains, dashing and spraying over the stones; or we crossed a rough bridge of pine trees over a cascade which bounded over the rocks far below; then would come a level road through pine forests for a few miles; again we went up hill round the side of a mountain, only to descend again far down into the valley, shut in by large trees and cool even in the heat of day, but never out of sight of huge mountains, principally covered with fir.[79]

Despite the hardships of such a journey Guillod could still see the beauty of the countryside. That he could do so suggests that he was content and enjoying the challenge. He was perfectly happy with the outdoor life, as hazardous and uncomfortable as it may have been, and he met the challenges of the frontier with cheerful courage. When he arrived at the goldfields he immediately set about buying a claim and digging for gold. For someone trained as a chemist, gold mining in the wilds of British Columbia would have been punishing work. However, Guillod was not a man to contemplate failure and, despite the fact that he knew nothing about mining, took to the miner's life and its attendant hardships with gusto. He did not baulk at the 12-hour days of physical toil: 'I got on first rate at pick and shovel, and then went to wheeling up an inclined plane, which as the barrows were very rough homemade things, with solid wood wheels, was frightfully hard work, but I stick [sic] to it like a brick.'[80] So determined was he to be successful that, despite failing at the first attempt at gold mining, having to break stones to earn a pittance, and trek and paddle back to Victoria for the winter where he arrived with barely the shirt on his back, Guillod returned to the Cariboo for a second attempt to strike it rich.

Presumably he had better luck the second time, as in 1863 he became part owner of a sawmill, thereby establishing himself as an independent man. Guillod was extremely proud of his achievement in reaching the Cariboo. On his first excursion he spent four months trekking to, and working on, the goldfields. In his letter to his mother he boasts of having 'seen The Elephant' as the Cariboo was known among the miners, and reports that 'my health has been first rate' and 'my spirits were not at all damped'.[81] Guillod had strong views on manliness and what it took to succeed on the frontier. In a preface to his journal he issued a challenge and a warning to other young men:

> No doubt there are thousands of our city youths who would as readily leave the comforts of a quiet home and face the hardships of a mountain journey bad food and short commons, hail and rain and storm, mosquitoes and sand flies with as good a heart and as patient an endurance, shewing the sterling qualities of the Saxon race; but there are also thousands who would not be able to do so; and it will be well for every one who is tempted by the glittering prizes which are held out by the Cariboo and its rival Goldfields, to consider deeply whether they have got the right stuff in them and will be able to bivouac in wet blankets and cook a pancake in a hailstorm,

without regretting the snug featherbed and comfortable chophouse of the West end and the city.[82]

In Guillod's view there are two types of men – those who possess 'the sterling qualities of the Saxon race' and those who do not. Endurance and optimism, the strength and willingness to face frontier hardships are foremost amongst these qualities. The frontier will bring out the manliness in British men. But a man needs to be sure he has what it takes before going; not all Saxons have the 'sterling qualities' in equal portion. In making this distinction between men, Guillod is obviously placing himself on the side of the manly Saxons in contrast to the unmanly, stay-at-home Saxons. On his own account, Harry Guillod personified the manly virtues. He possessed unextinguishable self-confidence, he was strong and self-reliant, and was not daunted by setbacks.

Guillod's journal was not published. The only reader was his mother, although she probably circulated it amongst the family. This restricted readership makes the inclusion of the above passage, with its exhortative and admonishing tone, curious. Who is Guillod trying to convince? He is obviously trying to impress his mother and family, and perhaps by demonstrating his manly attainments, justify leaving home. Perhaps Guillod's main audience is himself and the journal is an exercise in boosting his own sense of manliness. After all, what does his mother care for men who prefer comfortable beds and chop houses? Guillod is exalting in his self-perception as a 'manly' man, and reinforcing this by contrast with those he regards as unmanly. Guillod's journal is a deliberate work of self-construction. He saw the British Columbia frontier as a suitable site for the construction of Harry Guillod, the 'manly' man. Additionally, he wanted those who meant most to him know of his manliness.

Arthur Neame was probably more qualified than Viscount Milton or Harry Guillod for a frontier career. Neame had trained as an engineer, but deciding that there was 'not much for them' in England, he and his brother Frank emigrated to Queensland in 1870, and in 1871 took up land 'quite on the outskirts of civilisation', on the Herbert River inland from Cardwell.[83] What 'not much for them' actually meant is not clear. Neame had worked for a number of engineering firms in London before deciding to go to Paris to learn French and, unlike other British men who went to the frontier (e.g. Leslie and Bushby in Chapter 2), he had engineering qualifications, so employment *per se* may not have been the issue.

That they decided to emigrate suggests that they were looking for something more than a mere occupation, namely, the opportunity to prove themselves as independent men in a challenging environment. Further evidence for this is suggested by the poem at the beginning of the reminiscences:

> I hear the tread of pioneers
> Of nations yet to be
> The first low wash of waves, where soon
> Shall roll a human sea.[84]

The poem indicates that Neame was motivated by a sense of imperial mission, that he felt the obligation, suggested by Said, to settle and develop distant lands, as well as a desire to build an independent life. Neame's reminiscences portray a British man, armed with only fortitude, perseverance and sense of empire, overcoming physical danger and a hostile environment, and finding independence on the frontier.

On arriving in Brisbane, Neame wasted no time in leaving for less settled parts, travelling to Jondaryn on the Darling Downs and then to another property a further 200 miles out. At first Arthur Neame disliked colonial life, finding the hotels in Brisbane 'very rough and uncomfortable...I found the private boarding houses much pleasanter'.[85] Once out in the bush he was forced to adapt to the rough outdoor life, which he quickly did. A few weeks on a sheep station demonstrated that discomfort was relative. Sleeping in a slab hut, where his hand could go through the space between the slabs, was a 'luxury' and 'a great treat...as most of my time whilst at this station was spent away on the run sleeping either in a tent or under the sky'.[86] While he was initially unprepared for rough accommodation, Neame knew that he would have to do hard, physical work: 'I quite expected whilst here we should have work given us to do, as I understood that everyone who went to the Colony was expected to lend a hand at anything that was required.'[87] Beginning his frontier career on a sheep station 200 miles west of Roma, he had every opportunity to put his understanding into practice. In three months on the station he built fences, cooked, herded sheep, mustered and branded cattle. He observed transient men carrying their swags. With clothes and provisions rolled in a blanket, and a quart pot and tin mug fastened to the roll, Neame admiringly thought, 'You are then quite independent of everyone and everything.'[88] Admiring though he was of the perceived independence of the swagman, the independence Neame had in mind would see him as an employer of labour, not an employee.

Preferring sugar to sheep, Neame and his brother were keen to go to North Queensland, 'anxious to settle down' in Neame's words, and were advised of the dangers: 'Before we left Brisbane we were told that we should most likely be killed and eaten by the Blacks, or else by Crocodiles, & if not we should die of fever, the coastal districts all suffered much from Malaria.'[89] Undeterred, they arrived in Cardwell and immediately set about looking for suitable land. This took longer than expected, and Neame did contract malaria, but eventually the pair successfully applied for 1,280 acres on the north side of the Herbert River.

Neame's reminiscences provide an almost day-by-day account of how he and his brother built a cane farm out of the scrub. They faced numerous difficulties and hazards. Cardwell was two days away and supplies and materials had to be brought up the Herbert River in a boat or punt. They were constantly harassed by the Aborigines whose land they had taken. The almost impossible project Arthur and Frank had taken on is illustrated by this account of a not untypical minor misadventure:

> The punt came down we loaded it and started for the plantation at 11 p.m. ran on a snag in the dark, and made a hole in the bottom, so had to run her aground on the sand bank, sent the boat up to the camp to fetch a man with tools to stop the hole, but could not float here again till the following night for want of water, got her off just at high tide with much trouble, but could not get any further up the river & had to remain till the following night, when we started at 1 a.m. & got within 300 yards of our landing at 5 a.m. but could get no further, the tides being very poor, tried to get her further with the day tide at noon, but only succeeded in getting her 100 yards. We floated the punt at 3:30 a.m. unloaded her, and started at 7 a.m. for the vessel, arrived there about 11 a.m., loaded and got back within 200 yards of the landing at 6 p.m. when we were aground. Got punt across in the morning unloaded and started off for the vessel, but grounded in Humbug reach & had to wait for the tide, reached the vessel at 4:30 p.m. loaded and waited for the tide, started at 2:30 a.m. reached the plantation & unloaded.[90]

If there was one manly quality Neame possessed it was perseverance.

Life was all work, except for Sundays and Christmas Day. Neame does not record any social life, and perhaps there was none. Recreation, such as it was, usually involved hunting, an archetypal masculine pursuit.[91] Neame was stoic, and this is reflected in his matter of fact writing style. Despite the hostile environment and the incredibly long and strenuous working days, Neame perseveres. He never expresses any frustration, fear or anxiety. There is no question of quitting the enterprise. Hacking a cane plantation out of the bush gave the brothers all the chances they needed to exercise or acquire their manly qualities. Strength, perseverance and fortitude were required, generated and put into action. Neame went to the colonial frontier to be an independent man, to establish himself in the world, and ultimately he succeeded. He made two return trips to Britain and on the second, in 1882, he married Jessie Harrison. They returned to North Queensland in September the same year, only to sell the plantation. Over the next 14 years he migrated back and forth between Britain and North Queensland, actually repurchasing the plantation from the company to which he had earlier sold it. The brothers continued to operate the plantation and mill until 1896 when they sold it to the Colonial Sugar Company for £120,000, and Neame returned to England for good.

Arthur and Frank Neame were typical of the middle-class men who came to the Queensland frontier. They were well educated, but devoid of skills which might be useful on a sheep or cattle property, or on a cane farm. Nevertheless, they adapted quickly, not hesitating to take on tasks for which they had no experience. Neame's reminiscences, like John Tod's, betray no doubts. In his memoir, Neame never wonders if he made the right decision to leave England, and never considers giving up, despite the tremendous difficulties and hardships. Bereft of opportunity in Britain, Arthur and Frank Neame revelled in the hard-work frontier life, putting into effect the manly virtues of stoicism and perseverance.

Neame's is a more humble, matter-of-fact account of frontier life than Milton and Cheadle's or Henry's. Yet all the tropes of frontier life are there: the inhospitable environment, disease, savage natives, unrelenting hard work, mishaps and adventure. There is an addendum to the main manuscript titled 'Lectures Given by Arthur Neame to Schools in England', which is an abridged version of his life in North Queensland. There is no indication where or how many times Neame delivered lectures on his life, but in them he conveys the same story of hardship, hard work and perseverance contained in the main manuscript. He thus disseminated a picture of frontier life consistent with that constructed by the other men in this chapter. As a result of his endeavours, Neame became a prosperous man. He and his wife had two sons, and employed a governess to look after them. They travelled widely, and could afford to go to the United States and Europe by saloon class. When he returned to England for good in 1897, having sold the plantation for a second time, he did not work again. He was able to lead a very comfortable, middle-class existence – he had achieved full independence. While he does not make an explicit connection between his work on the plantation and his prosperity, the message to his school audience was clear: manly independence awaits all those who have the self-reliance, endurance and strength to meet the challenges of the frontier.

When they went to the frontier, many men left relatively sedentary lives to embark upon physically demanding careers. Equipped with unshakeable confidence and a will to succeed they went to the colonial frontier to build a manly life, to gain independence and to put into practice the masculine codes valued by metropolitan society, but for which that society could provide only limited outlets. They took on the challenges the frontier offered, constructing the masculine status to which they aspired and revelling in the experience. They expected to be tested and were not disappointed. The trials and ordeals encountered were not seen as obstacles or hindrances. They were opportunities for practising and achieving manliness, which men found gratifying and rewarding. In their memoirs and journals men recorded and sometimes embellished their manly deeds, demonstrating to themselves and others that they had had fulfilled the requirements of the manly ethos.

However, once achieved, manliness could not be taken for granted. White British manliness had to be constantly reasserted and defended against the challenges of the frontier and alternative versions of masculinity. At the same time not all men were successful in their frontier endeavours. The frontier, as well as providing opportunities for the performance of manliness, put manliness under pressure. Not all men were the noble, manly pioneers of frontier mythology.

4
Men without (White) Women

> I hate isolation. To set out alone on a long trip makes me feel like the small child who, lingering behind, screams for fear of being abandoned; or like the squadron horse, on scouting work, that frets to go back to the other horses. Nearly always, on rough journeys, one has a companion, a partner; and a partner means safety and cheerfulness and the surety of proper camps and fires and meals. A lonely man, panting to get to his journey's end, pushes on too hard, tires himself, travels too late into the falling dusk, and is exhausted as he makes camp.
>
> I cursed Carter as I dug my axe into log after log and found them all rotten; and every pole and even every twig seemed rotten too. And at that twinge of despair the horror of loneliness came upon me, and I looked up the mountain, and over the misty, white-caped sea, and round upon the scattered tangle of fallen timber on the mossy rocks – and the sight was dreary, the abomination of desolation.
>
> (M. Allerdale Grainger, *Woodsman of the West*)

Manliness is an active construction. A conscientious and sustained effort is required to maintain one's manly status, and the frontier provided the stage on which men could perform and refine manly skills. However, the frontier also posed challenges to the manly ideal. One of these was the remoteness of the frontier, and the concomitant loneliness and isolation, which could undermine manly self-esteem and self-control. Hostile physical environments, isolation and hard times could reduce men to despair and alcoholism. Paradoxically, loneliness and isolation could enhance domestic ties, and men could form new bonds to replace the old.

Fears of loneliness were not unusual. They were shared by many men on the frontier and arose out of their physical remoteness from their families and friends, poor communications and their inability to alter their situation in the short term. Miles Fairburn, in *The Ideal Society and Its Enemies: The Foundations of Modern New Zealand Society 1850–1900*, identifies social isolation as the 'prevailing tendency' in that frontier society.[1] This was primarily due to the large tide of immigrants who went to New Zealand during this period, severed as they were from their networks in metropolitan society and having been in the colony an insufficient time to build new ones. There were also a host of secondary causes. The frontier expanded so quickly that most colonists settled in new areas where they were strangers to one another and there were no institutions to facilitate meeting and mixing. The temporary nature of employment meant that men were transient, often travelling from one brief employment to another, preventing them from establishing 'mateship' bonds. Households were geographically isolated, and an 'extreme individualism' hindered the growth of local institutions.[2] The result of this combination of factors was pervasive loneliness and despair. The frontier tested men's stoicism and perseverance, and not all men could cope. Life on the frontiers of British Columbia and Queensland could be equally solitary.

Victoria was three to six months from England by ship and overland communication with eastern Canada also took months. Sailing time from England to Queensland was similar and Brisbane is 1,000 kilometres from Sydney. The settlements of far North Queensland are even further from Brisbane. Towns and villages in Queensland and British Columbia were small and dispersed, and many men did not settle in one location. This remoteness placed strains on individuals and relationships, and it had implications for the practice of manliness and the gender order.

Men could be profoundly affected by the absence of their familiar domestic environment, of family and loved ones, by the isolation and remoteness of the frontier. The remoteness and isolation of the frontier challenged the manly ideal and its performance in a number of ways. Firstly, the physical hardships of the frontier tested men's stoicism and perseverance. Hard work, a poor diet and poverty could lead men into despair, tempting them to forsake the frontier life which had held out much promise. Secondly, frontier life could lead to profound emotional deprivation and loneliness, which damaged men's self-belief.

Paradoxically, the separation from family and loved ones that frontier living entailed could accentuate desire, as husbands and wives strove to maintain relationships. Thirdly, many men sought comfort from the harshness of the frontier in alcohol, the excessive consumption of which was characteristic of frontier life. The frontier undermined the sobriety demanded by the conduct books, and the lack of sobriety on the frontier suggests a loss of manly self-control.

Finally, the isolation and remoteness of the frontier could both intensify and undermine the normative heterosexuality implicit in the masculine ideal. The absence of white women did not necessarily mean that white men were celibate. For men predisposed to homosexuality the frontier provided the opportunity to shed some of the constraints imposed by the dominant versions of masculinity. For others, the isolation and loneliness of the frontier led them to seek comfort in the company of other men by forming close homosocial relations, some of which may have been homosexual. In all, these factors demonstrate that on the frontier, many aspects of the masculine ideal were diluted, and reality and ideal did not necessarily coincide. Not all men were able to construct a manly identity, nor did their experiences become part of frontier mythology.

On the Queensland frontier there were few occupations lonelier than that of shepherd. Loggers or miners usually worked as members of a team.[3] Although they were remote from family and friends, they were surrounded by other men and were rarely alone in the strict sense of the word. Shepherds, on the other hand, were not only cut off from family and friends, but were often isolated from all human contact for weeks at a time. Not all men were cut out for shepherding. Before heading to North Queensland Arthur Neame recorded in his reminiscences:

> I found this shepherding very lonely work, and also very fatiguing... you must try to imagine yourself in a hut and no other habitation, or human being within three miles, and only then another little hut with one man in it... it is not suitable work for young people, so when the overseer came around 9 or 10 days after I went there, I asked him to send someone to relieve me, as I could not be responsible for the lambs any longer; many of the old shepherds are more or less mad after living by themselves for a number of years.[4]

Neame recognised the potential dangers of isolation early, and his shepherding career was brief. He avoided the psychological consequences that afflicted others and turned to cane farming with his brother, an occupation apparently more conducive to achieving manly independence, and potentially less lonely. Isolation could play tricks on one's mind. George Carrington worked as a shepherd in the Queensland bush on and off for three years. It did not take long for the isolation of the bush to have an effect. Left alone with 800 sheep he wrote of his first night in the bush by himself. When sleep would not come, his thoughts turned to the dangers of the bush:

> First of all, I began to think what a long way off I was from my fellow men, at least from men of my own colour, cut off entirely from assistance should I require it. Supposing I was taken ill, suppose the blacks attacked me, I might shout for help, no one could hear me. Then I began to argue that this was all nonsense, I was well and strong, and there were probably no blacks anywhere near. It was foolish to annoy myself with such idle speculations, I had better go to sleep, but it was no use; all the horrible stories that I had ever heard thronged to my recollection: of men attacked by savages and murdered, of ghastly corpses subjected to frightful mutilations, of dead men lying unregarded and found days after in lonely huts.[5]

Perhaps the isolation of frontier life was playing tricks on Carrington's mind. Certainly he appears to be unnerved by his isolation and the perceived danger posed by 'blacks'. To allow his 'foolish' fears to overwhelm him would be to lack manly courage and he tries to allay his fears by mocking them, but to no avail. There is a racialised aspect to his unmanly fear: on the Queensland frontier, danger is black. Carrington was cut off 'men of my own colour' and endangered by black 'savages' who engage in barabarism. In this passage the relationship between Indigenous masculinity and white manliness is evident. In Carrington's imagination, black men are savage and uncivilised, the antithesis of white manhood. However, Carrington's fear shows that the manly superiority supposedly possessed by white men is very shaky indeed.

Carrington found the monotony of shepherding 'sickening', 'apt to dull the faculties, both of mind and body'.[6] Shepherding and its attendant loneliness had a reputation for producing strange characters:

> The professional shepherd is easily known by his general abstracted and neglected appearance, and his lounging habits. He is strange and 'cranky' in his ways too. Indeed squatters assert that the

best shepherds are those who are more or less mad, and consider a little crack in the understanding to be a great qualification. Shepherds...talk to themselves, to their materials, to the gum trees.[7]

The experiences of Neame and Carrington illustrate a contradiction in frontier manliness: shepherding required the manly virtues of stoicism and perseverance, and yet at the same time could lead to madness. In the mid-nineteenth century madness, medically labelled 'hysteria', was regarded as a feminine affliction. Mental instability in men was therefore unmanly.[8] The practice of manly stoicism and perseverance – which on the frontier meant enduring isolation and loneliness – is turned upside down. Manliness was undermined by frontier conditions. What in other times and places would be regarded as manly leads to unmanly behaviour.

In 1863, R. Henderson was employed as a shepherd, carrier and labourer on a property at Auburn 140 miles 'up the country' from Dalby. The remoteness of this station is indicated by the fact that it took him over a month to get there from Brisbane, travelling by foot and dray. He kept a diary for the year he was engaged, making a weekly entry of the work and the weather, and of his hopes, often unrealised, of letters from his family:

February 22nd Sabath

Another man and I have been ingaged [sic] all week putting up the fence that the flood swept away and in the bush sometimes for days cutting rales and forks for the fence. Yesterday we had a fine days ride about twelve miles to mend a yard, a sheep yard which we did in about 9 hours then we had a fine ride home. I killed a sheep it was a fine days sport to me. I had a fine bath in the river today it is fine and deep and I injoyed [sic] it very much but my great anxiety is to know how William and bellow and gessie are all getting on. I have gote [sic] no letters yet and I weary very much for them.[9]

Finally after four months his relief at hearing from his family is palpable:

Sabath 26th of April

Monday was a happy day for me for I got 7 letters – 3 from jeannie 2 from father and 3 papers 1 from William and 1 from W Mcfarlin. I was happy to here [sic] William got work at the saw mill. I sent a letter next day to William and I expect an answer shortly. It was the happiest week I spent in Australia. I hope and trust letters will be oftener.[10]

Thereafter Henderson received letters every month or so. However, this was insufficient to ease his sense of loneliness. In nearly every weekly entry he pined for letters from home – the isolation was the most difficult part of frontier life. One senses he felt very much like Grainger's child who feared abandonment. Henderson stuck assiduously to the tasks he was given, 'manly' tasks which required strength, perseverance and self-reliance, but which failed to distract him from his solitary state.

Two men on the frontier of British Columbia who strove to fulfil what they believed were their masculine obligations and who consequently struggled with isolation and loneliness were Robert Harkness and James Thomson who travelled to the Cariboo goldfields in 1862. Their response to the challenges of the remoteness of the frontier of British Columbia and the concomitant isolation from their families is revealed in a series of poignant letters written to their wives detailing both the psychological and physical demands they faced. Harkness and Thomson sketch a picture of frontier males who were far from the rugged frontiersmen stereotype of popular culture, and their letters can be read as a journey of self in which the competing notions of masculinity and allegiance to family are played out. The challenges arising from a sense of geographical remoteness undermined both writers' sense of manly self-esteem and self-control – so important in the male public sphere – while at the same time strengthening their attachment to the domestic sphere.

At the beginning of their journey Harkness and Thomson, as mid-Victorian males, appear to subscribe to the prevailing patriarchal ideals in which the male is the provider and therefore protector of the family unit. Their letters also construct an image of them as loving husbands and affectionate fathers. While they were optimists who were willing to do what was necessary to provide for their families, neither man conformed to the conventional image of the North American frontiersman. Harkness was a shopkeeper and Thomson a baker, more used to wearing aprons than buckskins. The frontier would test their physical courage, endurance and fortitude, demanding of them those attributes central to the Victorian masculine ideal. They also had to struggle to reconcile their actions with devotion to family. Their time on the frontier illustrates a paradox in dominant model of manliness: the centrality of the family and of a companionate marriage that was central to the mid-Victorian gender order was undermined by the fact that in order to provide for their families, Harkness and Thomson had to leave them, an act which potentially sacrificed their relationships and emotional life in order to practise the more ostensibly virile 'masculine' attributes. Furthermore, the performance of the masculine virtues failed to yield any benefit. Their letters show that neither man achieved wealth nor manly independence. Arguably, the frontier for Harkness and Thomson was a place of trial and tribulation, not of self-realisation, and both were impoverished and diminished by the experience.

In his autobiographical novel *Woodsmen of the West*, M. Allerdale Grainger describes the risks faced and the fear felt by men on the frontier, surrounded by a strange and threatening country, and remote from the familiar and reassuring people and places of home. Grainger recounts the occasion on which he had been sent to procure supplies for a logging camp, a journey that could easily take him a month or more alone. He was well aware of the risks, and had spent some time apprising the camp boss of these in a futile attempt to avoid the journey. A day into his trip 'the horror of loneliness' and the 'abomination of desolation' came over him. As luck would have it, he was joined by two loggers from a rival camp bound in the same direction, and he did not have to face the wilderness alone. Later he engaged two men and a boat to help him return to camp with the supplies.

For Grainger, the very landscape was threatening, exacerbating his isolation, emphasising his vulnerability. Loneliness can trigger primal fears and irrational, bestial responses. Loneliness produces not only psychological dangers, but physical dangers as well, as the lonely man feels compelled to push himself beyond his limits, to somehow overcome his isolation through exertion. While Robert Harkness and James Thomson were never absolutely alone on the frontier – in the sense that there were no other people around them for an extended period – they experienced severe emotional trauma arising from isolation from their families. Grainger had no family that he wrote of, nor did he write of strong bonds with fellow woodsmen. He would have been content simply to have one human companion. Despite these differences in circumstances, Grainger's story, together with those of Harkness and Thompson, suggests that isolation and loneliness were common among frontier men.

Robert Harkness, who had owned a general store in eastern Ontario, was a member of the largest of the several groups of 'Overlanders' which journeyed across the Canadian prairies, and over the Rocky Mountains to seek fortune on the Cariboo goldfields of British Columbia in 1862. Compared to the published diaries of other Overlanders, Harkness' letters are more personal and possess an intimate and revelatory voice that public narratives do not.[11] He describes the trip as 'a great task' and despite the hardship he expresses pride in his undertaking:

> In a fortnight more we will be at Fort Edmonton & then our real hardships begin, but I have grown so tough that I don't expect to mind it. I have lost at least 20 pounds of flesh since I left home but still I am perfectly healthy. In these long days & and in this northern clime daylight comes very early & we are up every morning at two o'clock & travel two or three hours before breakfast. What think you of that?[12]

Why did he choose the overland route as opposed to the alternatives – via the southern tip of South America and San Francisco, or across the Isthmus of Panama? A number of explanations are possible. He may have simply been unable to afford a boat ticket. Perhaps he derived a sense of security from travelling with a group of like-minded men. For Harkness the journey may have been as necessary and important as the gold mining. This was a quest to prove his manhood. Harkness undertook his journey as a test which, if he succeeded, would redeem past failures. In an undated letter Harkness says of group leader Thomas McMicking that 'like myself he was unfortunate in business'.[13] In 1864 he acknowledged his relief that 'enough had been collected on my accounts to pay Moran the interest due and got all the payments postponed another year'.[14] Harkness goes into no further detail, but these lines suggest that his general store had not been a success. Business failure, debt and possibly lack of local opportunity meant that Harkness had lost his role as the family provider.

The Cariboo goldfields provided Harkness with a way of recuperating his fortune, and salvaging his tattered sense of masculinity. In this sense it could be argued that in Harkness' letters home he reveals his attempt to conform to established masculine stereotypes in being a provider, a man of fortitude, a family man and a courageous adventurer. Finding gold is central to this myth for it is this success which will enable him to financially support his dependents and maintain a home. In order to find gold he must exert his physical strength. It also meant leaving the family for four years. This led to in a psychological conflict resulting in stress and anxiety. This is evidenced in his letters home, but at the same time, his professions of love for his wife and family are not only undiminished but are intensified.

While he was away every letter Harkness wrote expressed his love for his wife and children and his desire to be eventually reunited. At the early stage of his journey but already homesick, he wrote to Sabrina from Detroit:

> I am more homesick than ever I was in my life before but if I had a letter from you it would half cure me. I could sit down and read it over and over again and almost imagine I had it from your own dear self. But although I haven't heard from you I must keep writing to you, I have nothing to do and I can think of nothing but the 'loved ones at home'. Do you know it hardly seems possible that I am really gone to stay away from you for such a length of time. I feel at times as if I were dreaming but I know it is too true that I am not. Well, Sabrina my dear, it must be put up with.[15]

On 9 May 1862 en route to the Cariboo goldfields of British Columbia, Harkness wrote to his wife:

> While assured of your love I care not for the world besides and O Sabrina I cannot express my gratitude for the confidence you repose in me... this separation has at least one compensating quality; but for it we should probably never have known the real depth and intensity of our love for each other. I think so and feel so tenderly towards you that it seems to me I can never say another unkind word to you and I hope I never shall. I'll not ask your pardon for those that are past for I know they are forgiven. True love cannot harbour unkind thoughts of its object.[16]

These passages suggest that Harkness subscribed to the ideal mid-Victorian domestic life (or at least its rhetoric), embracing marriage and a loving family in which the male is the breadwinner and the woman the nurturer.[17] Harkness missed his wife and family a great deal, and his love for Sabrina was profound and it would seem that she also wrote to him in very affectionate terms. Though separated by a thousand miles or more, he was confident that faith would nurture their love. Harkness hints at some past quarrel, but is sure that harsh words have been forgiven. Robert and Sabrina would be apart for four years. During this time Harkness wrote to his wife whenever circumstances allowed and 12 letters survive in the public archive.

What did the children think of him? Only one voice from the family endures in the form of a letter of daughter Mary Dell Harkness to her own daughter, written in 1952. Although she was not born until after his return, Mary wrote of her father: 'I am proud of the letters he sent home. They bespeak a generous and affectionate heart.'[18] While Mary is not reflecting on her father's absence, nevertheless, such sentiments suggest that he was loved by his children, and his absence wrought no long-term adverse effect on his relationship with them. The ideals of family and domesticity are obviously central to Harkness' letters. In his letter of 28 June 1864 he wrote:

> It is you and you only that can confer happiness on a husband who, whatever his faults, is most sincerely and devotedly attached to his wife, and who, though in the third year of his adventurous ramblings, has been uniformly faithful to his marriage vows. I take no special credit to myself for this, it should mark the conduct of every man endowed with a proper degree of self-respect and no man could love and esteem his wife as I do mine and yet be deliberately false to her.[19]

Harkness' fidelity to his wife conformed to the Christian precepts of the Victorian era and was clearly integral to his personal feelings of manhood and to his idea of right conduct. This was not necessarily the norm on the British Columbia frontier. A lack of women of their own race did not necessarily mean that white miners went without sex. Mixed-race relationships between white men and Indigenous women were widespread.[20] Over the years Harkness' yearning remained undiminished:

> Do you remember the 25th of June 1856? Day ever dear to me, that on which she whom I so truly and faithfully loved deigned to become 'all mine own'. Perhaps I have fulfilled my trust unworthily, but at least, my Nina, I love you, if possible more truly and tenderly now than on that memorable day.[21]

While all the letters contain similarly effusive passages, there are also clues that relations between Harkness and Sabrina were not always characterised by such strong, loving feelings. The extracts below suggest marital conflict, harsh words and discord concerning Harkness' plan to venture to the Cariboo:

> O Sabrina nothing but a pressing necessity induced me to leave a home blessed with all the affection the most craving heart could desire and I hope I shall not be very long absent from it.[22]

> ...our petty difficulties. What a depth of love lay concealed beneath them and how well we know it now![23]
>
> I don't think you'll ever doubt me again, it seems to me that my sincerity will be too apparent to admit of doubt.[24]

The letters these extracts come from were written over the entire period Harkness was away. It seems that marital discord, or at least financial difficulties – 'pressing necessity' – weighed on his mind for a very long time. Harkness' effusions of love – 'all the affection the most craving heart could desire' – appear in part to be attempts to make up ground that was lost between him and Sabrina, though that does not mean that they are less than completely genuine. His words suggest that he and Sabrina had quarrelled – 'our petty difficulties: what depth of love lay concealed beneath them' – perhaps over the business and perhaps she did not embrace his plan to go to British Columbia, and may have felt that he was deserting her and the children. Furthermore, Harkness' letters reveal a certain 'asymmetry' or lack of proportion in his feelings for his wife and family. This is not to suggest that his words are inappropriate. The term 'asymmetry' in this context refers to the actual or conceptual distance separating one individual from another.[25] In this case, the further Harkness gets from his family in time and distance, the closer he gets to them psychically or emotionally. The distance between him and Sabrina intensifies his emotions and language:

> If only you knew how anxious I am to see you, your utmost cravings for my love would be gratified.[26]
>
> O my own, my loved my precious wife, 'tis a weary life apart from you'.[27]
>
> Could gold buy me love such as yours? Could gold buy children such as ours? No, verily. And with such a wife & surrounded by such children I envy no man.[28]

Obviously, what is missing here are Sabrina's letters to Robert. One wonders if she reciprocated his love with similar intensity. One can only imagine what her feelings might have been during their separation. A little of her experience is revealed in Harkness' letters: it seems that she did not entirely approve of his venture, and is often desperately short of money. In his own letters, Harkness tells her a good deal about his life on the frontier, but there is little which indicates much understanding of her predicament:

> You told me in one letter that I, as a father, couldn't appreciate your feelings as a mother in being separated from your children. That's cool certainly. What till you get to be a father before you judge.[29]

There is a hint of the stern paterfamilias in these lines. There appears to have been no question that Sabrina or the children would accompany Harkness to the Cariboo. Rather, Sabrina stayed at home and looked after the children. While he was away Sabrina had a job – she taught at the school in Dixon's Corner, Ontario, which itself indicated a failure on the part of Harkness to support his family. Harkness obviously felt that her teaching was undesirable as he wrote in 1865 that 'I hope the money I sent you arrived safely and that you will not be obliged to teach anymore'.[30] When Harkness eventually returned from the Cariboo he took over her job at the school. Thus he reasserted his authority as patriarch and breadwinner while Sabrina's place in the domestic sphere was confirmed.

In the early stages of his journey Harkness had cause for optimism. On 22 April 1862 he wrote: 'I suppose you have read the *Globe*, I got hold of one here yesterday and was gratified to see the favourable accounts of British Columbia.' On 23 July 1862 he wrote: 'That there is plenty of gold on the Saskatchewan and that rich diggings will yet be discovered I have no doubt.' Optimism was mixed with stoicism:

> It is dark and damp, with a very cold wind blowing hard, so cold, in fact, that I was obliged to put on two coats and wrap myself in my blanket and stay in the tent all day to shelter myself from the piercing wind. These things, of course, however, I expected and can bear them with tolerable patience if I could only be assured that my dear loved ones were comfortable at home.[31]

Eventually, stoicism would give way to despair. Evidently, Harkness also feels guilt for leaving his family. Nevertheless, he displayed some amount of resolve and expects his wife to do likewise. That he felt guilt and resolved to repress his feelings illustrates the tension between the domestic ideal and adventurous masculinity. At first Harkness seemed to revel in the physical challenges his trek entailed:

> The first night we camped out ice formed on a lake nearby more than a quarter of an inch thick but I haven't suffered any from cold. I am

now sitting under a tent with a piece of board on my knee for a writing table so you must be lenient towards my poor writing. I am up every morning before 5 o'clock; what do you think of that for Bob?[32]

However, as the journey unfolded, it was not only the pain of separation that struck Harkness hard. Perhaps more predictably, the frontier asserted physical demands that must be met and endured. Starting at five o'clock in the morning he and his party walked until ten or eleven and then stopped until one or two o'clock and then started again. They travelled until six or seven o'clock, ate and went to bed. They got up the next morning and started the process all over again, usually covering ten miles a day.

The frontier's physical demands became more strenuous and Harkness struggled:

> Often we have to take off our shoes, roll up our pants and help push the cart through mud holes. Yesterday we crossed the Assiniboine in a scow taking one ox and cart at a time and pulling over by a rope. We don't travel on Sundays and both ourselves and our cattle are very glad to get a rest but today is very dreary and dispiriting.[33]

As Harkness had been a shopkeeper, such strenuous physical exertion must have been difficult, to say the least, and it obviously exacted an emotional toll. The trek must have strained his reserves of stoicism and perseverance, and the temptation to turn back must have been strong. The monotony and routine of frontier life and its negative emotional toll did not end once he reached the Cariboo: 'I wish I had something more cheering to write but the fact is I am quite out of spirits. I have been three months now in this miserable town [New Westminster], I have worked whenever I could to get a days work, yet haven't so much as made my board.'[34]

Throughout these letters, when he writes of separation and the physical severity of the journey, there is a strong sense of exile, of the psychological anxiety which accompanies the uprooting of one's foundations to wander in the wilderness. A year into his sojourn, the Cariboo was clearly not what Harkness expected. In 1863 he wrote from Richfield on the goldfields and there was no mention of earning a living from gold mining, let alone striking it rich. One letter of 1864 conveys Harkness' feelings of exile and isolation:

> It is now nearly two years since we separated, two long, weary years such as I hope never again to see in my lifetime. If all we have

endured is not to benefit us in any money point of view, be it so, we shall, at the least, the better enjoy our domestic pleasures from having experienced the pain of being deprived of them. I confess that I am weary, weary of our separation... it would cause me no very serious regret if I never again saw Canada, though I should as soon think of settling in the moon as in this country. I am now very much like my father, stern and unsociable, speaking to nobody and asking nobody to speak to me. No play, no mirth, no jollity of any kind, all work and somberness.[35]

Harkness appears to have undergone a transformation in outlook. The optimistic tone of earlier letters has given way to despair. British Columbia no longer holds any attraction – the frontier is as alien as the moon. It seems that Harkness' frontier experiences have ultimately narrowed his focus to the domestic. Harkness' experiences and focus on his family call into question the public/private divide that supposedly delineated masculine and feminine spheres. As John Tosh points out, men's power has relied heavily on their ability to pass between the public and private spheres. He argues that as a social identity, Victorian masculinity was constructed in three arenas – home, work and the all-male association. Not only did creating a home establish the conditions in which private life could prosper, it was also an important stage in gaining recognition as an adult male. Providing for the home and one's dependents was a key element of manhood.[36] It seems that Harkness' life was strongly conditioned by the Victorian ideal of domesticity and it is as a husband and father that he most identifies.

Harkness was not alone in his experience. He had friends, but the frontier goldfields were not treating them very well either: On 28 June 1864 he wrote: 'Charley Bowen is still on Lowhee Creek, prospects of getting anything there are not very brilliant. Josh Bowen and Aus McIntosh are both working in the Montreal claim. Gilbert Munro has been making shakes but is not likely to do so well this summer as last.'[37]

Frontier British Columbia constructed a broad male culture that fostered same-sex social, emotional and sometimes sexual bonds. Illness and death often made these bonds explicit and the dissolution of male friendships could cause considerable pain.[38] However, the depth of Harkness' friendships is not easy to fathom. These men were obviously his friends as they are mentioned in several letters. It is not clear whether he knew them in Ontario, although he seems to take it for granted that his wife knows who they are. Although Harkness shared a shanty with another man named Nicholls, he explicitly states they ate and slept apart. Despite the common quest and common hardship among these men, the letters give only very matter-of-fact reports of their comings and goings. Harkness expresses no sense of a collective consciousness, nor any hint of mateship. He may have been something of a loner, or the matter of factness in the passages about his friends could indicate a masculine reserve in expressing feelings towards other men. Either way, it appears he did not form close emotional ties with others. For Harkness, the masculine frontier environment did not alleviate his sense of loneliness and isolation, nor help him achieve redemptive manliness.

The last letter in the collection is dated 28 April 1865. Harkness had been away for three years when he wrote from New Westminster:

> I have been three months now in this miserable town, I have worked whenever I could get a days [sic] work, yet haven't so much as made my board. I live all alone in a little cabin for which I pay $4 per month rent. I hired to go to work on a road on Monday, at $40 per month and board. If I can get three or four months steady work the proceeds will enable me to reach home.[39]

He has clearly given up hope of making any kind of fortune on the goldfields. He has not been able to provide for his family, which was the main reason for his journey. All he hopes for is his fare home. Four years on the British Columbia frontier did not yield the masculine status it was supposed to. Manliness could be elusive. Rather than comprising a stable core of qualities and behaviours, the requirements were continually changing. Is one's male status determined by how one cares for one's family, or by how one performs the muscular virtues in a hostile environment? What if the former depends on the latter? Harkness found that he could no longer keep up the performance. The pathway to manliness was strewn with many obstacles. Over the four years he was in British Columbia these obstacles became insurmountable.

Compared to Robert Harkness, James Thomson had a relatively easy journey to the Cariboo, sailing from San Francisco. As a 22-year-old baker's apprentice from Aboyne, Aberdeenshire, he left Scotland in 1844 to start a new life in Canada. While Aberdeenshire was a relatively prosperous county, as a result of famine in the Highlands and the subsequent evictions of crofters from their farms, it experienced a net increase in population as Highlanders filtered into coastal centres. This would have made the employment market difficult and Thomson may have emigrated due to unemployment at home.[40] His early years in North America reflect the transient nature of life for men in new societies. On arriving in Canada he worked as a baker in Montreal. In the spring of 1845 he moved to Edwardsburgh on the St. Lawrence River where he continued to work as a baker. In 1849 he went to Chicago to work in the office of a timber firm. In California in 1850 he mixed gold mining with timber getting and baking. By 1853 he had made enough money to visit Scotland, buy a farm in Edwardsburgh and marry.[41]

Thomson's journey to the Cariboo began on 8 May 1862. He wrote in his diary: 'got on Board "Pacific" and sailed at 4 p.m. Ship dreadfully crowded with passengers, oxen, mules, horses and sheep. Passed out at Golden Gate strong head wind.'[42] He had chosen one of the sea routes rather than travel overland. On 13 May he arrived at Esquimalt Harbour on Vancouver Island and walked the three and a half miles to Victoria. After catching a boat to the mainland he did, however, walk for 37 days from Fort Yale, at the head of navigation on the Fraser River, to Keithley's Creek which flows into Cariboo Lake. Although he walked up to 22 miles a day, Thomson's diary conveys little of the physical hardship experienced by Harkness during his trek. The diary records 'the trail in some places very steep going zig zag up & down', 'mosquitos very bad', and 'trail for 4 miles very bad with mud holes and fallen timber', which, while daunting, falls well short of the severity of Harkness' journey.[43] In contrast to Thomson's description, Harkness wrote to his wife from Fort Edmonton:

> We travelled every day but one and were continually wet. Our walking was all wading, the whole country was under water for miles at a time we plodded along through mud and water sometimes up to our ancles [sic], sometimes up to our armpits. We had to build no less than eight bridges over streams so swollen by the rain that we couldn't cross them otherwise. At night we had to make willow beds to keep us out of the water & in the morning we often found ourselves lying in puddles 3 or 4 or perhaps 6 inches deep.[44]

Despite 'discouraging accounts from the mines...causing many to return home and throw a gloom upon others', Thomson, like Harkness, retained a sanguine outlook: 'To the upright there ariseth light in the darkness may it be so with us.'[45]

However, Thomson's diary records how his first attempt to strike gold ended in failure:

> June 24. Commenced sinking hole in bed of creek. Gravelly hole very hard.
>
> June 25. White frost this morning, quite cold, rain P.M. hole down about 6 feet.
>
> June 26. Hole full of water. Bailed out and got down about 10 feet from bed of creek.
>
> June 27. Hole half full of water. Bailed out enlarged and timbered. Got no lower than yesterday. Very hard picking. Dry all day.
>
> June 28. Got down about 12 feet. Still hard clay and gravel. No gold. Fine dry day.[46]

This failure does not dent his optimism which is reflected in his appreciation of the scenery:

> June 29. Beautiful morning. Sun shining bright and clear. Tent pitched in a beautiful spruce grove, Elpin Creek rippling past in new channel we have made for it. Lofty mountains each side, thick timbered towards summit. Sides green with willows, grass and wild rhubarb, weeds gooseberry bushes spruce pine and poplar trees.[47]

Optimism, however, is one thing, fulfilment is another, and in gold mining Thomson was ultimately no more successful than Harkness. After this initial unsuccessful attempt he and his companions set out for Antler and then on to Williams Creek where they were equally unsuccessful. The cost of provisions being exorbitant, Thomson and a number of his companions returned to the Forks at Quesnel, and then on to Williams Lake, leaving the remaining members of the party to continue prospecting. In Williams Lake he and his companions obtained work building a clay oven and sawing timber.[48] It was from Williams Lake that Thomson wrote to his wife Mary. This letter reveals that he was undergoing similar emotional privations to Harkness. Loneliness, anxiety and desire are intermingled with a matter-of-fact account of his journey from Victoria to Williams Creek. Most difficult is the fact that he has not received letters from home: 'Not a word have I heard from the loved ones at home since the morning of 7th of April. Amidst all the toil and anxiety and privations experienced in this country that is the hardest of all to bear.'[49]

The letter is in two parts. The first part is written so that Mary may show it to friends if she wishes. The second part is for Mary alone, and it is here that Thomson most reveals his emotional trauma:

> Oh Mary were you by my side I have much that I would like to say. Mary I have thought of you more, prayed for you more, and if possible loved you more this summer than ever before. Volumes could not contain all the thoughts I have of home and the loved ones there. Mary I often wish that I had more of your courage and energy and resignation to battle with the disappointments in life. I sometimes wonder how I ever came to leave a kind and affectionate wife and all that the heart of man could desire of a family to sojourn in this land.[50]

Like Harkness, Thomson misses his children:

> I suppose the children have forgotten all about Pa. Tell them I have not forgotten them. I have got a Bible lesson for them to learn, I hope to hear them repeat it yet. Oh if God would enable one to return and hear Minnie repeat that verse I would be a happy man. It is the 2nd verse of the fourth chapter of Micah (omitting the first and the last clause). May God bless all, and bring us to that land, where farewells are unknown.[51]

Even though prospecting has been a failure Thomson, like Harkness, finds comfort in thinking about his children, in focusing on the domestic. He also finds comfort in his religion: 'I cannot say that I regret coming to this country for God has softened my heart and enabled me to see myself in the gospel glass as I never did before, and I never yet have been able to get over the conviction that God in His providence pointed it out as my duty to coming [sic].'[52] God's approbation notwithstanding, returning home without gold is not a prospect he relishes: 'Mary, I really hardly know what to think about this country I cannot make up my mind to remain long away from home and then to think of returning without making something, to be as poor as when I left and in debt besides, and it might be laughed at into the bargain is hard to think of.'[53]

It is clear that, like Harkness, Thomson left eastern Canada to redeem his family's fortune. He too chose a muscular path to redemption. He too experienced not only failure in his quest, but also the emotional deprivation consequent on leaving loved ones behind. Furthermore, he felt he lacked the manly virtues, virtues which he felt, paradoxically, that his wife possessed. In this letter to his wife Thomson's intensity of emotion and language, magnified by distance, is similar to Harkness'. There is the same sense of exile, anxiety and loss. There is also the same focus on the domestic, on the family as life's centre or anchor. Unlike Harkness, Thomson appears to have found some comfort in religion, although the spiritual comfort God might provide is countered by the temporal humiliation he may face at home. Failure to provide for his family, to achieve financial independence, was something that he could not countenance.

The stories of Robert Harkness and James Thomson illuminate the effect of distance on men's attempts to achieve manhood by acting out the manly ideals of the mid-nineteenth century. Harkness' and Thomson's letters to their wives enable us to see how two men saw themselves in relation to their environment and to their loved ones. Loneliness on the frontier was common, and extreme isolation from one's normal social and domestic environment could undermine the manly ideal in a number of ways. Emotional deprivation and personality change were often the result. Distance magnified emotions and heightened desire towards those with whom one had closest affinity, often leading to dysfunction rather than independence. The letters of Harkeness and Thomson illustrate how *dependent* on their families some men were, a dependence which undermined the ideal of the breadwinner and patriarch. Like M. Allerdale Grainger, they were remote from familiar and comfortable homes and experienced pangs of anxiety and despair. As for Grainger, the frontier for Robert Harkness and James Thomson was a place of trial and tribulation, not a realisation of their manliness.

The experience of Charles Hayward as recorded in his diary provides a contrast to the trials of Harkness and Thomson. Hayward was a carpenter who emigrated to Vancouver Island in 1862, and in a relatively short time he had established himself in his trade in Victoria. Arriving in Victoria on board the *Shannon* on 7 May 1862, Hayward was confident that 'industry and perseverance will eventually work one to a position'.[54] He obtained employment within a week of landing, but this seemed to him an inordinate amount of time. The day before he found the job he wrote that he was 'very much perplexed' at not immediately finding work.[55]

By June he was taking small jobs on his own account and these jobs grew to the point where he became self-employed. On 12 September he was able to record: 'Like this opportunity of making money that I may have to prepare for my beloved wife.'[56] Like Thomson and Harkness, Hayward was separated from his wife (Sarah), whom he had left behind in England. Like them, Hayward missed her – 'my precious jewel' – a great deal, and he prays that God will 'hasten the time when I shall meet my love'.[57] Unlike Thomson and Harkness, Hayward did not seek his fortune at the Cariboo mines. Several times during these months he prepared to go, but the horror stories he heard from returning failed miners convinced him that life was better in Victoria: 'Met more of Shannon folks down from Cariboo. Broken in health and spirits.'[58]

Hayward's experience was altogether different from that of Thomson and Harkness. Preferring the relative comfort of Victoria, Hayward chose a different path to manly independence, involving less risk but more certain reward. In Victoria, Hayward was an active church-goer and taught at the Sunday school. Most of the time he lived with a friend from the journey out, identified only as 'Tom'. He lived in a house as opposed to camping under the stars in all weather. With the blessing of the Anglican Bishop he helped establish a 'Young Men's Society'. While it had a large transient population as men passed through on their way to the goldfields, by the time Hayward arrived Victoria had become an established town, the seat of colonial government and had a settled but growing population. While not the backwoods, Victoria, nevertheless, constituted a liminal zone, a place of transition on the edge of the metropole. Only a few years earlier it had been a Hudson's Bay Company fort.

Although separated from his wife, Hayward had the support of church and friends to ease his loneliness. The networks that he had lost were replaced by new networks and transplanted social institutions. Frontier life did not bring on an identity crisis. Hayward did not need an arduous journey to prove his manhood (his sea journey from Britain was, on the whole, rather pleasant). Nor does it seem he was seeking redemption for having failed as a breadwinner previously. Nevertheless, it is on the frontier that he sought to establish his manly independence. He seems a model for William Cobbett: in his diary he faithfully recorded his weekly earnings; he abstained from alcohol; and he attended church at least once every Sunday. Eventually, he purchased a house in Victoria.

On 6 September he is able to write in his diary: 'Weather fine – hard work. Spirits good. Prosperity'.[59]

Nevertheless, Hayward's manliness contained a paradox similar to Harkeness' and Thomson's. On 5 October he writes: 'But what loss I feel I have sustained in losing my dear Sarah. How worldly minded I became by my strivings to be rich without the balancing influence of her pious and affectionate companionship. Hasten the time when we shall meet again.'[60] The demands of manly independence seemed to be at odds with the domestic ideal and companionate marriage. Hayward's anguish was, fortunately, short-lived: Sarah was able to join him in January 1863.

It was not only Hayward's efforts to become a self-made man that was seemingly at odds with the domestic ideal. Sarah too had plans for independence of her own. She had been a schoolmistress in Britain – one of the few 'respectable' occupations open to women. In 1864 she founded and was principal of the Fort Street Academy, a school for young ladies, which operated until 1871. Sarah also taught at the Anglican school, Angela College, and in August 1872 she became principal of the girls' department of the public school in Victoria.[61]

Charles opened a contracting business in partnership with a Robert Jenkinson which later expanded into the ownership of a factory producing timber fittings such as windows and doors – and coffins. So profitable was the latter that he entered the undertaking business in 1867. By 1870 the business of the BC Funeral Furnishing Company had grown to such an extent that undertaking became Hayward's full-time occupation. Hayward was extremely active in the public sphere, serving two terms as an alderman, as a school commissioner from 1885 to 1898, and as Mayor of Victoria from 1900 to 1903. Hayward also was a founding member and vestryman of the Church of Our Lord and a director of the BC Protestant Orphans Home.

Charles and Sarah had nine children, but their family and domestic life could not have conformed to the mid-Victorian middle-class ideal. Charles, as an independent man, could clearly move between the private and public spheres at will. But so, it seems, could Sarah, which was less usual, but not unknown.[62]

Though white women were scarce on the frontiers of Queensland and British Columbia, non-white women were not. In the absence of women of their own race, many white men sought companionship and sex with Indigenous women. Many, though not all, of these relationships were exploitative. Many white men used Indigenous women solely for sexual gratification, sometimes in return for trinkets, tobacco or alcohol, sometimes in conditions of sexual slavery. The exception was on the fur trade frontier of Rupert's Land, as the western portion of British North America and what are now the northwestern states of the United States were known. Numerous Hudson's Bay Company and North West Company fur traders formed long-term relationships with Indigenous women, and fathered and supported mixed-race children.[63]

In terms of conforming to an ideal of manhood, sexual relations with Indigenous women, be it in Queensland or British Columbia, signified a manifest departure from the norms of the metropole. In mid-Victorian Britain the middle classes believed that sexual activity should be disciplined and discreet and espoused control for men and chastity for women. Sexual behaviour was, like work and sobriety, a marker of distinction between the middle class, the aristocracy above them and the plebeians below. The gentry and aristocracy held more liberal attitudes than the middle classes, which regarded aristocratic sexual behaviour as debauched.[64] Working-class men particularly, and apprentices and artisans, belonged to a bachelor libertine culture which differentiated between 'good' girls one would marry and other women with whom they could have sex.[65] In general women were alleged to lack passion and, as passionless beings, supposedly possessed a greater capacity to control the irrational and potentially subversive repercussions of uncontrolled sexuality. Men, on the other hand, were seen to be sexually undisciplined, insistent and dominant.[66] On the frontiers of Queensland and British Columbia the behaviour of many men justified this characterisation.

Adele Perry has examined how beliefs about First Nations women and their relationships with white men in British Columbia were discursively constructed and characterised as dangerous and inimical to the establishment of a respectable white settler colony.[67] Mixed-race relationships were not confined to the fur trade. Perry's research shows that sailors, prospectors, building, industrial and retail workers entered into long-term partnerships with First Nations women, some in conventional Christian unions, others not.[68] Many mixed-race relationships were exploitative and temporary – some white men deserted their Indigenous partners without any pangs of conscience. Violence was also a feature of these relationships; not only between the individuals involved but between whites and the Indigenous peoples generally. Many relationships were facilitated by the exchange of cash or goods desired by Indigenous women and men, a feature which perhaps underwrote the transient nature of these partnerships.[69]

White male attitudes towards Indigenous women in British Columbia were mixed and contradictory. George Blair found them repulsive, but not all white men did:

> By the way the Squaws or Cleuchmen as they are Called in the Chenook Dialect have a filthy habit of Sitting in the Streets and picking the Creepers out of each others head and eating them, yet there is scarsley a White man in the place but keeps one of these dirty filthy disgusting Cyprians.[70]

Dr John Helmcken was very attracted to, and eventually married, Governor Douglas'eldest mixed-race daughter Cecilia. He had quite a different view of Cecilia to Blair's view of Indigenous women on the streets, describing her as 'one of the prettiest objects I have ever seen: rather short but with a very pretty graceful figure – of dark complexion and lovely black eyes'.[71] Unlike the women observed by Blair, Cecilia would have been raised in a manner likely to appeal to a British gentleman on the lookout to establish himself in colonial society. Her 'dark complexion and lovely black eyes', the product of the Indigenous side of her ethnicity, were obviously an attraction to Helmcken, not a deterrent. C.E. Barrett-Lennard felt that he was 'bound to acknowledge that I have sometimes seen faces which might be described as pleasing, as well as not ungraceful figures, among the younger women, but a due regard for truth obliges me to add that their charms, if any be discoverable, a very short-lived'.[72] Barrett-Lennard's heavily qualified appraisal of Indigenous women points to the ambivalence with which they were viewed – and used – by white men.

In Queensland it was not uncommon for Aboriginal women to offer themselves to white men, or be offered by their husbands. Far from being prostitution, this was the way Indigenous people established kinship ties and reciprocal relations. Few white men recognised this and after sleeping with an Aboriginal woman would deny any further obligation or duty. This would result in conflict which was only resolved by violence. But apart from failing to recognise Indigenous customs, many white men kidnapped and raped black women. This was known as 'gin busting' and one station in Queensland had nine Aboriginal women confined behind fencing for the use of white station hands.[73]

The sexual abuse of Aboriginal women in Queensland was underpinned by attitudes towards them that were at best condescending and often outright contemptuous. At the waspish end of the spectrum white settler Rachel Henning described an Aboriginal woman as a 'queer object' because she was dressed only in a man's shirt.[74] At the more misogynistic end the Reverend Henry Stobart described Indigenous women as 'old hags' and the 'lowest stamp of the human race'.[75] Charles Eden believed that 'gins', as Aboriginal women were called, were the 'root of all evil'.[76]

In the mid-1840s colonial men outnumbered women in Brisbane by three to one, and in the pastoral district of the Darling Downs the ratio was five to one.[77] Pastoral worker William Telfer recognised what this meant for Indigenous women and men:

> The scarcity of white females was the cause of the men on the different stations taking black females as wifes [sic] this accounts for so many half-castes in the Collony [sic] also a great many of the squatters in those days had black females on their stations as Companions and if the poor aboriginals said anything about their women they were shot down by the Squatter and his men.[78]

Shepherds and squatters often held Indigenous women captive, preventing escape by chaining them, sometimes for long periods while the whites were away. Clergyman Frederick Richmond labelled the behaviour of white men towards Aboriginal women as 'unblushing animalism'. This behaviour only occasionally met with condemnation:

> A case was heard, when a 'gentleman' was accused of having shot a black fellow because he would follow him. The reason why the poor fellow followed him was because the gentleman was taking away the blacks [sic] wife, tied up to a chain to his wagon. He was acquitted, the judge remarking, 'Thank God gentlemen that is not my verdict.' No jury in the North would have convicted.[79]

In a similar case described by Charles Eden, in which two brothers, referred to by Eden only as the 'Gs', entered the camp of a group of Aborigines, 'took a fancy to a certain gin' and dragged her to their dray to which they secured her with a bullock chain around her ankles. When the woman's husband and others tried to release her, Edward G shot the husband, killing him. According to Eden when the case went to court Edward was acquitted.[80]

The miscegenation referred to by William Telfer was despised by white colonists:

> I have seen a half or three-quarter caste white child, a girl, rolling in the ashes. If anything could have violated our best instincts which

belong to us as a race, those which regard life and its transmission as sacred, it was this. The child's face was pathetic... she with the blood of England's best was growing up a savage, with degraded savage mates.[81]

For many white men on both frontiers, Indigenous women were merely chattels which they could treat with impunity in whatever manner they chose. Anne Mc Clintock has argued for a connection between conquering land and conquering women, and her argument appears to be supported by the sexual behaviour of white men in Queensland.[82] As with the land on which they grazed their sheep and cattle, white men simply took what they wanted, and shot any Indigenous man who stood in their way. Freed from the constraints of family, friends and church, many white men repudiated norms of restraint and self-control, vindicating the belief that essentially they were sexually undisciplined.

For some, the strain of isolation and hardship could only be relieved by obliterating the present with rum or whisky. In his study of the New Zealand frontier, Fairburn cites the use of alcohol as one of the survival techniques used to combat loneliness, to block out the 'psychic pain of social isolation'.[83] Men in Queensland and British Columbia used the same technique.

In Queensland, alcohol was a central part of the male lifestyle – few occasions, public or private, were considered successful unless copious quantities of alcohol were consumed.[84] George Carrington described the scene at an annual race meeting in the bush and observed: 'A sprinkling of the squattocracy who held themselves aloof, and drank themselves blind drunk in their own exclusive booth.' Apparently, 'the horses attracted very little attention... and the serious business of the day was not very long in beginning: "well old boy what'll you drink," "come on and have a nobbler." This was the constant burden wherever you might happen to be a listener.'[85] Carrington further recalled some of the shepherds he met:

> One Cambridge man; one Trinity, Dublin, one ex-lieutenant in the army, educated at Rugby, who carried the Queen's colours (so he said) into the Redan, and buried the dead afterwards; one Oxford man (myself); one old Wintonian; and two Germans. All these men (myself excepted) used to drink frightfully when they got the chance. About once in three months, they would demand each his cheque, and ask leave of absence for a few days: and they would return at the end of a short period, minus money, and often minus horse, saddle, bridle, clothes and blankets.[86]

It would seem that on the Queensland frontier class affiliations could be fluid – in more than one sense of the word. The listing of these men's schools and universities indicates that for Carrington class is important. In his mind the manhood of these men and their class are inextricably linked. It was obviously common for higher-class men to ostensibly lose their status. Yet the university (class) background of these men remained integral to their manly identity and important enough for Carrington to include in his memoirs. The implication is that getting as drunk as these men did is repugnant to their upper-class masculinity, and repugnant to Carrington's sense of manhood. Carrington's testimony suggests that such drinking habits were not uncommon, that these men were not an aberration. Manliness could obviously be brittle.

The reputation of working-class men as hard drinkers was reinforced on the frontier, and employers often had difficulty in ensuring a sober workforce. Canegrower Frank Neame found that his men would go to great lengths to get a drink:

> On Nov 23 the men had a large quantity of grog out from Cardwell and most of them were dead drunk for the next day or two, we tried to put a stop to this by forbidding the boatmen to land any grog, but they got over this difficulty by landing it further down the river and telling the men where to find it; the next thing was to get rid of the chief offenders, and we then discovered that two men were actually keeping grog on the place to sell to others, they were promptly cleared out, and then I gave notice that any man not at his work 7 o'clock on Monday mornings would be dismissed, as they used to go up the river on a Saturday afternoon and drink until they were thoroughly intoxicated, and not turn up again until sometime Monday.[87]

While for the (lapsed) members of the upper classes heavy drinking was indicative of a failure of manliness, the same behaviour among working-class men on the frontier was consistent with working-class manliness.

Charles Eden attributed the heavy drinking of frontier men to the absence of women:

> I take it an educated man begins to deteriorate as soon as he gets beyond the reach of ladies' society; carelessness in dress gradually creeps in, then greater license of tongue, whilst a yearning after any

new face causes a man to associate with a well-known blackguard rather than be alone. The whole *morale* of the man becomes lower in tone, and then few escape the grog shop which is yawning to receive them in its fatal embraces.

For some men at least, the self-discipline required to be manly did not run very deep. Without the civilising influence of women, men were at the mercy of whatever temptations lay in their path. 'Educated' men were particularly vulnerable, and were not the paragons of manly virtue popular discourse would have them be.

British Columbians emulated their southern hemisphere counterparts. Historian Perry remarks that 'drink...was indelibly marked on British Columbia's homosocial culture'.[88] In the early 1860s, with a population of less than 5,000, Victoria had 85 licensed inns.[89] Robert Melrose, a servant of the Hudson's Bay Company in British Columbia, argued that heavy alcohol consumption was the norm on Vancouver Island: 'It would almost take a line of packet ships, running regular between here and San Francisco to supply this island with grog, so great a thirst prevails amongst its inhabitants.'[90] One of the remarkable features of his diaries for 1852–1855 are the number of entries where he quantifies how drunk he and his associates were on particular occasions. For example, the entries for 9 and 10 September 1854 include 'P. Bartleman ¾ D. The Author ¾ D. John Instant ¾ D. Thomas Williams ¾ D. Jack Humphrey ½ D'.[91] Arthur Bushby was of the opinion that 'you can have no fun here...unless you are half screwed'.[92] In one journal entry he noted: 'So jolly I'll be hanged if I can write.'[93]

Governor Douglas described drunkenness as 'the crying and prevalent sin of this colony'.[94] In a masterpiece of understatement HBC's Dr John Helmcken remembered that 'drunkenness was not infrequent'. On one occasion a group of sailors had acquired a cask of whisky and had proceeded to get themselves very drunk. Governor Douglas ordered the seizure of the cask which the sailors had hidden under the floor of their house. Armed with a sword, Helmcken, Douglas and others confiscated the liquor and Douglas ordered that it be emptied into the street. Aghast that their libation was literally running down the gutter the men 'threw themselves on the ground to drink it as it ran or collected it in holes – some on their knees scooped it up in their hands, others lay down and sipped it from the earth!' Helmcken ended this spectacle by sprinkling tartar emetic on the whisky and before long the drinkers were vomiting up what they had drunk.[95] Amongst this sin, however, there was a glimmer of redemption. Emigrant carpenter Charles Hayward recorded in his diary on 13 October 1862 that he attended a lecture on 'Total Abstinence' at the Wesleyan Chapel in Victoria. Hayward was extremely gratified by the large attendance and hoped that 'many poor victims of intemperance be rescued'.[96]

It seems that alcohol was like sex. Freed from the constraints of metropolitan society, some men allowed their passions to take over. The self-discipline that was supposedly a hallmark of manliness was thrown aside. Perhaps it never had a strong purchase in the first place.

Many men of British Columbia and Queensland apparently had not absorbed the exhortations of the author of *Letters to Young People Single and Married* regarding drink, nor had fathers like William Leslie to advise them. Obviously, some men could not find within themselves the requisite manly qualities, nor could they acquire them. Instead, they attempted to cover up their deficiency with alcohol. As Catherine Murdoch has noted: 'Alcohol abuse was a male attribute that destroyed masculinity.'[97] Paradoxically, excessive alcohol consumption appears to have been the norm among frontier men, which is probably why some men turned to drinking. They could conform to at least one of the norms of frontier manliness, if not to the manly ideal as conceived in Britain. Indeed, for Melrose and Bushby drunkenness appeared to me a badge of manly honour.

Some men coped with remoteness from family and friends and the hardships of work and frontier life by making alternative personal and domestic arrangements, and developing close bonds with other men. In Australia, such arrangements were the source of the mythical concept of mateship.[98] In its most common form mateship refers to the close bonds between two men, bonds which, according to Russel Ward, arose out of 'the hazards and hardships, but above all the loneliness of up-country life'.[99] Ward surmised that mateship was based on the typical bushman satisfying his 'spiritual hunger by a sublimated homosexual relationship with a mate, or a number of mates, of his own sex'.[100] Ward's speculation about sublimated homosexual relationships may be a bit coy. Anne O'Brien argues that in small North Queensland towns in the late-nineteenth century, which had predominantly male populations and where heavy drinking was the principle recreation 'the boundaries between homoeroticism, homosociality and homosexuality were likely to be particularly porous'.[101] In short, not all men chose to sublimate their sexual desire merely because of the absence of women. One visitor to the frontier districts of New South Wales in 1848 observed that among pastoral workers 'it is no wonder...that in such a state of society, deep seated vice should exist, and that abominable offences be practiced to an appalling extent'.[102]

Adele Perry has described how men in British Columbia, living without women, joined together to create households, devising various arrangements for the sharing of household chores.[103] This often required men to learn skills and tasks that were unfamiliar, with varying degrees of success. One farmer's '"meat, fish and potatoes were poor", but "his bread was the crowning atrocity"'.[104] According to Robert Aldrich, homosociality, sometimes veering towards homosexuality, was a fact of life in the early colonial world: 'If the full gamut of emotional and sexual contacts between men are included, it is probable that a considerable cohort had feelings or experiences not strictly conforming to European and Christian precepts of sexual propriety.'[105] One pair of men who found life without women to their liking were Reginald Pidcock and his companion 'Fred', for whom separation from their home in England and the isolation of the frontier was something of a boon. The story of their partnership provides a different picture of frontier isolation to that of the men above, and illustrates an alternative way of coping with and combating isolation.

In early 1862 Reginald Heber Pidcock of Surrey boarded a Royal Mail Steamship at Southampton bound for Vancouver Island. While he ultimately married and operated a saw mill where the town of Courtney is now located, earlier he led a freewheeling life of adventure in the wilderness of British Columbia and Vancouver Island, accompanied by a partner to whom he assigns the pseudonym 'Fred'. Pidcock's journal of 1862 is an account of their year's adventures: travels to the Cariboo goldfields, accounts of the characters they encountered and their journey back to Victoria. The greater part of the journal, however, is taken up with a description of their time in a then remote location, known as Comox, in the north of Vancouver Island, where Pidcock and 'Fred' shared an idyllic existence camping and hunting, occasionally returning to a European or Indigenous settlement to trade venison they had hunted in return for other supplies. The journal reads like a boy's own adventure. After buying a canoe and outfitting themselves in Victoria they set off: 'Nothing could be wanting to perfect our enjoyment, the Scenery fair wind and lovely weather with the novelty of our position affords us intense pleasure. Fred went to sleep after a time at the bottom of the canoe while I steered and we went merrily along at the rate of about 6 miles an hour.'[106]

On their journey they called in at various European and Indigenous settlements. When they were not paddling their canoe Pidcock and 'Fred' hunted, and many pages of the journal are devoted to accounts of hunting expeditions.[107] No animal was safe: deer, trout, salmon, grouse, ducks and geese all provided sport and food. During their journey they established something of a domestic routine:

> We took it in turns to go out hunting, one going in the morning and the other in the afternoon. The one who stopped at home cut firewood, cooked the dinner and made bread. We never both went out at the same time as we did not like to leave our camp as Indians might have seen the smoke of our fire and found us out and no doubt robbed us.[108]

There is no precise statement of exactly how long Pidcock and 'Fred' lived in this manner. But indications are that they lived this way for at least five months. The most intriguing part of Pidcock's account is the nature of his relationship with 'Fred'. Pidcock gives no information whatsoever regarding 'Fred's' identity, merely stating one point: 'We bought a tent (that is myself and my friend who came out with me and who I shall call Fred for the future).'[109] No reason is given for the necessity for 'Fred's' anonymity, and one is left to speculate why Pidcock felt it necessary to conceal his friend's identity. 'Fred's' anonymity suggests that there is something covert about their relationship.

At the same time however, Pidcock clearly foresaw that his journal might be read by others. At the outset he states:

> The readers of this volume (should there be any) must not expect an elaborate account of the botanical or geological formations of the island. The book simply contains an account of various excursions on the sea coast, made in canoes, and inland journeys made on foot for almost the express purpose of fishing and shooting.[110]

As 'Fred' travelled from Southampton with Pidcock they obviously knew each other in England, and perhaps their journey was planned. While Pidcock states nothing directly, a number of passages in his journal suggest an extremely close bond. Early in their adventure Pidcock recorded:

> We had determined to camp for the night as the wind was increasing and in the prettiest and snuggest of the little harbours we put up our

tent and camped for the first time on our journey by ourselves and in the forest. As it was still early in the day I said I thought if Fred would keep camp I would go and try and shoot a deer... Fred liking to keep camp than otherwise I started for the bush.[111]

Later in their adventure, on returning to camp after having slain a deer, Pidcock wrote:

> I arrived in about an hour at our camp and had to relate all my adventures to Fred who congratulated me on my good luck. I found that he had not been idle but had cut firewood and cooked our supper and deferred eating our venison until it was cold. We had a most comfortable camp and sat rather late over our fire and then turned in for the night.[112]

After a day when they had both been hunting:

> It was nearly three o'clock before we got back and we were pretty hungry as we had breakfasted at daylight, so the steaks soon disappeared and we felt very much better afterwards. We cut our firewood and made all snug for the night, piled on more wood and laid down and talked over the days' work.[113]

In the first extract the words 'by ourselves' suggests that Pidcock and 'Fred' were more than just individuals travelling together. It suggests that they shared an identity as a couple and had found something they had been seeking *together*. Implicit in Pidcock's words is a sense of satisfaction that they had arrived in this isolated place away from others. The fact 'Fred' liked to keep camp rather than go hunting suggests that he and Pidcock shared a mutually agreeable division of work. 'Fred' is prepared to adopt a domestic role – cutting firewood and preparing meals – while Pidcock goes out in the bush to hunt. It is as if they have adopted the 'separate spheres' model to regulate their relationship, with 'Fred' adopting the feminine role and Pidcock the masculine role, although 'Fred' does occasionally join Pidcock hunting. At the end of the day, they enjoyed each other's company and engaged in pillow talk over the day's events. The repeated use of the word 'snug' also suggests that Pidcock was describing a particular sort of arrangement or relationship. 'Snug' is synonymous with 'cosy' and 'homely'. Pidcock's use of this word suggests that he and 'Fred' had set up a secure and comfortable home and enjoyed a relaxed intimacy, not only in their physical surroundings, but also in their relationship.

From these intriguing, but admittedly limited, indications, it seems possible that Pidcock and 'Fred' were in an intimate relationship, that they had a strong and exclusive commitment to each other. Looking back with modern eyes it is tempting to conclude that they had a homoerotic relationship. But these events must be understood in the context in which they occurred, and not judged by today's standards. Present definitions of 'homosexual' and 'heterosexual' are specific to our own historical period, and behaviours that are considered 'homosexual' today have not always been seen as such. While there have always been those whose primary sexual attraction has been to their own sex, throughout history men have confessed their love for each other without embarrassment and without erotic feelings.

It is equally likely that Pidcock and Fred were simply close mates who relied upon each other for companionship and security, sharing a sense of adventure and combining their resources to enjoy a life free of responsibility and commitment for as long as they could. John Beynon argues that for many nineteenth-century writers the British Empire was the location of 'masculinist imaginings' in which men could enjoy homosocial friendships in physically demanding and arduous circumstances far from what they saw as the harmful influences of the 'feminine', that is, the family and domesticity.[114] Perhaps Pidcock and 'Fred' were a prototype for Robert Louis Stevenson and Rider Haggard. If they did have a homoerotic relationship, it is pertinent to ask how the frontier contributed to its development.

While there is an extensive literature on the history of homosexuality and, as Neil Miller observes, although homosexual relations appear to be commonplace in many all-male societies – prisons and military units for example – there is little documented evidence about their existence on the frontier.[115] In Australia, a number of historians, relying largely on legal sources, have revealed that on the Australian frontier same-sex relationships, often involving physical sex, were common. Like Aldrich, Perry observes that there is no clear line which definitively separates the homosocial from the homosexual and reviews a number of cases which indicate that colonial British Columbia was a society that tolerated a certain amount of male-to-male sex.[116] In Britain there was far less tolerance of same-sex activity.

In nineteenth-century Britain physical homoerotic relations were unacceptable. A severe legal regime buttressed a social norm in which homosexuality was seen as antithetical to an industrialised, Christian society. By encouraging emotional connectedness between men, homosexuality defied the precepts of competitiveness and self-restraint, was inimical to the ideology of the family and, according to David F. Greenberg, was gradually medicalised and pathologised as abnormal.[117] Sodomy or buggery was part of a range of non-procreative sexual acts which were not only legally prohibited, but that, in the interest of maintaining masculinity as a 'social status', was vilified as unmanly and effeminate.[118] There is an important distinction to be made between the traditional concept of buggery and the modern concept of homosexuality. Buggery was an act that was seen as sinful in nature, as something which should be reviled and judicially punished. It was not, however, like the modern concept of homosexuality, seen as a characteristic of a particular type of person.[119]

While in the early-nineteenth century, men and boys could indulge in emotionally charged but platonic relationships, the law imposed strict sanctions on 'sodomy' and 'buggery', and trials proliferated after 1800.[120] Based on a 1533 Act of Henry VIII, under English law the 'Abominable Vice of Buggery' was punishable by death.[121] In 1828 Home Secretary Robert Peel amended the English buggery law. Despite abolishing the death penalty for a range of other offences, Peel retained it for buggery. What did change was the need to prove the emission of semen for the act of buggery to be deemed complete. After the Peel amendments this was no longer necessary, proof of penetration being the only criteria to be satisfied.[122] In 1841 an attempt by Lord John Russell to abolish the death penalty for 'unnatural offences' failed due to lack of parliamentary support.[123] The death penalty was finally removed from the statutes in 1861 to be replaced by the less severe but hardly permissive sentence of ten years to life.[124] Despite the severity of the law as it appeared in the statutes, its application waned as the century progressed. While more than 50 executions occurred in the first 30 years of the nineteenth century (the military was particularly harsh on offenders), no one was executed after 1836.[125] This could be a reflection either of juries being unwilling to convict or of judges being unwilling to impose the maximum sentence. Either way, it is indicative of a softening of social attitude, in that buggery, while a serious crime which should be punished, was no worse than many other crimes.

In the colonies, the law followed the English example. When Queensland became a separate colony in 1859 the laws which pertained to buggery were adopted from New South Wales. Homosexual offences were specified in 29 VIC No 11. Sodomy was serious enough to be dealt with by the Supreme Court, but lesser offences, such as indecent assault or attempted sodomy were dealt with by the District Court. The words sodomy and buggery were interchangeable, and also referred to bestiality. Clause 62 stated that persons 'convicted of the abominable crime of buggery, committed either with mankind or animal' should be imprisoned for any length of time from ten years to life, as was the case in England. Clause 63 dealt with attempted sodomy and sexual assault of males and animals. This could earn an offender imprisonment from three to ten years, or imprisonment not exceeding two years with the option of hard labour.[126]

In British Columbia the legal position also reflected the laws of Great Britain. Under the proprietary rule of the Hudson's Bay Company British laws applied to Vancouver Island and British Columbia (or New Caledonia as it was initially called). When British Columbia was constituted by imperial statute, the Governor was authorised to make laws and 1858 was stipulated as the date of reception of British laws.[127] Between 1849 and 1871 at least four men were charged with sodomy or buggery. The legal position reflected the views of at least some of the citizenry. Perry cites one letter writer who proclaimed that 'murderers, sodomites and burglars have few sympathisers in Victoria'.[128]

In view of the legal and social prohibitions, to be labelled a 'sodomite' in the early- to mid-nineteenth century was something to be feared. If Pidcock and 'Fred' engaged in physical sex, fear of the legal consequences would be reason enough to conceal 'Fred's' true identity. In Pidcock's diary there is no mention, even obliquely, of physical sex, nor are there any emotional outpourings or terms of endearment between Pidcock and 'Fred'. It seems possible that they could occupy any one of a range of places on a sexual continuum, from being exclusively homosexual, physically homosexual, being celibate homosexuals, exclusively heterosexual, bisexual or asexual, or indeed changing places on the continuum as desire and inclination dictated.

In her analysis of Gilbert White's mission to male-only communities in North Queensland in the late-nineteenth century, Anne O'Brien addresses the issue of male-to-male desire without sex. She draws attention to the problem of attributing to people feelings they were not conscious of at the time.[129] Nevertheless, restricting the definition of homosexuality to cases in which irrefutable evidence of physical intercourse can be found imposes an impossible burden of proof. What is important to realise is that the boundaries between homosexuality, intimate friendship and male bonding could be extremely porous and mateship could turn into sexual intimacy.[130]

Why did men form homoerotic bonds with each other? Bob Hay identifies three types of homosexuality. The first is commonly called situational homosexuality and occurs among primarily heterosexual men when there are few or no women available. Such homosexuality was prevalent during the convict era in Australia when men outnumbered women by as many as 20 to 1.[131] Such sexual relationships were consensual, unlike the second type identified by Hay, coercive or violent sex as occurred on the prison transports and in gangs. The victims of this predatory sex comply for their own safety and this is more of a survival strategy than a form of sexual expression. The third type of homosexuality that Hay believes was common was that practised among men to whom it was an essential and natural expression of their personalities.[132] To these three broad situations, which could apply in metropolitan social environments as well as on the frontier, can be added a number of factors more likely to pertain only on the frontier. Libby Connors has identified the seclusion of work and living space and the lack of external checks on private behaviour, combined with the practice of mateship, as factors which allowed 'alternative moral practices...to develop'.[133] Seclusion, lack of external checks and obviously mateship all applied to Pidcock's and 'Fred's' situation.

It cannot be known whether or not Pidcock and 'Fred' were sexually intimate. They obviously had a strong homosocial bond and enjoyed the freedom from social scrutiny their isolation provided. If they were not sexually intimate, they must have practised a remarkable degree of celibacy. On the frontier the controls and sanctions the law and society imposed were diminished by remoteness and the relative weakness of other institutions such as the church and family. Isolation and loneliness could undermine heterosexual normativity, pushing men together. The need for comfort could outweigh fear of social opprobrium. Therefore, for those men for whom inclination or circumstance made homosexuality an option, the frontier provided an environment in which they could conduct same-sex relationships relatively free from censure or persecution.

Not all frontier men become characters in frontier legends. Their attempts to live the manly ideal could be thwarted by frontier conditions. Loneliness was common, and extreme isolation from one's normal social and domestic environment could undermine the manly ideal in a number of ways. Emotional deprivation, personality change and alcoholism were often the result. Distance magnified emotions and heightened desire towards those with whom one had closest affinity, leading to dysfunction rather than independence. The frontier also provided opportunities for men to renegotiate some of the normative roles of their gender. Through both necessity and desire men constructed relationships which alleviated their sense of isolation, and provided some of the physical, emotional and sexual comfort they would normally receive in the family home.

5
Blacks, Chinks and a Pig-Headed German

> Blackfellows...consist of two distinct classes namely, Tame Blacks and Wild Blacks. The Tame blacks have picked up all the worst characteristics of the white man, and lost some of their own. They learn to drink grog and smoke; and become weak and lazy, content to live on the white man's scraps, rather than exert themselves to get their own living. These tame blacks are cunning and treacherous.
> (George Carrington, *Colonial Adventures and Experiences by a University Man*)

> The natives are hideously ugly and atrociously dirty: their customs are beastly, manners they have none.
> (Edmund Hope Verney to his Father, 15 May 1862, in Allan Pritchard, ed., *Vancouver Island Letters of Edmund Hope Verney 1862–65*)

British men of the mid-nineteenth century not only took their gender practices to the Queensland and British Columbian frontiers, they took their racial beliefs as well. One of the things British Columbia and Queensland had in common in the mid-nineteenth century was large Indigenous populations. Like George Carrington and Edmund Hope Verney, most white commentators had very little to say about Indigenous people that was favourable. Not only were Indigenous people in general racially denigrated, the masculinity of Indigenous men was contrasted with and found wanting against white hegemonic standards.

As R.W. Connell has argued, varying masculinities exist and are practised in diverse environments and historical periods, and arise from the interplay between gender, race and class. Understanding how these multiple masculinities are constituted requires an examination of the differences in and relationships between the different types, as well as the interplay of these types with other social variables.[1] In other words, masculinities can vary across class and race, and one type of masculinity can be defined by how it differs from an alternative type. Arguing for what she terms a 'historical-materialist' approach to the analysis of colonial masculinity, Mrinalini Sinha has called for an examination of the mutual constitution of the colonisers' masculinity and the effeminacy of the colonised as a practice of colonial rule.[2]

The frontiers of Queensland and British Columbia are sites which provide ample material for such an examination. In these places white British men constructed Indigenous and other non-white masculinities as the antithesis of their own ideal. In constructing non-white, non-British masculinities as inferior and 'uncivilised', British men were defending and affirming the version of masculinity they had absorbed in Britain. This exercise was fundamental in exerting British dominance over these frontiers, part of a strategy to 'extirpate savages from their native soil in order that it may be peopled with more intelligent and civilised race of human beings'.[3]

An analysis of contemporary texts including official reports, travel and anthropological writing from both Queensland and British Columbia reveals the systematic and in some cases calculated construction of Indigenous and other non-white men as embodying an 'uncivilised' masculinity. Discursively constructed 'truths' about Indigenous men – that they were 'unmanly', uncivilised and sexually depraved – were used to justify their dispossession and conquest. Such practices have been labelled 'aboriginalism', a form of discourse which 'produces authoritative and essentialist truths about Aborigines, characterised by a mutually supporting relationship between power and knowledge'.[4] Such 'truths' about Indigenous men buttressed white male masculinity and power, and facilitated the dispossession of Indigenous people.

In their opinions of Indigenous people Carrington and Verney reflected the anthropological orthodoxy of the mid-nineteenth century. At that time, among Europeans, 'race' had assumed primacy as a framework by which the natural and social worlds could be understood. Benjamin Disraeli in *Tancred* had a leading character explain that 'all is race; there is no other truth'.[5] Scottish anatomist Robert Knox in his *Races of Men* announced that 'race in human affairs is everything, is simply a matter of fact, the most remarkable the most comprehensive, which philosophy has ever announced. Race is everything: literature, science, art – in a word, civilisation – depends on it.'[6]

The emergence of race as a primary category of humankind had its origins in a reaction to Enlightenment thinking, the institution of slavery and the advance of the biological sciences in the eighteenth and nineteenth centuries. The Enlightenment philosophies believed that nature had endowed all humans with rationality and sociability. They believed in an immutable human nature that was common to all peoples. Divisions among humankind were either artificial or largely irrelevant in comparisons to the commonalties. There was a belief in human unity and equality, and human differences, whether physical or cultural, were not differences in kind but only in degree.[7]

Modern racial discourse originated as it was realised that the Enlightenment view of unity and equality did not appear to be the natural state of the world. Difference and inequality were manifest, and 'racial' explanations appeared to account for social and cultural differences.[8] Following Kant's arguments in *Critique of Pure Reason*, conservative Romantic thought posited that human beings possessed an unchanging inner essence which was unaffected by culture or society. This essence was manifested through the idea of race. Racial essence was not a universal formulation – different strands of humankind possessed different racial essences. Allied with Romantic ideas of community and belonging, race enabled community to be defined by exclusion. In a world where social differences were important and not eradicable, race had significant explanatory and justificatory power.[9]

At the end of the eighteenth century, the study of human races had become the key field of scientific investigation. By the middle of the nineteenth century racial science was firmly established, and was used to support the belief that certain groups of humans were intrinsically superior to others. Scientists concerned with race were not unified by common beliefs about the origin of races. Monogenisists believed that all humans had a common ancestry and belonged to a single biological species. Polygenisists, on the other hand, believed that each race, far from having a common ancestor, so varied in their physical, moral and mental characteristics as to constitute distinct biological species of their own. Regardless of where they stood on questions of the singularity or plurality of human species, all racial scientists believed that race was a permanent and natural phenomenon of enormous explanatory power.

Colour was regarded as the most salient characteristic differentiating various peoples. Robert Bernasconi points out that Kant relied almost exclusively on colour for his classification of races.[10] European involvement in the African slave trade was a crucial factor in the development of a colour hierarchy. The term 'white' arose in the seventeenth century as a descriptor for European explorers, traders and settlers who came into contact with Africans and the Indigenous people of North and South America, and implied an array of physical and cultural indicators of European difference.[11] Blackness, on the other hand, was negatively associated with the degraded position of slaves. Over time, a black skin was taken to be an external sign of inner mental and moral inferiority.[12] To the extent that whites considered themselves superior to everyone else, one obvious way of ordering the racial hierarchy was along a continuum of white to black. Arguments for the biological inferiority of non-whites constituted the dominant discourse in debates about race. Race was constructed as a biological category, and it was asserted that whites were biologically superior.

But, not content with merely explaining the physical differences between groups of humans, scientists sought to explain what they perceived to be the superior 'civilised' position of white Europeans and the inferior 'uncivilised' position of non-whites, especially black Africans and other people with dark skins (like the Australian Aborigine). In the early decades of the nineteenth century, phrenology provided 'proof' of the inferiority of non-whites. Phrenology actually lost favour as the century progressed, but it bequeathed to racial science the belief that the human skull and the brain it housed held the evidence of racial superiority and inferiority.[13] By the middle of the nineteenth century everyone shared the belief that in fundamental ways the white race was superior to all others. Race was seen as a natural but immutable ladder of merit and achievement. The racial hierarchy developed by European scientists was regarded as a reflection of the excellence of European civilisation and the impoverished nature of other cultures. This view had widespread appeal because it accorded with Europeans' view of themselves and appeared to be based on scientific measurement. In the racial discourses emerging during the nineteenth century white Europeans located themselves in a privileged position as the inheritors of the cultural legacy of the Greeks and Romans. The classical revival which commenced in the seventeenth century valued whiteness, as well as the facial features and physiques believed to have characterised the ancient Greeks and Romans.[14]

But not only was whiteness understood as one attribute distinguishing some humans from others, it became a condition of humanity. Whiteness was universalised: 'To be white was to be human, and to be human was to be white.'[15] Whiteness was the human universal that no other race attained. All other races were inferior, falling short of the universal, and therefore of humanity.[16] What is more, whiteness did not pre-exist the construction of non-Europeans as other. White, European self-construction was fundamentally linked to the discursive production of others.[17]

Discourses of race were accompanied by discourse of civilisation. This discourse of 'civilisation' – a belief in human progress grounded in the conditions of social and economic life, a progress of knowledge, social organisation and morality – arose from the work of the philosophers of the Scottish Enlightenment. Relying on the narratives of the European explorers of the American continent for their empirical evidence, the Scots invented a history in which Indigenous people were morally inferior. Every human institution, they maintained, developed along an unbroken continuum and provided evidence of the laws of man's original nature. Progress meant upward growth for the better. As man and his institutions developed they became more 'social'. Social, technical and moral progress were identical; the progress of the individual was to be measured in terms of the progress of the society which gave him his social being.

From their studies of 'primitive' societies such as that of native Americans, the Scots concluded that in becoming civilised men had gained more than they had lost; and that the act of civilising, for all its destruction of primitive life, put something better and more noble in its place. Primitive life had its positive aspects and its negatives, the product of the society which produced them. Savage courage, fortitude and freedom could only be developed in a primitive society. The negatives included hardship, cruelty, warfare, lack of religion and learning. Both good and bad qualities were part of a social whole which should slowly evolve towards something better. Civilisers, that is, Europeans, were agents of that evolution and progress. Savage life and civilised life were worlds apart, separated by centuries of cultural history and different environmental situations. The principles of a savage society were built around hunting and war, and its members could develop no further than their lives let them. The idea of history as progress made it possible to understand early cultures as morally inferior. Uncivilised peoples were uncivilised because of their isolation and the overpowering effect of the environment.[18]

Industrial capitalism and evangelical Christianity shaped the British conceptualisation of 'civilisation' in the late-eighteenth century. The conceptualisation of the philosophers of the Scottish Enlightenment always had Christianity at its base. The 'Idea of Progress' they formulated explained how God was revealing Himself to man and how man was progressing to higher civilisation, leaving his savage state behind him.[19] The idea of civilisation as formulated by the Scots was extended to include the operation of industrial capitalism, representative political institutions, a middle-class standard of material well-being, self-discipline and sexual restraint, and Protestant Christianity – the same factors that determined the gender order.

Gender was an essential element of civilisation.[20] Advanced civilisations could be identified by the degree of their sexual difference. Men and women of the civilised races had evolved obvious sexual differences. Civilised women were 'womanly' – intuitive, sensitive, nurturing. Civilised men were the most 'manly' ever evolved – strong, self-disciplined, providers for and protectors of their families. In contrast, gender differences among savages (i.e. non-whites) were blurred. Savage women were aggressive, carried heavy loads and performed 'masculine' hard labour. Savage men were emotional and were unable to restrain their passions. They were capricious and attacked women instead of protecting them. They failed to care properly for their children. The strong sexual differences of the British middle class's doctrine of the separate spheres were assumed to be absent in savagery, but were regarded as an inherent and essential aspect of higher civilisation.[21]

The most influential understandings of civilisation were those which both assumed and asserted white male supremacy. Scientific theories corroborated the belief that racial difference, civilisation and manliness all advanced together. Mid-nineteenth-century ideas of civilisation conflated biology and culture. They understood race to have 'a mixed biocultural character'.[22] White men believed that non-whites were biologically incapable of attaining civilised manliness. Most biologists assumed that the only way human races could evolve towards a higher civilisation was for each generation to incrementally advance, and to genetically pass learned characteristics on to their offspring. In this way whites felt scientifically justified in believing that no racially primitive man could possibly be as manly as a white man. Primitive men would require many generations to slowly acquire manliness and pass these civilised capacities on to their offspring.[23] Thus manliness was constructed as simultaneously cultural and racial. Europeans had inherited the capacity for manliness from their ancestors. Non-Europeans could never be manly, because their ancestors had never developed that capacity.

British social scientists led the way in asserting the cultural and moral superiority of white men over non-white men, and to their eventual dominance. In 1864 Darwin's friendly rival Alfred Russell Wallace wrote:

The intellectual and moral, as well as the physical qualities of the European are superior; the same powers and capacities which have made him rise in a few centuries from the condition of the wandering savage with a scanting and stationary population to his present state of culture and advancement, with a greater average longevity, a greater average strength, and a capacity for more rapid increase – enable him when in contact with the savage man, to conquer in the struggle for existence, and to increase at his expense.[24]

Anthropologist John William Jackson believed that

to affirm that a Negro is in every way as good a man as a European, is to deny the historic testimony of five thousand years, seeing that in all that time no negro nation has ever, either with or without assistance, reached the civilisation achieved by the great centres of Caucasian civilisation.[25]

Not only were whites superior to non-whites, but Britons were ranked first among European 'races'. In 1859 Charles Kingsley addressed the Ladies Sanitary Association:

Of all the races on earth now, the English race is probably the finest, and it gives not the slightest sign whatsoever of exhaustion; ... it is a duty, one of the noblest of duties, to help the increase of the English race as much as possible, and to see that every child that is born into this great nation of England be developed to the highest pitch to which we can develop him in physical strength and beauty, as well as in intellect and virtue.[26]

In Kingsley's mind, the fine attributes of the English race were embodied in the English male. It was a duty to develop in *him* the virtues of white civilisation.

Nineteenth-century anthropologist Louis Figuier depicted the English racial type as a blend of

subtlety to will; hence his practical power; being strong and able, he acquires a confidence in himself which easily degenerates into pride, and saves him from smallness of character. He is neither obsequious nor prone to flattery; ... he keeps his word, and considers that he would be dishonoured in breaking it; but he makes the best of his advantages. For him, life is a struggle for triumph, without regard for those who are unable to contend, and who succumb in the attempt. He asks no pity, and gives but little; he cannot be called cruel, for cruelty is a form of weakness; but he does not hesitate to suppress an enemy, when to do so would be productive of material advantage.[27]

In all of these examples, the white European is male. The virtues of the white race are embodied in and exemplified by men, and the apex of these virtues was British manliness. On the frontier, race, gender and the discourse of civilisation operated in tandem to advance the dominance of white British males. On the frontier, individual action was not enough to ensure the survival of the masculine ideal. What was also necessary was the demolition of alternatives, or rather the construction of alternatives as inferior. Using the discourses of race, gender and civilisation as a foundation, white men constructed the Indigenous men of Queensland and British Columbia as unmanly, denying them any possible claim to equality of status with the colonisers. It was through the discursive construction of Indigenous people as 'other' that the dominant white manly self constructed itself. This white, male self-construction was fundamentally tied to the discursive production of others – it did not pre-exist that process.[28]

From the outset, most Europeans regarded the Indigenous people of Queensland and British Columbia as inferior beings. In his 1778 description of the Indigenous people of Nootka Sound on Vancouver Island, Lieutenant James King, who sailed on Cook's third voyage, was clearly unimpressed with the appearance of the locals:

> It will require the assistance of one's imagination to have an adequate view of the Wild, savage appearance & Actions of these first Visitors, as it is difficult to describe the effect of gestures & motions. Their dark coppery colour'd bodies were so cover'd over with filth as to make it a doubt what was really their proper Colour; their faces were bedaub'd with red and black Paint & grease, in no regular manner, but as their fancies led them; their hair was clot'd also with dirt, & to make themselves either fine, or frightful, many put on their hair the down of young birds, or platted in it sea weed or thin strips of bark dyed red.[29]

The maritime fur traders of the eighteenth century were the first Europeans to have regular encounters with Indigenous British Columbians. The prevailing view among this group is illustrated by the account of Alexander Walker. According to Walker the native of the northwest coast of America had many 'unfavourable features of Character'. He was suspicious, deceitful and treacherous:

> The life of a savage is mixed with uncertainty and deprivations: but its excitements and habits are dear to him. Custom and ignorance are necessary in our Eyes to reconcile the savage to his existence. How differently does he view the situation! Every attempt to reconcile him to the Ease and luxuries of civilised life have failed. After enjoying them for a short time and when he has had the option of enjoying them for Ever, he has preferred the hardships of his former state, and to cover himself again with the skins of Wild Beasts.[30]

King's description makes it clear that he had no hesitation in passing judgement on Indigenous people, even before he had had any communication with them, let alone taking time to learn about their way of life. As a fur trader Walker probably had more extended contact, but his opinions are similar to King's. Neither man is able to accept the different (from their own) habits and customs of the Indigenous people. Walker and King are utterly convinced of the material and moral superiority of their own culture that any deviance from or rejection their way of life horrifies them.

Several generations of contact did not change European views. Almost 75 years later colonist Charles Bayley had his first view of native Americans. He found them to be 'the most hideous beings as they appeared to us imaginable'. He thought native dress was 'grotesque' and 'many of them in a nude state which to the eyes of our passengers was anything but agreeable. One young lady bursting into tears at the sight.'[31] Ten years later native British Columbians had forsaken nudity, but were still offensive to the eyes of Europeans. Harry Guillod's preconceptions took a jolt: 'A journey out here soon destroys all romantic illusions with regard to the Indians; instead of anything noble they are dirty, immoral and fond of tawdry finery.'[32] The Reverend Lundin-Brown was sure that Indigenous British Columbian men knew that they were less manly than whites. Of an encounter between an Indigenous chief and Europeans he wrote:

> He could easily see that in the matter of *physique* those men were very different from his fellow countrymen. His eyes fell on lithe and stalwart frames, on countenances full of intelligence and self-reliance. A type of character so unlike the Indian, who alone is nothing,

however brave he may be at times in company with others, could not fail to strike our chief.³³

Like Walker and King before them, Bayley, Guillod and Lundin-Brown cannot see anything of worth in Indigenous culture. In Lundin-Brown's description can be seen the conflation of physical and moral characteristics postulated by the racial theorists: whites have 'lithe and stalwart frames'; therefore they are intelligent and self-reliant. Indians, it is implied, are the opposite.

Anthony Trollope utilised bestial imagery and the Regency fop in his description of Queensland Aborigines who assumed the manners of whites: 'To my eyes the deportment of the dignified aboriginal is that of a sapient monkey imitating the gait and manners of a do-nothing white dandy.'³⁴ One way of keeping adult male Aborigines subordinate was to deny their adulthood by referring to them as 'boys'. When Ernest Henry departed on a trip from Mt. McConnell Station with another white man, a Mr. Devlin, they took with them 'but one black boy. We call them all boys, regardless of age; ours was probably, some 23 or 24 years old.'³⁵ In his account of this trip, Henry does not remember the boy's name, even though the 'boy' had single-handedly fought off an attack by unfriendly Aborigines intent on killing him and stealing the party's supplies.³⁶ Charles Eden also adopted the practice of calling adult male Aborigines 'boy'. In his account of Edmund Kennedy's trek to Cape York, Eden wrote, 'This course was adopted, and the leader, accompanied by three men, and the boy Jackey-Jackey, left the camp at Weymouth Bay on the 13th of November 1848.'³⁷ In offering Jackey-Jackey's account of the Kennedy expedition, Eden wrote:

> I extract Jackey-Jackey's evidence in full, not only because it will give the reader a good idea of the manner in which the civilised blacks express themselves, but because it will also show him that affection, gratitude, and devotion are to be found in the hearts of *some* [sic] of a race that are too often heedlessly credited with the opposite qualities... there is a deep pathos in the poor savage's rugged sentences that I venture to think can hardly fail to interest the reader.³⁸

Having called into question Jackey-Jackey's maturity, Eden effeminised him (and Aborigines in general), by attributing to him qualities regarded by Victorians as womanly virtues. At the same time, despite Jackey-Jackey's selfless actions, he remained a savage whose 'rugged' command of English is presumably further evidence of his lack of manliness and civilisation.

In the nineteenth century Queensland attracted a number of writers and adventurers who recorded colonial life. The descriptions of the Indigenous peoples of Queensland penned by travel writers A.W. Stirling and Charles H. Allen are typical of the European perspective. In *The Never Never Land: A Ride in North Queensland*, Stirling recorded his impressions of Queensland Aborigines, offering a stark contrast to Figuier's Englishman. He notes that 'amongst the human family the Australian black occupies the lowest place'. Exactly how low, however, could only be understood by 'ocular demonstration'.[39] In their dress, their accommodation, eating habits, physical appearance and religion, Stirling found that Aboriginal men embodied the complete antithesis of British standards and values. They were dirty, lazy and sexually promiscuous. Stirling not only observed the difference between Indigenous and European ways of life but considered that their lifestyle put Indigenous people on the lowest rung of humanity.[40] In his account of frontier life in Queensland, Allen found that 'of all the wild men of the earth, the Australian savage is one of the most degrading and uninteresting; and, without any exception, all the tribes who inhabited the great southern continent before the arrival of the white man, were living in a state of only just removed from that of the beasts of the forest'. Aboriginal men were undependable, untrustworthy and were of the 'very smallest intellectual development'.[41] Aboriginal men were as far removed from 'civilised' manliness as anyone could be.

Even when particular attributes were regarded positively, it was in a heavily qualified form. Virtues, which in a white man would be unhesitatingly praised as noble, were diluted by qualifiers such as 'savage', 'rude' or 'primitive' when possessed by Indigenous men. Of the Indigenous people of British Columbia, traveller C.E. Barret-Lennard noted:

> In common with all their race, they possessed the savage attributes of a wonderfully passive endurance of hardship and suffering, and a stoic indifference to torture and death when inevitable, which amounts to a kind of rude heroism.

In contrast British men were depicted as being of unqualified merit.[42] Clergyman Frederick Richmond wrote of the white men of the Queensland frontier: 'Still we may claim we are an imperial race, if that will make us zealous to go on in this new age, as our fathers did in the past. One must admire the cool courage, boyish spirit and push of our successful men.'[43] Nehemiah Bartley in *Australian Pioneers and Reminiscences* praised the manly qualities of settlers and squatters such as Patrick Leslie ('brave, chivalrous, fearless of danger'), Claudius Whish ('well-set, handsome, disciplined') and Joshua Bell ('enterprising, honourable').[44] Aborigines on the other hand were brutal, crafty and vicious.[45] Integrity, honour, determination, courage, competitive spirit – these were the attributes that white men possessed and Indigenous men lacked.

There were some exceptions to these views, but positive depictions were rare. Arthur McConnel recalled: 'The Durundur and upper Mary River blacks were a fine lot of people – the boys first rate stock hands and some of the gins good workers around the homestead.'[46] However, even in this relatively positive appraisal, the use of the derogatory word 'gins' indicates that Arthur McConnel thought that Indigenous people were inferior to Europeans. Writing of his adventures in British Columbia, Kinahan Cornwallis rendered a panegyrical depiction, evoking the image of the noble savage:

> But is society in a healthier state than when nature reigned in an undisturbed, unmolested sovereignty; when the savage was lord of all, and he rang out in strains triumphant and the chilling whoop of victory, the enchanting and unsophisticated song of freedom, unconscious of a blighting future; when his native glee was boundless, and the thought of a world beyond never broke through the sunlight of his imagination, nor darkened the horizon of his happiness?[47]

Later he describes the Indigenous people of British Columbia as a 'valiant race' possessed of 'unsophisticated honesty and generosity'.[48] Such overblown descriptions are as racist as those openly hostile to Indigenous cultures. What Indigenous person could possibly live up to the image painted by Cornwallis? If Cornwallis's noble savage was what Europeans were expecting when they went to the frontiers of Queensland and British Columbia, it's little wonder that Harry Guillod's 'romantic illusions' were shattered.

In their descriptions of the Indigenous people of British Columbia and Queensland Europeans exaggerated the separation of the white and non-white races. They did so to make the point, to themselves, that the Indigenous people were distinct and other than themselves, and inferior. White settlers feared being reduced to the level of 'savages' and tended to emphasise characteristics that established their separateness from Indigenous British Columbians and Aborigines, rather than those that demonstrated their common humanity.[49] In the North American context Roy Harvey Pearce argues that for the settler wanting to establish and advance a civilisation on the frontier, the Indian was the symbol of something that he must not allow himself to become.[50]

The production of stereotypical 'truths' about Indigenous people also took more systematic, official forms. The colonial Queensland Parliament's 1861 *Native Police Force Report* is an example of 'aboriginalism', the effect of which was to subordinate Indigenous men by depicting them as practising an uncivilised form of masculinity. The Select Committee of the Legislative Assembly was established in May 1861 by the Queensland Parliament to 'enquire into and report on the organisation and management of the Native Police Force; and to further enquire into and report how far it may be practicable to ameliorate the present condition of the aborigines of this colony'.[51] While the purpose of the *Report* was ostensibly to enquire into the efficiency of the Native Mounted Police (NMP) and the condition of Aborigines, it had the effect of constructing Aborigines as inferior, unmanly savages, producing 'truths' (or reinforcing existing 'truths') about Aborigines that would become incontestable and which thereby maintained the power and control whites exercised over them.

The NMP was a force constituted to ostensibly 'protect' Aborigines from white settlers. In reality it was an arm of a colonial project – the aim of which was to dispossess Aborigines of their land. The main function of the NMP was to 'remove' groups of Aborigines from squatters' 'runs' (the term used to describe the portion of land used to graze sheep or cattle). A detachment of the NMP would consist of a white officer, and six to eight Indigenous troopers, recruited from outside the geographical region the detachment patrolled, so that they would have no attachment or association with the Indigenous people they were 'protecting'. Typically, a detachment of the NMP would receive a complaint from a squatter that Aborigines were committing 'depredations' against the squatter's stock. This may have meant that Aborigines were spearing and taking a sheep or bullock. It could have easily meant that Aborigines were merely congregating on the squatter's run, probably as they had done for centuries. The NMP would locate the 'offenders' and 'disperse' them. 'Disperse' was the euphemism employed to describe the killing of Aborigines. More often than not no attempt was made to positively identify the group responsible for the alleged depredation – any group that the NMP came across was 'dispersed'. No attempt was made to verify a squatter's complaint. His word was simply taken as fact.[52]

The Select Committee, composed almost entirely of squatters, heard evidence from witnesses who themselves were mostly squatters, as to the operations of the NMP, the racial constitution of the force and its deployment. It also solicited the opinions of these witnesses as to the habits, lifestyle and ceremonies of Aborigines, taking particular interest in witnesses' knowledge of what it termed 'borees'. The Committee was chaired by Robert Ramsey Mackenzie, a squatter who initially had runs in the New England district and who later took up land in the Burnett district, and who was Member of the Legislative Assembly for Burnett.

Squatters and other landowners were the largest category of witnesses (15). A number of these witnesses were also members of the Queensland Parliament. Other witnesses included three white officers of the NMP, three senior public servants, two missionaries and one doctor who was also a coroner and a magistrate. No women or black troopers of the NMP were called as witnesses; nor were any other Aborigines. In short, everyone involved in the enquiry was white, male and British. More than half of the witnesses and all but one of the Committee relied for their livelihood on land expropriated from Aborigines. None of them gave it a thought. Six witnesses were employed by the government, or were drawn from the parliament in which the Committee members and some of the witnesses sat. The structure of the enquiry was weighted entirely in favour of white, male, colonial interests.

Most of the evidence given to the Committee was oral, although a few witnesses also tendered written statements, copies of letters and other documents. Some of the oral evidence given to the 1858 enquiry of the New South Wales Parliament into similar matters was included in the *Report*. Therefore, most of the evidence in the report comes from stories – the witnesses are narrating their experiences of Aborigines and the NMP. Much of the evidence is anecdotal and second-hand – the lack of direct experience with either the NMP or particular aspects of Aboriginal life was not an impediment to expressing an opinion. Michael Taussig argues that it is through stories rather than ideologies that people define their world. It is in 'the rumour, gossip, story and chit-chat where ideology and ideas become emotionally powerful and enter into active social circulation and meaningful existence'.[53] It is primarily through stories, which were often little more than rumour or gossip, that the

Aborigine was constructed as savage, sexually depraved, cannibalistic and treacherous – in short as the 'ignoble savage', incapable of being educated or Christianised.

The evidence of C.M. Frazer is illustrative, not only of the anecdotal and hearsay nature of much of the evidence, but also of one of the sub-themes of the enquiry and Report, the alleged cannibalism of Aborigines:

> 40. *You don't know anything of your own knowledge with respect to their cannibalism at that time?* Not of my own knowledge, except what the blacks have told me.
>
> 41. *What have they told you?* They have told me that very often if they can't get cattle, or they don't happen to have any other food, they will kill one of their tribe and eat him. They generally kill a black gin; that is what they have told me.
>
> 42. *Have you any reason to believe that is correct?* I think so. I think it is very likely.
>
> 43. *Have you ever heard that they kill children?* Yes.
>
> 44. *More frequently than grown up people?* I could not say that – whether more frequently than grown up people or not.
>
> 45. *Then, in fact, you have no doubt that the practice of cannibalism prevails?* I have not the slightest doubt in my mind.[54]

Cannibalism was high on the Committee's list of concerns. Echoing Frazer, Mr. J. Davies testified (incredibly):

> 14. *Have you noticed that any of these blacks are cannibals?* The whole of them are.
>
> 15. *Without doubt?* I believe so, but I should not like to say they are all cannibals all over the interior. As far as I have been – and I think I have been six or seven hundred miles to the north – they are all cannibals.
>
> 16. *You must have often seen them eating the blacks?* I have seen them eat hundreds of them.[55]

Other witnesses who testified that Aborigines practised cannibalism included Captain John Coley, squatter A.W. Compigne, squatter J. Fraser and Thomas Petrie.[56] Some witnesses claimed they had witnessed cannibalism. NMP Lieutenant Fredrick Wheeler testified:

> 72. *Did the native Police leave the bodies lying where they were shot?* Yes, but it was some distance in the scrub. The blacks heap up a quantity of wood over the dead bodies. In fact, they generally eat them, I have seen them eat them.[57]

However, such first-hand experience on the part of witnesses, if it is to be believed, was rare. One witness testified to the contrary. Squatter Jacob Lowe testified:

> 101. *Do you know if they are cannibals or not?* No I do not.
>
> 102. *Do you know that they carry about their dead for a considerable time?* Yes. The gins carry their own offspring occasionally for twelve months after they are dead.
>
> 103. *How you no idea for what purpose they carry their dead?* No.
>
> 104. *Do you know that, for a certain time after death, the bodies are carried about, and that the males of the tribe dip their fingers in portions of their bodies and suck them?* I don't believe anything of the kind.[58]

Whether or not Aborigines practised cannibalism is not the point argued here. The point is the potency of cannibalism as a discursive weapon employed against Aborigines to depict them as savages, the antithesis of civilised white man. Eating one's fellow humans is, to Western minds, one of the most abhorrent acts in which an individual can indulge. If it could be shown that Aborigines practised cannibalism, that they were in fact addicted to it, then it could be argued that they were beyond civilisation. Indeed, 'addiction' was the picture presented in the *Report*, concluding as it did that 'credible witnesses shew that they are addicted to cannibalism'.[59] This is despite the fact that there were witnesses (albeit a minority) who testified that they did not believe Aborigines practised cannibalism, and that most witnesses were far from being credible, relying as they did on second and sometimes third-hand information.

Equally abhorrent to the Committee and witnesses were the 'unnatural acts' allegedly practised by Aborigines at their 'borees'. Fewer witnesses were prepared to state that they believed Aborigines committed 'unnatural acts'. Squatter Carden Collins was an exception:

42. *Do you know that at the borees, where they met for the purpose of admitting boys to the privileges of manhood, they are guilty of unnatural crimes?* Yes.

43. *Whence do you derive this knowledge?* The blacks have told me so themselves.

44. *Had you any reason to believe that they told you the truth or otherwise?* I believe they told me the truth, as they had no object to gain in deceiving me. I merely asked them what was done on those occasions, and they told me. The natives rather seem to glory in it than otherwise – they laugh at it.[60]

Despite the lack of witnesses prepared to testify about the sexual practices of Aborigines, the Committee was consistent in questioning many of the witness in this regard.[61] In fact it could be very persistent in its desire to uncover 'unnatural crimes', prepared to rhetorically transverse a large section of the frontier in the hope of doing so:

99. *Have you ever heard that at the corroborees or borees of the blacks they commit any unnatural crimes?* I have not.

100. *Do you think that if they did such things you would have heard of it?* I think so.

101. *Have you not been on the Mcleay River?* I have not resided there, but I have been on that river.

102. *In the Port Macquarie District?* Yes.

103. *You know something of the manners and habits of the blacks there?* Yes.

104. *Have you travelled through New England and the Beardie Plains district?* Yes.

105. *Have you travelled through the McIntyre District?* Yes.

106. *You have lived on the Logan sometime?* Yes.

107. *And have had opportunities of seeing the blacks there and knowing their habits?* Yes.

108. *You have been on the Dawson for sometime, and in the Burnett District?* Yes, several years.

109. *And also on the borders of the Port Curtis District?* Yes.

110. *You have been in the neighbourhood of borees – you have seen the blacks going to and from them?* Yes.

111. *You have never in any of these districts heard anything of the kind?* Never.[62]

There is a distinct pattern of questioning regarding 'unnatural acts' throughout the 'Minutes of Evidence' by which the Committee sought to establish Aborigines as sexually depraved. The sexual vilification of those one wanted to subordinate was not a new tactic. Richard C. Trexler's study of the Iberian conquest of South America reveals that accusations of sodomy against native American males was a tactic employed by the Spaniards to justify the conquest of the former. Sodomy was characterised by literary, religious and governmental commentators as 'nefarious', 'unmentionable' and 'abominable'.[63] It is an inescapable principle that discourses of sexuality and gender are about power and subordination.[64] This attempted construction by the Committee of Aborigines as sodomites was a further discursive weapon with which white males sought to maintain their superiority and power over Aborigines.

Aborigines were also constructed as rapists and murderers who went unpunished. The Committee questioned humanitarian Dr Henry Challinor, also a magistrate and coroner:

77. *Were there not a rape and an atrocious murder committed within four or five miles of Brisbane by a black – comparatively civilized?* I heard from the public reports that a German woman had been murdered and robbed, but I was not aware that a rape had been committed.

78. *You said murdered and robbed?* That I knew from report.

79. *Are you not aware that a warrant was out for that man, and that he was not taken?* I believe so. I myself issued a warrant for a blackfellow, for killing a gin, on an inquest I held.

80. *Were there not two comparatively civilised black boys executed for atrocious rapes on German women?* I believe I was one of the Committing magistrates.

81. *That is within your knowledge?* Yes.

82. *Was there not a rape or violent assault committed by blacks between here and Fortitude Valley within the last two or three years?* I could not speak positively on the subject, but that brings to my mind an

attempt to commit rape, which comes within my own knowledge, in the neighbourhood of Ipswich.

83. *Then it is within your knowledge that blacks do occasionally commit rape?* I believe it to be so – such cases have occasionally come before me.[65]

This persistent questioning about alleged rapes by Aboriginal men was a feature of the Committee's investigations. Similarly, it persistently questioned witnesses about the murder of a number of white men, who had been accompanied by Aborigines, in a boat on Moreton Bay. According to the Committee no action was taken to apprehend the Aborigines, whom it presumed to be guilty. This alleged failure was contrasted with what the Committee saw as the zeal with which the white authorities prosecuted white men who had murdered Aborigines. But while many witnesses testified in support of the Committee's assertions, not all were prepared to be led:

54. *In your experience, has it been the case that murders of the blacks by the whites have been taken more notice of such cases as I have mentioned?* In my experience it has been quite the reverse: I have never known until lately *any* notice taken of the murders of blacks.[66]

The *Report and Minutes of Evidence* contain two central themes: Aborigines' lack of civilisation and the necessity of a black police force led by white officers to 'protect' Aborigines and whites from each other. The report produced an array of 'truths' about Aborigines, each of which was used to demonstrate that they were 'uncivilised' and incapable of 'civilisation'. Aborigines' lack of civilisation is simultaneously the prism through which all 'facts' are viewed, and the inevitable conclusion to which these same 'facts' led. These 'facts' or 'truths' included Aboriginal 'depredations' on white property were 'inevitable', therefore the need for a 'protective' force; Aborigines would not work in a regular and dependable manner; their borees were events where they planned their 'outrages'; Aborigines were often not punished for the crimes they committed; they were treacherous, violence perpetrated by whites on Aborigines received a disproportionate legal and press response; they were superstitious; they were not susceptible to Christianity; and they caused their own demise. Each 'truth' produced about Aborigines – that they were cannibals, that they committed 'unnatural' acts, that they could not be Christianised – were weapons in a discursive war of sustained subjugation. These 'truths', which constructed the Aboriginal 'other', in themselves constituted dispossession just as much as the direct violence these 'truths' legitimated and sanctioned. Moreover, fundamental to the construction of Aborigines as 'savages' was the depiction of Aboriginal men (and the Aborigine was almost always male), as lacking the 'civilised' masculinity of white men, and embodying a savage, 'uncivilised' masculinity, which was the antithesis of mid-nineteenth-century masculine values.

The production of these 'truths' was a reflection of the paranoia of whites. The enquiry and *Report* attempted to control and denigrate Aboriginal men through the cultural elaboration of the ignoble and unmanly savage and white fear that the savage might not be controlled. Even when evidence was presented contrary to these 'truths', the Committee was able to maintain its discursive tack, as the testimony of Augustus Rode illustrates:

> 30. *Then you cannot give this Committee a single instance in which you succeeded in civilizing the natives or making them useful?* I will give you an instance of one of my travels. I was travelling with two or three of my friends in company with some blacks and I got ill. Some of my friends prayed for my recovery which was observed by the natives, and they believed that it was in answer to their prayers that I got well. That was their impression. Well, some time after one of the natives became ill, and after we had returned to the station one of them called upon my friend and asked them to pray for the recovery of the black, referring to the circumstance of their praying for me, and of my getting well again. I think that must have made some impression upon them. This circumstance was repeated three or four times.
>
> 31. *Do you not think a good deal of that arises from their superstitious feelings?* I cannot say.[67]

In the view of the Committee, when a white man prays, he is a Christian, when an Aborigine prays he is superstitious.

The press response to the report was not favourable. The *Brisbane Courier* believed that 'a more piquant farce was never enacted'.[68] The *Guardian* described the report as 'lame and impotent'.[69] Both papers doubted the motives of the Committee and believed that it only sought evidence which confirmed its preconceived notions of Aborigines and the NMP. The *Maryborough Chronicle* thought the report was a 'mouse' in contrast to the 'mountain in labour' that went into it.[70] In general, the press portrayed the Report as a whitewash of the NMP and its violent tactics. However, while there was a degree of sympathy for Aborigines (this 'benighted race', in the words of one letter writer), the press and public did not take the Committee to task for its representation of Aborigines as uncivilised or unmanly. The concern of the press was the 'efficiency' and conduct of the NMP, and the taxpayers' funds that maintained it.

In the eyes of white British males, the Indigenous men of Queensland did not measure up to British standards of manliness. By the middle of the nineteenth century, the idea of the 'noble savage' was dead, replaced by images of degenerate, emasculated races. This stereotyped imagery of the ignoble, unmanly savage justified the surveillance and management of Indigenous people by whites, and bolstered white male self-image. It provided a rationale for the use of the NMP to suppress the black population of Queensland. 'Truths' about Indigenous people were in fact white constructions, and reflected back to white men the savagery that they needed to maintain their status as 'civilised' and 'manly'.

Aboriginalism' was a discursive tactic employed by white men in British Columbia as well as in Queensland. Numerous commentators – travellers to British Columbia writing for a British domestic audience – believed that their visit qualified them as anthropologists. Part of what they wrote was merely descriptive of the Indigenous way of life: how canoes were made, the practice of flattening baby's heads, the geographical disposition of various tribes. However, the lack of 'civilisation' amongst the Indigenous people in general and the unmanliness of Indigenous men in particular were common themes. John Emmerson published his impressions in *British Columbia and Vancouver Island: Voyages Travels and Adventures*. Relying on 'science', Emmerson believed that 'phrenologically speaking, the development of the North American Indian is of a low order, the animal propensities preponderating greatly over the intellectual faculties. He is crafty, thievish, and treacherous.'[71] Emmerson believed the various tribes possessed 'different classes' of facial features, which revealed the Indigenous character: 'There is the broad flat face with a vacant childish expression, and the sharp featured with ferocious countenance.'[72] He noted that Indian men detested manual labour, and made their wives carry heavy loads.[73] Manly British men would never exploit their wives in this way.

William Carew Hazlitt, grandson of essayist William Hazlitt, devoted considerable space to native British Columbians in his ponderously titled book, *British Columbia and Vancouver Island, Comprising an Historical Sketch of the British Settlements in the North-West Coast of America and a Survey of the Physical Character, Capabilities, Climate, Topography,*

Natural History, Geology and Ethnology of that Region, with a Map. Hazlitt's survey is indeed as comprehensive as his title promises. He found the physical resources of British Columbia, soil, flora, fauna, climate eminently favourable for British settlement and exploitation, but was far less impressed with its inhabitants.

According to Hazlitt, one tribe, the Talkellies, were physically and morally filthy. They had 'untutored minds' and were addicted to gambling and falsehood.[74] They were gross and brutal. The fact that they preferred their meat putrid divided them from civilisation.[75] To the extent that some tribes were less brutal and more moral than others, Hazlitt supposed it to be due to their contact with Europeans. Such a tribe were the Talkotin. In Hazlitt's view they displayed a 'superiority in general conduct and behaviour' compared to the Talkellies, no doubt due to 'considerable intercourse with whites'.[76] Citing a Mr. Dunn, Hazlitt distinguished between the tribes of the northeast and those 'in the countries of the Columbia and New Caledonia' (as British Columbia was originally known). In the latter region 'the natives do not lead the same solitary and ferocious lives' of the northeastern tribes: 'They are endowed with a greater capacity and quickness of apprehension; are more pliant and tractable in temper; appreciate more the talents, attainments, and social arts of the white man; and are fonder of imitating their customs and principles.' Even when he praised Indigenous men, Hazlitt did so in terms which elevated white civilisation, feminising Indigenous men as 'pliant and tractable'.[77]

Hazlitt described the tribes of Vancouver Island as cruel, bloodthirsty, treacherous and cowardly. They were incapable of being taught and had no religion, only superstition. He found their ceremonies disgusting and 'not worthy of the inquiry of an ethnologist'.[78] Like Emmerson, Hazlitt could discern the unmanly Indigenous nature from their physical features. The native men of Vancouver Island, in Hazlitt's discerning eye, had a long nose, high cheek bones, a large ugly mouth, very long eyes and their foreheads were 'villainously low'.[79]

What the Queensland Legislative Assembly's Report did for the Australian Aborigine, Gilbert Sproat's *Scenes and Studies of Savage Life* did for Indigenous British Columbians. Gilbert Malcolm Sproat, businessman, government agent, Indian reserve commissioner and magistrate went to Vancouver Island in 1860 to establish a sawmill on Alberni Inlet. After a display by his ships' cannons, forcing the local Aht people to move, he established his own settlement and from there made his observations. *Scenes and Studies of Savage Life* purports to be an account of the 'condition and customs' of the Aht people of northern Vancouver

Island. However, like the Select Committee Report, it is little more than an attempt to denigrate the culture and character of an Indigenous people in order to justify violence and dispossession. In particular it is the Aht men who are the victims of Sproat's amateur anthropological work. According to Sproat, when compared to Englishmen, Aht men are deficient in every respect. These deficiencies are apparent from puberty, when the 'visage of the men assumes the composure, and displays the cold serious traits of the savage'.[80] The face of the Aht male shows all the vices, especially anger, cunning and pride.[81] The Aht male is also mentally deficient compared to Englishmen. When faced with difficult questions 'the mind of the savage then appears to rock to and fro out of mere weakness, and he tells lies and talks nonsense'.[82] Of course, over a period of time the mental powers of the Aht could be improved by education, but the problem as Sproat saw it was that the people would vanish before their education was complete.[83]

While the Aht male did possess some virtues (he displayed strong love for his children), he failed to attain the standards of the Englishman.[84] His vices, on the other hand, far exceeded English vices. In summary the Aht male displayed a want of observation, a great deficiency of foresight, extreme fickleness in his passions and purposes, was habitually suspicious, and had inordinate love of power and display, the last being a curious criticism coming as it did from an agent of the British Empire. Furthermore, Aht men were noted for their ingratitude, vindictiveness, cold-bloodedness, absence of religious faith and extreme indifference to human suffering.[85] Aht men completely lacked the courage, stoicism, integrity, honesty and perseverance supposedly embodied by the British male. In their lack, Indigenous men were closer to the wild beasts which they hunted, than they were to civilised and manly Britons.[86] The white settlers are, by contrast, 'the finest looking men' Sproat had ever seen, and are described as 'stalwart handsome fellows'.[87] According to Sproat, the Governor of Vancouver Island, Sir Arthur Kennedy, embodied all that was manly in the white settler, and provided a stark contrast to the native: 'The Governor is a soldier-like man, with a resolute handsome face, and a firm voice.'[88]

The views of Emmerson, Hazlitt and Sproat are representative of the attitudes prevailing among white settlers and reflect the race consciousness of the time. The Indigenous male of British Columbia was in no way similar to the British male. Indigenous men had none of the virtues and all of the vices of British men. As in Queensland, white men constructed 'truths' about Indigenous men in order to uphold their own status as civilised and manly. White men reading Emmerson, Hazlitt or Sproat could be confident that they were morally and physically superior to Indigenous men, and therefore had the right, indeed the obligation, to take control of Indigenous lands and 'civilise' the wilderness.

Indigenous men were not the only group of men subordinated and marginalised on the frontier. In Queensland and British Columbia, non-white male colonists were also denigrated, and placed on a rung in the masculine hierarchy that was well below that of the white Briton. Chinese men in particular were subjected to organised violence, political and economic restrictions and discursive vilification which depicted them as unmanly and as inferior human beings. The purpose of these tactics was to make life so difficult for them that they would abandon the colonies, or preferably not arrive in the first place, leaving the British in complete possession.

Chinese men first came to Queensland when pastoralists on the Darling Downs sought labourers to solve a labour shortage resulting from the cessation of transportation in 1839. The pastoralists had relied on 'ticket of leave' or 'expired' men and by the late 1840s they were desperate for a new source of labour. In the middle of the nineteenth century, a Chinese diaspora formed as men left the southern districts of Fujian and Guadong for destinations in the Pacific and Southeast Asia, including Australia. Fujian and Guadong were undergoing economic crises, and Chinese men were looking for opportunities abroad.[89] In 1848 fifty-six Chinese labourers arrived in Queensland aboard the *Nimrod* and initially received an enthusiastic welcome. These labourers were incorporated into the existing labour structure of the Downs.[90] The Chinese, although initially intended as relief from a short-term labour shortage, quickly became essential workmen in low-paid jobs or jobs that were too boring or menial for whites. They worked as shepherds, shearers, gardeners or domestic servants, their employers maintaining that these were the only jobs appropriate.

In 1867 gold was discovered at Gympie, and was followed in 1868 by finds at Ravenswood, in 1871 at Charters Towers and in 1873 on the Palmer River. These discoveries brought in a huge influx of Europeans and Chinese. Prior to the discovery of gold on the Palmer River there were over 2,000 Chinese in Queensland, most of whom had arrived from the southern colonies. Increasing numbers headed for North Queensland with the Palmer River rush so that by 1876 there were over 17,000 Chinese on the northern goldfields. Their numbers were overwhelmingly male, as they were in British Columbia.[91]

Attracted by the Fraser River gold rush, approximately 2,000 Chinese, initially from the United States, arrived in British Columbia in 1858.[92]

In 1859, the numbers of Chinese increased considerably as a recruitment system was organised to transport labourers and merchants from Hong Kong to Victoria via San Francisco. By 1860, following the discovery of gold in the Cariboo, almost 4,000 Chinese lived on the mainland colony.[93] The overwhelming majority of Chinese in British Columbia were males who ventured abroad to earn money for their families in China. In 1867 there were only 52 women among 1,995 people of Chinese origin in British Columbia.[94] The numbers of Chinese on the mainland could fluctuate with the vicissitudes of gold mining. Most worked at placer mining, a form of mining that required little capital, sifting the sand and gravel of creek and riverbeds, and reworked diggings abandoned by whites.[95] Not all Chinese immigrants ventured to the mainland in search of gold. Some remained in Victoria, where they established themselves as importers and general merchants. Chang Tsoo was the first Chinese immigrant to go into business, opening a laundry.[96] The resulting Chinatown was known disparagingly as 'Little Canton'.[97] In 1860 the Chinese population of Vancouver Island was 1,577.[98] However, these numbers were small compared to the situation 20 years later when 17,000 Chinese, between 1881 and 1884, half from China and a substantial number from the United States, arrived in British Columbia to work on the Canadian Pacific Railroad.[99]

Chinese were an incongruent presence on Queensland and British Columbian goldfields when measured against European norms. They differed markedly from Europeans in their physical appearance, dress, diet, customs and work habits. They tended to live in separate communities, and were little inclined to adopt local norms and customs. Racial prejudices, white fear of difference and perceptions of unfair competition for gold led to the subordination and marginalisation of Chinese men. Tactics of subordination were practised by politicians, the press and white miners – in short, by white men at every level of frontier society.

For example, in the Queensland election of 1888, Sir Samuel Griffith of the Liberals and Sir Thomas McIlwraith of the Nationals both adopted strong anti-Chinese positions.[100] As whites regarded Aboriginal men as degraded and immoral, so did they regard Chinese men. A white miner wrote to the *Brisbane Courier,* accusing Chinese of practising unclean habits and spreading disease:

> The effluvium which greets the olfactory nerves on passing through is abominable. The filth must be the means of generating those dangerous noxious vapours that cause typhoid and other fevers which are so

fatal to life. I trust the authorities will see the necessity of appointing a sanitary inspector, for these celestial gentlemen have already a nest of pigsties in the main track close to the township and adjoining the site for the crushing machine which imparts everything but a pleasant sensation in the sense of smell to those who are unfortunately compelled to pass that way.'[101]

The use of the word 'gentlemen' in the derisory manner adopted clearly indicates that this white miner believed that Chinese men were most definitely not gentlemen. According to Charles Eden, all miners 'had a horror of Chinamen, but I doubt if half of them could tell you for what reason'.[102] As was the case on other Australian goldfields, in Queensland Chinese miners were despised for their industrious habits and for their supposed vices which included smoking opium, fouling watercourses, 'unnatural' sexual practices and debasing white women. Chinese miners were frequently the victims of violent attacks by white miners, as Eden describes: 'Should any unfortunate Celestials show their flat faces on a gold filed, a cry of "roll up" passes from hole to hole, up come the occupants, and if Johnny is not wise enough to beat a hasty retreat he stands every chance of a bloody coxcomb.'[103] Eden's patronising descriptors of Chinese men – 'Celestials' and 'Johnny' – indicates where he placed them in the masculine hierarchy.

The *Northern Miner* of Charters Towers doubted not only Chinese but also Pacific Islanders' claim to humanity, and articulated fears of interbreeding:

> Kanakas and Chinese are distinct types of the genus Homo – some would go so far as to deny that they belong to the human family at all. There is no affinity between them and the men of the Caucasian race, and miscegenation of races so physically antagonistic must inevitably degrade the higher race.[104]

Journalist William Lane was particularly vituperative. Writing of the Chinese quarter in Brisbane, he urged readers of the *Boomerang* to

> burn down this joint and all the other joints and with it every one of those yellow devils who, with their mask like faces and fawning guise and patient plodding ways and superb organisation ... will wreck the manliness of our men and the womanliness of our women and will bury our nationality in a deadly slough of sloth and deceit and filth and immoralities from which the vigorous white man now shrinks in horror.[105]

In the white imagination, Chinese men were barely human, let alone manly. They occupied an entirely different place in the gender order, one that threatened British manliness (and womanliness) with extinction. No white man would live like a Chinese man, and white men instinctively rejected Chinese vices. Chinese men were dirty, lazy and immoral, the antithesis of the 'vigorous' white man. Chinese men were often referred to by snide nicknames such as 'the wily Celestial' or 'Chinkey', and universally christened with the sobriquet 'John', thereby denying them individuality and confirming their unworthiness as men.[106]

The discovery of gold in British Columbia in 1858 not only brought an influx of white males from California, Oregon and Washington, it also brought anti-Chinese sentiment that had been fostered in American mining towns and elsewhere. Chinese men were not allowed on the Cariboo goldfields.[107] Local miners threatened to drive them out of the district and on one occasion white miners drove a group of Chinese miners off the Hudson's Bay Company's ship the *Otter*.[108] The editor of the *Colonist*, Amor de Cosmos, maintained that there was a position for the Chinese miner on the goldfields, but he added that the white miner was 'more civilised, more energetic, and more valuable'.[109]

Gilbert Sproat, whose interests were not confined to the Aht, penned views that were representative of white anti-Chinese sentiment in British Columbia, and typical of the contradictions in white views which saw the Chinese as simultaneously inferior and superior. Sproat wrote of the Chinese worker:

> The long continued, uniform operation of over-mastering external conditions, has compelled him, and it has also enabled him, to subsist on the very least which his case will merely maintain the nerve force that drives his muscular machinery... The repression of the natural development of the man, which ought to be moral and intellectual as well as physical, together with an inherited inaptness, prevents his advancing much beyond the ways and means which the passion of self-preservation inspires and stimulates.[110]

The Chinese worker was therefore an immutable alien, intellectually inferior, at best an economic resource, but superior for the machine-like labour he could provide. In both colonies, much of the animosity towards Chinese men was based on economic fears. It was widely believed that Chinese workers hoarded their money and sent it back to China. It was believed that they spent as little of their money as possible, thereby failing to invest in the longer-term interest of the community (the fact that most of the Chinese were men without their families reinforced this idea). Most important to white workers was the fact that the Chinese were prepared to work for lower wages than whites, thereby endangering white prosperity.[111]

Unfortunately for the Chinese, they arrived in Queensland and British Columbia at a time when the cultural and moral superiority of whites was held to be a universal and immutable truth, and a consciousness of race had a strong hold on the popular imagination. Indeed, the presence of large numbers of Chinese outside of China for the first time was a significant cause of this discourse. In both colonies the Chinese were victims of stereotyping. They were regarded as unclean, failing to adhere to the sanitary conventions of white society. The Chinese were perceived as threatening pestilence and disease; they thrived in overcrowded housing, were addicted to gambling and opium, and were deceitful, cunning and sexually perverse. For these sins they were vilified by politicians and the press and despised and feared by the general population.

In British Columbia the attitudes of whites towards Chinese immigrants were not uniformly negative. Travel writer C.E Barret-Lennard thought that they were 'frugal, persevering and abstemious'.[112] Naval officer Edmund Hope-Verney considered: 'They are a wonderful race, generally keeping very much together and patient and enduring. I never saw a Chinaman looking otherwise than contented, and I never saw one the worse for drink. And there they were today, toiling and plodding along but withal cheerful.'[113] Newton H. Chittenden, in providing advice for would-be settlers in British Columbia, admired a Chinese community in Tranquille:

> I went three or four miles up the stream, and was much surprised at their extent and production. From twenty to forty Chinamen have mined here for several years and are evidently doing very well. The first one whom we asked to show us some gold, brought out several packages containing an ounce or more in each. They build log cabins, cultivate gardens, raise chickens and live here the year round on the best the country affords. An oven was shown me made of rocks and mud, where they occasionally roast a whole hog, usually on their national holidays. Mr. Fortune says that they frequently go home to China and bring back their relatives with them.[114]

To these observers, the Chinese immigrant was a positive addition to the colony. In their industry, perseverance and frugality they appeared to be the ideal settlers, forming vibrant and enduring communities. The qualities the Chinese male possessed were similar to the British ideal. What accounts for this difference in attitude? One possible explanation lies in the fact that Verney, Chittenden and Barret-Lennard were temporary visitors to British Columbia, not intending to settle permanently and not seeking to get rich quick on the Cariboo goldfields. They did not face economic competition for scarce resources from Chinese miners, nor were they intent on establishing permanent ties to the colony. White colonists and fortune hunters, on the other hand, needed to assert their dominance over competitors, be they Indigenous or Chinese. The construction of 'truths' about Chinese men served a similar purpose to the 'truths' that were constructed about Indigenous men. The depiction of Chinese men as unmanly facilitated and legitimised their economic and social exclusion.

The shortcomings of white men who did not conform to the homosocial culture of the frontier could be deployed to make those particularly keen to appear manly more so than perhaps they were. Such was the fate of the comically unfortunate Eugene Francis O'Bierne, who accompanied W.B Cheadle and Viscount Milton on their overland trek. In both Cheadle's journal and *The North-west Passage by Land* O'Bierne (or O'Byrne as it is spelt by Cheadle) embodied all the inadequacies and failings that an individual could possibly possess.[115] He was the living antithesis of the hegemonic masculine ideal.

O'Bierne made the acquaintance of Milton and Cheadle at Fort Edmonton, introducing himself as the grandson of Bishop O'Bierne and a graduate of Cambridge, Milton's and Cheadle's *alma mater*. He gained their confidence by revealing that he knew many of their friends and acquaintances and they were satisfied that he was a well-connected gentleman.[116] He persuaded them to allow him to join their party, a request they agreed to with some reluctance. Their hesitation was to prove, in their eyes, well founded.

In *The North-west Passage by Land* O'Bierne is depicted as helpless as a child and as displaying qualities antithetical to the frontier male. He was lazy: 'He was afraid to approach a horse, and when his help was required to load the animals, he was invariably missing.'[117] He was timid and fearful: 'Mr. O'B. was a man of most marvellous timidity. His fears rendered his life a burden to him. But of all the things he dreaded – and their name was legion – his particular horror was a grisly [sic] bear.'[118] He is an incompetent fisherman: 'Mr. O'B also attracted by the prospect of a meal more attractive than pemmican, essayed to fish; but he splashed around so restlessly, and met with so little encouragement, that he soon wearied of his employment.'[119] Cheadle summed up O'Bierne's character (or lack thereof):

> O'Byrne's assistance is nil; most hopeless fellow I ever saw; frightened of a horse, & shews very little disposition to help in anything without I ask it. Asks the men, rather tells them, to do little things for him, as if they were his servants & he an emperor. Does not even attempt to pack his own horse. I fear trouble with the men on his account. He is the greatest coward I ever saw, & I can hardly stop laughing at his continual questions as to the chance of meeting grisly bears.[120]

Despite representing, in Cheadle's words, a 'minus quantity' on the trail, in *The North-west Passage by Land* O'Bierne's manhood was represented as subordinate to the hegemonic manhood practised by Milton and Cheadle.[121] In their published account, O'Bierne's masculine failings provide comic relief:

> Before daylight he crept into the lodge for safety. Milton, dreaming at the time, woke up with a shout, and Mr. O'B. cried out in terror, 'Oh, dear! Oh, dear! This is perfectly horrible – what has happened? *It's only me – O'B. – don't shoot my lord!*' Everyone then woke up, and there was general commotion; but finding the alarm groundless, all returned to their blankets, except the unhappy cause of the disturbance, who remained sitting in the darkness, too discomposed for sleep.[122]

Throughout the book, O'Bierne is held up as a man of ridicule, while Milton and Cheadle are the heroic conquerors of the wilderness.

Non-British men too often occupied subordinate positions in the masculine frontier hierarchy. When a shepherd, who was German, said he could no longer look after his flock as he was ill and intended to leave them in the charge of Charles Eden, Eden was so angry that he forced the 'pig-headed German' into a river to send him on his way. Eden didn't believe that 'any Englishman would have done such a mean trick, but it is by shabby things of this kind that Germans have earned the appellation of "black fellow white man", as they are called by the black boys, who rank them in the same category as Chinamen'.[123] Anyone who did not conform to the standards set by the dominant male population could find themselves pushed to the lower rungs of the masculine pecking order.

The manly ideal was not merely a set of attributes to which men could aspire or conform. It was employed by white male British colonists as a discursive tool to subordinate and marginalise those, particularly Indigenous, men who were perceived to be lacking in the required characteristics. The construction of Indigenous masculinities as inferior to British manliness was a practice of colonial rule intended to facilitate the dispossession of Indigenous people. In official reports, travel literature and anthropological studies, Indigenous men were characterised as the antithesis of white British males. Indigenous men were variously depicted as lazy, sexually depraved, cannibalistic, treacherous and stupid. This was in contrast to white men who were industrious, brave, resolute and strong, and who embodied all the virtues thought to bestow manliness. Other non-whites, such as the Chinese, were also depicted as unmanly and racially inferior, in an attempt to marginalise them economically and ensure the domination of white colonists. If discursive means were insufficient, more direct physical means could be employed to ensure the dominance of white British males.

6
A Hand Prepared to be Red

> The white man's revenge is pure terrorism... In the war of the races... there is much useless slaughter, much that is not only not chivalrous but is absolutely revolting.
> (Frederick Richmond, *Queensland in the Seventies: Reminiscences of the Early Days of a Young Clergyman*)

Some men, and at times great numbers of men, engage in violent behaviour. It is overwhelmingly males who control and use violence. Pieter Spierenburg points out that in every historical context violent crime has been a predominantly male enterprise.[1] It is not only in crime, however, that male violence is expressed. Wars, slavery and conquest are inherently violent enterprises, and men have been at the forefront of these activities. So ubiquitous is male violence that John Archer argues that it should be considered a 'normal' characteristic of masculinity.[2] Similarly, Elizabeth Stanko argues that violent behaviour is neither deviant or abnormal but 'an ordinary part of life'.[3]

On the frontiers of Queensland and British Columbia violence was not only ubiquitous, but it was often considered manly. I argue that the manly ideal had within it the potential for violence. The manly attributes such as courage, strength, rationality and perseverance could be distorted to justify violence. Moreover, the ideals of reason, civilisation and progress, outlined in the last chapter, were often used to justify violence against Indigenous people. Violence could also have an economic face. 'Capitalist patriarchy', when exported to the frontier in the name of progress and development, had the potential to encourage male violence.

Brian Moon argues that theories of male violence which are based on biology or Freudian psychology are all predicated on the idea that violence can be understood as a product of the psychosocial construction of the individual male. According to Moon, one flaw with these theories is that they ignore the effect of culture on the development of the individual. Furthermore, as Moon suggests, such theories ignore the specific character of different forms of violence. Rape, wife-beating and war are all explained either by male anxieties arising from the rejection of the mother and the identification with the father or by learnt behaviour.[4] Whatever the nature of the violence, it is the nature of men as individual subjects that lies at its heart. As an alternative Moon proposes a Foucauldian analysis of violence in which the task is not to discover what it is about men that causes them, as individuals or collectively, to commit violence, but to establish how certain forms of masculinity are constructed with a tendency towards violence.[5] In this analysis the capacity of men to act violently is conditioned by their position within a specific social milieu or apparatus and by a discourse and ideologies which normalise and rationalise violence.

Moon's suggestion is useful in examining three aspects of frontier violence: firstly, the prevalence of violence in Victorian Britain; secondly, the nature of violence on the frontier, particularly interracial violence, and how acts of violence were construed as expressions of manliness; thirdly, the nexus between violence, civilisation and manliness. Violence in mid-Victorian Britain was far from universally condemned. Moreover, while the ideal of manliness did not explicitly embrace violence, male violence was normalised, and certain types of violent behaviour by and among men were not only tolerated, but expected and positively valued.

In Britain prior to the eighteenth century, male violence was often not prosecuted as there was an expectation that men would defend their reputation, position and manhood by fighting. Towards the end of the eighteenth century violent behaviour was increasingly frowned upon and punished by the law, and intolerance of male violence grew.[6] Nevertheless, according to Vic Gatrell, 'Violence in the nineteenth century was ubiquitous.'[7] He cites industrial disputes, popular recreation areas, the streets and the home as common sites of violence. In addition, there were regular moral panics about violence including that of Chartists in the 1840s, garrotting and trade union violence in the 1860s, and child abuse, hooliganism and armed burglary in the latter part of the century.[8] To observers such as Henry Mayhew and Charles Booth criminals appeared to form a separate social class. That class was the working class, and violence was constructed as a working-class problem.[9] It was a widely held belief that working-class adult males were prone to outbursts of physical violence.[10] The middle and upper classes, however, committed their own forms of violence. The systems of discipline in the public schools, both formal and informal, the institutionalised violence of the army and Royal Navy, the violence committed overseas in the name of the Empire and parental discipline are a few examples of the violence which pervaded these classes.[11]

Despite the growing intolerance towards male violence, there were deeply held beliefs and values in regard to a man's right to fight. Physical violence was a key component of male identity. Physical prowess was a key part of the manly ideal and the manly attributes of courage and strength could be easily translated into aggressive behaviour. Courage could equal not backing out of a fight, or being able to take care of oneself in a fight. Strength could equal having the physical capability to fight. Some inclination and skill in violence was considered to be desirable for boys. To be regarded as a 'real' boy, a boy had to display a willingness to fight when necessary. 'After all,' wrote Thomas Hughes, 'what would life be without fighting, I should like to know? From the cradle to the grave, fighting, rightly understood, is the business, the real highest, honestest business of every son of man.'[12]

It was held that men possessed instinctive aggression, and part of the progress from boyhood to manhood was the development of the appropriate use of physical force.[13] What was appropriate depended on assumptions about class, age, gender and context. It was accepted that middle-class men had the same innate capacity for violence as working-class men, but they were presumed to be able to exercise manly self-control and channel it into rugby and other sports. Violence deployed to defend the weak, to defend one's honour or in defence of the country, and Empire was considered just and honourable.[14] In mid-Victorian Britain violence, in one form or another, was an acceptable, even desirable, part of manhood. As they took the dominant cultural ideas about race and gender to the frontier, mid-Victorian men also took their ideas about violence.

On the Queensland frontier, the lack of legal and moral restraints which existed in the metropole, combined with the harsh living conditions, created an environment in which men could do things they probably would not have done in Britain. Raymond Evans has suggested that the 'demonstrable Australian historical characteristics' of 'environmental confrontation, convictism, frontier conflict and the more pervasive vicissitudes of settler colonialism might all be interpreted as encouraging a particularly aggressive, conformist mode of masculinity'.[15] From at least the late 1830s the Queensland frontier was a place where violence was endemic.

Violence was a key feature of the homosocial culture of Queensland. In 1867 the *Brisbane Courier* reported from Queensland's Gulf country: 'Men, who if they were in Sydney or Melbourne, would attend church and be ornaments of society, are to be seen with their shirts off, doing astonishing feats of fisticuffs.'[16] Marilyn Lake has argued that the Australian frontier was a threatening place in gender relations terms as well as in terms of violence and bloodshed between men of competing cultures. The dominant reality of the frontier was as a place in which women, especially black women, were in constant sexual danger from men. The freedom of movement enjoyed by frontier men gave rise to the 'marauding white man' who, Lake argues, is the true representative of Australian frontier masculinity.[17] Due to the isolation and harsh conditions on the frontier, domestic relationships were more violent than in the towns and cities.[18] Nicola Henningham has examined the ways in which representations of Aboriginal savagery constructed the North Queensland frontier as a place of danger where 'civilised' white men tested themselves against 'wild' Aborigines, and how the wider colonial community reacted to white male violence on the frontier. She concludes that violence was not confined to 'testosterone rich' men on the frontier, but rather permeated colonial society across the colony.[19]

Henningham's conclusion holds for cases within white frontier society. Men used violence to administer summary justice. On Exmoor station Biddulph Henning took matters into his own hands to punish a thief who had stolen blankets and other items from the shearers' hut. Avoiding the time and expense of sending the alleged thief to 175 kilometres to Port Denison (present day Bowen) for a committal hearing and then almost 600 kilometres to Rockhampton to give evidence, Henning had the man tied to a tree and flogged with 24 lashes. Henning did not administer the flogging himself (being a gentleman), but delegated the task to 'Pat, who is a stout Irishman'.[20]

Violent predatory sexual behaviour by white men was not only perpetrated on Aboriginal women. Colonial newspapers often carried stories of attacks on white women and girls:

> Anyone who reads the newspapers...can see the great amount of mischief that is being done, and cannot close his [sic] eyes to the great many cases that have not been made public in which faultless young girls have been led astray.[21]

One such case occurred in 1871, when a 12-year-old girl, Ammelie Weise, was sent to the head station at Hirst Vale near Dalby to collect supplies. She arrived home in tears and with her dress torn. She told her mother that a shearer had followed her from the station and had demanded a kiss. When she refused he told her he would 'see about that', forced her to the ground and assaulted her.[22]

In Queensland men lived and worked in a physical environment which, at least in comparison to the countryside of Britain, was violent. George Carrington experienced a storm 'like nothing I had ever experienced before':

> Every minute the storm increased in violence. The lightning kept up a continual crackling and growling, with, now and then, a loud explosion, which seemed to be only a few feet off. The air was full, as it seemed, of fire, which ran along the ground, and illuminated all things.... the lightning itself seemed to speak and roar.[23]

When drought killed hundreds of his cattle Richard Symes Alford always carried a revolver to put a beast out of its misery. Nature itself was cruel in its disposal:

> It was a pitiable sight to see the villainous crows perched on the backs of living helpless bogged cattle, and having pierced a hole in the side, eating the flesh away piecemeal. Dingoes could also be seen eating the same live cattle when hopelessly bogged.[24]

Arguably, such an environment desensitised and hardened men to such an extent that violence was internalised and naturalised. The cruelty of nature was emulated:

> Frank Coulson was there with his once famous racehorse 'Colonel', an old snow white animal with both forelegs heavily fired. That is an operation done with a hot iron passed across both sides of each leg below the knee in order to strengthen the sinews.[25]

Alford's 'Memoirs' contain graphic descriptions of the slaughter of hundreds of kangaroos, which he and others regarded as vermin. The introduction of sheep and cattle to frontier Queensland meant intense competition with the native wildlife for food and water. The kangaroos not only had to compete with these introduced species, but with their human owners as well. Alford organised battues, inviting men from all around to participate, and devising elaborate means to entrap and slaughter the native animals.[26]

This indifference to pain and suffering applied to man as well as beast:

> No very great value is set upon human life in the colony. Everyman is supposed to take care of himself, and the weakest goes to the wall. If a man meets his *death* in anyway, the principle thing is to get someone to take his place, and he is soon forgotten.[27]

The first settlers on the Condamine and MacIntyre rivers in Queensland experienced the same difficulties as earlier settlers elsewhere: resistance by Aborigines forced whites to give up their stations and resulted in punitive expeditions, commencing 50 years of violence.[28] The Maranoa district of Western Queensland was settled by whites only after a violent struggle with Aborigines, and the Gulf country of Northwest Queensland was a place of unrestrained violence.[29] Aboriginal resistance to white settlement was a 'manifest reality' of colonial life. Resistance may have been 'scattered and sporadic', but it was pervasive and generated an atmosphere of fear among whites on the frontier.[30] Evans has described the 'frontier situation' as 'a condition of severe and usually protracted struggle, where contending parties behaved towards each other in a manner analogous to the confrontation adopted in a situation of war'.[31]

A few words from a number of men of the Queensland frontier will serve not only to emphasise the prevailing culture of interracial violence, but to illustrate the ease with which frontier men accommodated violence in their lives as a routine and normal part of frontier living, and as an appropriate way of dealing with 'troublesome' Aborigines. From the Darling Downs in Queensland in 1841 George Leslie, younger brother of Patrick, wrote to one of his brothers: 'Walter being down the country I can't leave home but Ernest Dalrymple and a party are out hunting the Niggers. They have killed a great many white men in this part of the country and not many days pass at a time, without hearing of some man being killed.'[32]

In 1862, the proprietor of Mitchell Downs station on the Maranoa wrote to the Colonial Secretary to express his gratitude for the efforts of the Native Mounted Police:

> I do myself the honour of informing you that in accordance with instructions issued from your Office, the Native Police under Lieut. Morehead have thoroughly tracked and cleared this run of blacks

who had assembled and attacked one of my stations. With a diligence deserving of every praise, Lieut. Morehead succeeded after many days pursuit in overtaking and dispersing a portion of the mob to which the murderers belonged.[33]

Magistrate and Commissioner of Crown Lands Stephen Simpson reported to the Colonial Secretary:

> The Stations to the North of Brisbane are suffering considerably from the hostile proceedings of the Aborigines, who appear to be carrying out their vengeance in a very insidious manner by attacking any defenceless individual that may fall in their way. A Hutkeeper of Mr. Bigge was murdered a few weeks since & within these few days another of Mr. Balfour's; besides several other individuals have been attacked on their way from one station to another.[34]

In the 1840s accounts Aboriginal attacks were a regular part of Land Commissioners' reports.

In the journals and reminiscences of frontier men, violence against Indigenous people is rarely condemned. It was regarded as an unfortunate but unavoidable part of frontier life:

> The pioneers cannot be condemned for taking the law into their own hands and defending themselves in the only way open to them, for the blacks own no law themselves but the law of might. The protection of outside districts by the Native Police, was the only course open... The white pioneers were harder on the blacks in the way of reprisals when they were forced to deal with them for spearing their men or their cattle or horses even than the Native Police. But how were property and the lives of stockmen, shepherds, and prospectors in the north to be protected unless by some summary system of retribution by native Police or bands of pioneers?[35]

Violence on the part of white men was considered acts of manliness. Manly courage was regarded as an absolute necessity. It included the willingness to confront violent, or potentially violent, situations, particularly those involving Indigenous people. In his roll call of manly frontier men Oscar de Satgé named Henry Gregory as a 'first rate bushman'.[36] One of the virtues that made him so was his courage when others were afraid. de Satgé relates an incident when a group of Aborigines attempted to kill Gregory and rob his store in the middle of the night. Gregory 'accounted for two of the aggressors with his first rifle shot, and then went out and shot several others, thus liberating the cowardly hands that dared not come out of the store'.[37] Gregory was obviously defending himself and his property, but the point lies in de Satgé's characterisation of Gregory's actions as courageous in contrast to the 'cowardly' inaction of his employees. Gregory is portrayed as the 'real man', who did not shirk a violent confrontation, while the obvious implication was that those who hid were unmanly.

When Allan McPherson attempted to occupy Mt. Abundance Station, near present-day Roma, the resistance from the local Aboriginal tribes was violent and protracted. McPherson lost stock, stockmen and dray drivers to attacks from Aborigines protecting their land. Most of McPherson's men were extremely fearful of Aborigines, but he was not. Accusing his men of being faint-hearted cowards, McPherson declared that he was not afraid of confrontation:

> Some few blacks made their appearance in the evening, who fairly frightened the men into convulsions. I laughed at them as cowards and faint-hearted creatures, and, as I might have expected, got sulky looks, and expressive growls for my pains. To show them how little I feared the blacks, I told my men that in the morning I intended to start ahead by myself, and to camp out alone for two or three nights, exploring the water, and finding out the best spot for forming the head station.[38]

He was pleased to avenge the death of one of his shepherds:

> I must own that it was a great consolation to me in the first conflict we had with the natives (and it was not the only one before we reached the Mount two days afterwards), that my keen eyed friend Charley found on the person of one of the blacks who had fallen a pocket knife with the initials 'F.G.' engraved on the handle – being that of the poor hut keeper, John Gore, who had been brutally murdered, at the door of his hut, only a month before. Certainly in this case retribution was not swift, it was at all events sure.[39]

In his memoir McPherson contrasts himself to his men. They are insolent cowards; he is brave and resolute. They fear death at the hands of Aborigines; he practically invites the Aborigines to attack him. McPherson clearly considers himself more manly than his employees. What is more, he considers that violence employed for revenge is justified, and violent conflict over possession of land is an occupational hazard and not something to shirk. In these examples, when the frontier tested men's courage, they reacted with violence which was regarded as an expression of manliness. Gregory and McPherson are manly because they were not afraid to 'act', to employ violence, while those who are too timid to act are depicted as unmanly.

Chapter 3 analysed how, for Anthony Trollope, the squatter embodied all that was manly in a frontiersman. Energetic, brave and commanding, the squatter occupied the summit of manhood on the frontier. Further, according to Trollope:

> The Australian grazier cannot live unless he defend his cattle. The pilferings have not been petty, and in many districts, I believe in all districts, would have absolutely destroyed the flocks and made grazing in Australia impossible, had not the squatter defended himself either with a red hand, or with a hand prepared to be red if occasion required. The stealing of cattle by tribes of black men – or rather the slaughter of cattle ... has in many cases been accompanied by preconcerted attacks upon the stations; and these attacks are made in the absence of the owner, when his wife and children are there almost unguarded.[40]

Trollope continued:

> There is a strong sect of men in England ... who think that the English settler abroad is not to be trusted, except under severe control, with the fate of the poor creatures of inferior races with whom he comes in contact on the distant shores to which his search for wealth may lead him. The settler, as a matter of course, is in quest of fortune and is one who, living among rough things, is apt to become less scrupulous than his dainty brother at home.[41]

In Trollope's view, frontiersmen were fully justified in using violence against Indigenous people. He implies that they were manly for doing so, more manly than men back in England. Trollope suggests that the frontiersman, 'in quest of his fortune' and fulfilling his manly and imperial duty, is entitled to take whatever action he sees fit to achieve his aims. That he may have to use violence in the course of this quest makes him manlier than the 'dainty' men at home.

In Queensland successful forays against Aborigines were the subject of manly boasting. George Cain wrote triumphantly to his grandmother:

Niggers have been showing up to [sic]; frightened a shepherd in from his sheep at one o'clock in the morning last week. Guess there's some of them wont frighten any more shepherds. Yah! a charge of big shot that I shoot turkeys with will scatter 50 of them; only when they turn and show spears you must give 'em pepper.[42]

In a similar vein George Leslie wrote to his parents about the local Aborigines: 'We never allow them to come about the station or hold any communication with them except it be with a gun or a sword.'[43]

In short, Queensland frontier society was characterised by a large population of transient white men culturally and environmentally habituated to violence. Men used violence to assert dominance over each other, women both white and black, black men and their animals. Violence was perceived not only as a necessity for the transformation of Queensland into a white settler society, but as a desirable element of one's manly character.

The establishment of a white settler society on British Columbia was also a violent process. Adele Perry observes that in British Columbia 'the settlement process gave white men an "intimate knowledge" of violence and normalised the use of force to control others'.[44] 'Barroom and back alley' brawls were common, and mates would meet violence with violence in each other's defence. Violence was used to assert white male authority over women and Indigenous people and to solidify the male community.[45] It was a key part of the discipline maintained in the fur trade forts. Corporal punishment, in the form of flogging, was management's response to indolence and disobedience, perceived or real.[46] British Columbia's history is replete with examples of direct physical and other forms of violence against Indigenous people. The pattern of violence was set in the late-eighteenth century on the maritime frontier of British Columbia when British and American fur traders used violence as a trade tactic to such an extent that it became a common feature of the coastal trade between white and Indigenous people.[47]

In one incident a fur trader, Captain Kendrick, reacted to the theft of linen from his washing lines with severe retaliation. He seized two chiefs of the Haida allegedly responsible for the theft, tied them to a gun carriage, cut off their hair, painted their faces with a ludicrous pattern and threatened to kill them unless the Indians sold him their furs at a ridiculously low price, which they did. Two years later when he re-entered the area, the people remembered. Boarding his ship they took over the arms chest and forced the crew below decks. The ship's officers passed around their personal weapons and after a skirmish repelled the Indians.

Subsequently Kendrick's crew kept a constant fire on the Haida with cannon and small arms chasing them and 'making the most dreadful havoc by killing all they came across'.[48]

The land-based fur trade was predicated on co-operation between Indigenous people and the British. Nevertheless, the Hudson's Bay Company thought it best to leave the locals in no doubt who possessed the superior force, should force be required to maintain the trade. On arriving at Fort St. James in September 1828, George Simpson, Governor of the HBC in North America, entered the fort 'in the most imposing manner we could make for the sake of the Indians'.[49] When within hearing distance of the fort, a shot was fired, a bugle sounded and a piper began to play. The guide led the party, carrying the British flag; then the bugler and the piper, followed by the governor mounted on his horse. Behind the governor came two traders riding side by side, then twenty men in a line on foot, another horse and lastly another trader. As the group neared the fort it was welcomed with a brisk discharge of small arms and other weapons.[50]

The Fraser River gold rush of 1858 continued the violent trend. Thousands of miners went to British Columbia to get rich quickly and were intolerant, to put it mildly, of any 'savages' who got in their way. A transient population of Canadian, English and American miners became 'habituated to violence' as a means of removing what they considered to be an obstacle to their 'get rich quick' schemes.[51] One company of miners destroyed the winter provisions of a group of Indians at an unattended village on Okanagan Lake. The next day a group of unarmed Indians was massacred by miners.[52] Such was the extent of interracial violence on the goldfields that Governor Douglas feared that a 'war of races' would be the 'inevitable consequence of a prolonged state of misrule'.[53]

As in Queensland, manly courage was regarded as an absolute necessity:

> Courage is a grand thing in first confronting the savage; it inspires immediate respect, whereas the slightest faltering or manifestation of fear leaves the traveler at the mercy of those who can entertain contempt, and detect a want of bravery as readily as any vassal of civilisation, and who hold as valueless that which they are not awed by.[54]

Nor was frontier violence necessarily confined to physical force. It included extermination through other, indirect, means. In April 1862 a white man from San Francisco brought smallpox to Victoria.[55] The disease spread rapidly among the unimmunised Indian population of Victoria, killing them in large numbers. Instead of trying to contain the disease, white authorities dispersed the Indians, sending them north to the mainland from where they had come. This spread the disease to the interior where it wreaked its havoc:

> Smallpox has this year contributed a sad quota of death. During my stay here this disease, which had only just broken out when I arrived, spread so rapidly that, in a week, nearly all the healthy had scattered from the lodges and gone to encamp by families in the woods, only, it is to be feared, to carry away the seeds of infection and death in the blankets and other articles they took with them. Numbers were dying each day; sick men and women were taken out into the woods and left with a blanket and two or three salmon to die by themselves and rot unburied.[56]

In March 1864 William Brewster, a foreman on the Bute Inlet Road building project in British Columbia, believed a group of Chilcotin Indians may have stolen flour. Frustrated by their unwillingness to co-operate he took out a notebook and wrote down their names. The Chilcotins did not like to see their names written down. They were mystified by writing and their names were important to them, indistinguishable from the people who owned them. Writing down a person's name was like casting an evil spell on them. Brewster said: 'I have taken your names because you would not tell me who stole the flour.' All the Chilcotins are going to die. The whites will introduce sickness into the country which will kill you all.'[57] The Chilcotins understood what he meant – they knew with dread the effects of smallpox.

The weaponry of George Leslie, the epistolary gratitude of Edmund Morey, the actions of Captain Kendrick and the threat of smallpox made by William Brewster all of these occurrences were acts of violence perpetrated by white British males on Indigenous people. It is not only the obvious references to physical violence by Leslie and Morey that constituted violent conflict on the frontier. On both frontiers, the taking of Indigenous lands, the exploitation of natural resources and the construction of roads and townships destroyed Indigenous lives, just as surely as a bullet from a Snider carbine or a shell from the deck gun of a British gunboat. On the frontier, outside the constraints of conventional society and impelled by frontier conditions, many white men engaged in violent acts.

Frontier violence did not only come from the barrel of a gun. It was an inherent part of the imperial project, and the cultural assumptions of European conquerors formed a philosophical basis for the violent dispossession of Indigenous people. The previous chapter discussed the connection between civilisation and manliness. The concept of 'civilisation' entailed a belief in human progress, based on economic, social and moral improvement. Civilisation was a progressive, unbroken movement. Furthermore, Europeans were 'civilised' and non-Europeans or 'savages' were 'uncivilised'. Savages were uncivilised because of their isolation from Europe and the overwhelming effect of their environment. The idea of civilisation buttressed white male supremacy. 'Science' supported the belief that racial difference, civilisation and manliness advanced together. Primitive men could not possibly be as manly as white men.

Allied to this understanding of civilisation was the masculinist appropriation of the Enlightenment conception of reason. The Enlightenment of the seventeenth and eighteenth centuries was based on the belief that human reason could solve the problems of society as it had the workings of the natural world. The Enlightenment encapsulated a belief in the possibilities of progress, the willingness to question tradition and the practice of improvement – in short, civilisation.[58] As Genevieve Lloyd has argued, since the Enlightenment, reason has been assumed to be the exclusive property of men.[59] Connell argues that hegemonic masculinity is culturally linked to both authority and rationality, 'key themes in the legitimation of patriarchy'.[60] According to Victor Seidler, 'There is an emergent historical relationship between a particular conception of reason, progress and masculinity and this relationship has consequences... for our sense of gendered identity.'[61] Of the relationship between reason and masculinity Seidler continues:

> Because society has taken as its self conception since the Enlightenment a version of itself as a 'rational' society, and because reason is taken to be the exclusive property of men, this means that the mechanisms of the development of masculinity are in crucial ways the mechanisms of the development of the broader culture.[62]

In other words, as Western culture is 'rational' and since men possess rationality, they are therefore the carriers of this culture. This idea of reason and civilisation as the exclusive property of men found expression in the relationships between white men and Indigenous people, between coloniser and colonised. Men on the Queensland and British Columbia frontiers invoked reason, civilisation and progress as the *raison d'etre* for all forms of violence, direct and indirect.

An analysis of the official correspondence of William Wiseman, Commissioner of Crown Lands in the Leichhardt District of Queensland during the 1850s, demonstrates how discourses of civilisation and savagery, reason and unreason were used to justify violence against Queensland Aborigines. Wiseman's correspondence illustrates not only how these discourses were used to justify racial violence, but also their contradictory nature. In his official capacity, Wiseman was a strong advocate of force against the Aborigines in his district. His letters to his superiors in Sydney themselves constitute a violent act, informing Government policy and official attitudes towards Aborigines.

The information on Wiseman's background and his life in Queensland is piecemeal and in parts contradictory. There has been speculation that he was the illegitimate son of an English nobleman, that he was Oxford educated, well travelled and had spent a significant amount of the money given to him by his family.[63] He came to Australia in 1840 aboard the *Wilmot*, and disembarked in Sydney. Henry Stuart Russell records that he met Wiseman in Moreton Bay 'when the penal settlement had been established sixteen years'.[64] This would place Wiseman in Moreton Bay in the same year he arrived in Australia. However, another contemporary recordist, J.T.S. Bird, states that while Wiseman came to Australia in 1840, it was 'a few years later that he came to what is now Queensland'.[65] According to Russell, Wiseman was living at Eagle Farm, just outside of Brisbane with another man known to Russell, Stephen Simpson (who became Commissioner for Crown Lands at Moreton Bay). Russell says that they were 'in former days associates of old' and had travelled through Germany together. Russell describes both Simpson and Wiseman as 'men of no mean powers of thought, enriched by no superficial study, and tempered by experiences beyond the role of everyday life'; Wiseman was 'a kind host and chivalrous gentleman'.[66]

Some time after he arrived in Queensland Wiseman became Clerk of Petty Sessions at Drayton on the Darling Downs, where he owned a few shops.[67] He became acquainted with the Archer family, squatters who owned property in the Burnett district. He travelled north with the Archers to Gracemere in Central Queensland. In March 1855 he was appointed by the New South Wales Government as Commissioner for Crown Lands for the Leichhardt District and together with the Archers chose the site of the present city of Rockhampton. As Commissioner of Crown Lands he was the representative of the New South Wales Government, possessing great official power, particularly with regard to law and order. His task was to survey the district under his jurisdiction, subdividing it for tender to those who wished to take up land for pastoral purposes, to make recommendations regarding those tenders and to ensure that successful tenderers abided by the terms of their leases.

After Queensland separated from New South Wales, Wiseman continued as Commissioner for Crown Lands. In April 1864 he was appointed Police Magistrate at Rockhampton, a post he held until his death in 1871. His obituary in the *Rockhampton Bulletin* stated:

> His career as a whole on the Rockhampton bench has given general satisfaction to the public...his conduct on the bench was generally marked by that spirit of impartiality which becomes a dispenser of justice, and his judgment was seldom in error. He was an excellent classical scholar, and a remarkably well read and well informed man. He was also a man of considerable experience, having before coming to Australia resided for some years in Germany and Italy, and moved in the best society both in Europe and England.[68]

It would seem that Wiseman belonged to the British upper class. Whether he went to Oxford or not he was very well educated, and his education was rounded off with extensive travel on the Continent. He was obviously regarded not only as a gentleman, but one with a strong sense of service and public duty. With friends such as the Archers and squatter Arthur Hodgson he moved in the best colonial circles. In short, it could be said that Wiseman was the archetypal British gentleman, a model product of the mid-Victorian upper class.

On 28 August 1855 Wiseman wrote a lengthy report to the Chief Commissioner of Crown Lands in Sydney. His views on the relative levels of civilisation between the British and Aborigines are evident from the following extract:

> I also think the first murder in a new country is generally committed by Blacks, nor can I recall to my mind in these Northern Districts an unprovoked or wanton attack by a squatter on Aborigines, the whites by education disposed to kindness and benevolence, whereas on the contrary the savage is by nature greedy and prone to steal, feels no compunction on committing murder, is generally addicted to pillage

those who treat him kindly and treacherously attempts the life of such as he knows will not shoot him thinking as they do that such conduct proceeds from fear.[69]

In Wiseman's eyes the contrast between whites and Aborigines could not be more stark. By virtue of their education, a 'civilising' process of learning and moral training, white Englishmen are disposed to kindness and benevolence. 'Blacks', on the other hand, being deprived of 'education', and therefore civilisation, are ruled by 'nature' and are consequently murderous, greedy, treacherous savages for whom no atrocity is impossible. There is an obvious dichotomy in this extract in the opposition between civilisation, or 'education' as Wiseman terms it, and 'nature'. In Wiseman's view these categories are mutually exclusive, occupying extreme positions on a continuum of civilisation. However, these categories are inextricably intertwined and mutually defining. 'Civilisation', which is positively valued, can only be understood in opposition to 'nature', which here is negatively valued. This dichotomy served to sustain the superiority of the white males, and to suppress Aborigines.

In another letter dated 5 January 1856, Wiseman, commenting on frontier violence, stated:

> Such a state of hostility is undoubtedly the natural consequence of the occupation of the soil by the white race. Without trying to disparage the character of the Savage whose conduct under the circumstances is quite natural, I may be allowed to observe that such behaviour is not in accordance with the habits of civilised life and is totally inconsistent with the policy of the white race.[70]

Wiseman is at least perspicacious enough to recognise that resistance by Aborigines is only to be expected when invaders try to occupy their land, though this does not give him pause to think that white men should halt their invasion. This extract contains a number of contradictions and disruptions. A disruption can be seen in the use of the word 'natural'. Here he appears to be using the word 'natural' in a different sense to that in the first extract. In the extract above the word 'natural' seems to mean 'only to be expected', whereas in the first extract it was used in opposition to 'civilisation', as something caused by nature. Here Wiseman's words begin to unravel and become contradictory. On the one hand he is saying that the Aborigines' hostility against the whites is only to be expected, on the other that their hostility is uncivilised.

He also says that he has no wish to disparage the 'Savage', when in fact the very use of the word 'savage' is in itself disparaging. He again invokes a dichotomy between Aborigines and whites when he says that the hostility of Aborigines is 'totally inconsistent with the policy of the white race'.[71]

Further on in the letter Wiseman warns of the consequences of not using force against Aborigines who commit 'outrages': 'The repeated success attending their outrages on the whites occurring throughout the Leichhardt and neighbourhood without being followed with adequate punishment so emboldens them that more loss of life will probably ensue.'[72] Wiseman is silent on the violence perpetrated by whites on Aborigines. In his position he could hardly have been unaware of what his fellow Britons were doing. His omission of these details in official correspondence must have been deliberate. Such a deliberate omission hides a threat to the superiority of white civilisation. If whites are as violent as Aborigines, what claim to superiority could they make?

In further correspondence Wiseman wrote:

> The savage cannot understand the benevolence and humanity inculcated by the Christian religion. Intimidation is the only principle of dealing with them... They respect the man who with rifle in hand demands 'an eye for an eye and a tooth for a tooth'. Strict retaliation in killing any member of the tribe when the actual murderer cannot be secured is the principle in force amongst the savages themselves.[73]

Wiseman is again saying that Aborigines are uncivilised, this time because they did not have the benefit of Christianity. What is more, Wiseman is clearly advocating the use of violent force against Aborigines, when previously he argued that violence was uncivilised and against the policy of the white race. While clearly contradictory, such force was justified because 'destiny proclaims the certainty of the future triumph of the white race and the final extrepation [sic] of the aborigines'.[74]

Wiseman's views are representative of the prevailing racial attitudes of the time. He is utterly convinced of the superiority of the white race and he has no compunction in advocating violence against Aborigines in order to take over their land. While that much is reasonably obvious, what is less obvious is the function his words perform. Wiseman's letters are weapons, loaded with masculine reason, and deployed in the maintenance of a power relationship of which violence was the primary instrument.

In the mid-nineteenth century white male superiority was seen as a civilising force and was one of the drivers of the colonising impulse.[75] Colonised people lacked reason. They were able to establish a relationship with reason only through a relationship with a white man – they had to be subordinate to a dominant white male. The legitimisation of colonial power was tied up with the legitimisation of male superiority. Gender and race were intertwined in the formation of a dominant white European masculinity. Therefore, in Wiseman's advocacy of force against Aborigines, the creation of white superiority goes hand in hand with frontier violence. Violence is an instrument of masculinity, a strategy of male power. If white British males were the bearers of civilisation, there was an obligation on the part of native peoples to accept it. Wiseman could not understand the refusal of Aborigines to accept British civilisation. If civilisation had to be imparted by force, so be it. If savages resisted with their own force, then greater force should be used to punish them. It was the duty of the dominant white masculinity to assert authority whenever and wherever it was needed – to, in Wiseman's biblical quotation, seek 'an eye for an eye and a tooth for a tooth'.

In the late-eighteenth century the British conceptualisation of 'civilisation' was influenced by the emergence of industrial capitalism. Capitalism drove economic and social progress. The world of business and commerce in nineteenth-century Britain was an exclusively male domain, and one's manly status could be, in part, dependent upon one's success in business or the professions.

A number of scholars have theorised the connection between masculinity or patriarchy on the one hand and capitalism on the other. Zillah Eisenstein has labelled the interaction between capitalist economic structures and other patriarchal structures 'capitalist patriarchy'. She defines capitalist patriarchy as 'the mutually reinforcing dialectical relationship between capitalist class structure and hierarchical sexual structuring'.[76] This means that capitalism and patriarchy are neither autonomous systems nor identical: they are mutually dependent. The accumulation of capital both accommodates itself to patriarchy and helps perpetuate it. Patriarchy provides a system of control and order through its imposition of a sexual hierarchy while capitalism, driven by the pursuit of profit, is fed by this system through its appropriation of women's labour and in the historical shift in production from the domestic to the public sphere.

Furthermore, Jean Lipman-Bluman argues:

> Males learn that society's goals are best met by aggression, by actively wrestling their accomplishments from the environment. Force, power, competition and aggression are the means. Achievement, males are taught, is measured in productivity, resources and control – all the result of direct action. In the Western world, the importance of self-reliant, individual action is systematically inculcated in males. To be masculine requires not only self-reliance and self-control, but control over people and resources.[77]

Many of the virtues required to be manly and the virtues required for success in a capitalist economy – self-control, self-reliance, action – are identical. Moreover, according to Lipman-Bluman, aggression is a primary ingredient for male success.

The colonial frontier was a place where capital could find new outlets for expansion and profit. It was a place where competitiveness, force, aggression and control over people and resources were considered vital for success. One capitalist who saw such opportunity on the British Columbia frontier was Alfred Pendrill Waddington. Waddington brought these values to bear in his business projects, principally the construction of the Bute Inlet Road, which facilitated the absorption of British Columbia into the Western world and helped exert and maintain power and control over Indigenous people. The building of the road also precipitated an orgy of violence on the part of Indigenous people and a police and military response from whites culminating in the judicial killing of a number of Indigenous men. The building of the Bute Inlet Road illustrates how colonial capitalism could generate frontier violence.

Waddington was born in London in 1801, the son of a merchant and banker. He was educated in England, France and Germany, and attended the University of Göttingen. His first business venture was with his brother Thomas, with whom he operated a foundry. This was the first in a string of failed business ventures. Attracted by the gold rush in California, Waddington borrowed money from another brother, Frederick, and sailed for California in May 1850. In California his fortunes changed. By 1854 he was a partner in the wholesale grocery firm of Dulip and Waddington in San Francisco. When gold was discovered on the Fraser River in British Columbia in

1858, Waddington went north to Victoria to open a branch of the business there.[78]

In 1861 the miners who had worked their way up the Fraser River discovered gold in the Cariboo country. These goldfields were a long way inland and the canyons of the Fraser River made transportation difficult and expensive. Waddington conceived the idea of building a road from one of the inlets along the coast to the Cariboo. Such a road would give Victoria a virtual monopoly on trade with the new mines, trumping its mainland rival, New Westminster, which was situated on the lower reaches of the Fraser. Waddington formed the opinion that Bute Inlet offered the best prospects as a starting point for a road. From there a route could be established 'which must eventually become the shortest, cheapest and easiest line of communication with the northern mines'.[79]

With a group of Victorian investors, Waddington formed the Bute Inlet Wagon Road Company with a view to building the road and obtaining a Government charter to charge a toll for the movement of goods along it. The charter was granted by Governor James Douglas, apparently with some reluctance due to Douglas's own project to build a road from New Westminster.[80] Construction of the road started in 1862. Thus began a significant intrusion into Indigenous land. The road was to traverse lands inhabited by the Homathko, Euclawtaw and Klayoosh people. The greatest part of the country, however, was the home of the Chilcotin. The road was pushed inland for 23 miles before the onset of winter.

In April 1863 Waddington returned to Bute Inlet to find a large group of Indians from the various tribes camped on the ground on which he wished to establish a town site. He first alienated the Chilcotin by informing them that they would not be needed to pack goods and equipment, Waddington having brought mules for that purpose. For many Indians packing goods for whites was a sought-after occupation, earning them blankets, firearms and food. The second affront came when Waddington required the Chilcotin and others to move from their established and preferred campsite so his surveyor could lay out the township that would bear Waddington's name.

However, Waddington would come to need the Chilcotin. At approximately 30 miles inland the canyon of the Homathko the river became virtually impassable, and the country beyond it inhospitable. A reconnaissance party became lost for 23 days, returning to Bute Inlet mere skeletons and barely able to walk. A new route had to be found and the Chilcotin were now needed to pack supplies and equipment. Instead of treating the Chilcotin as valuable allies, Waddington and his men treated them with contempt. The Chilcotin were of the view that Waddington should feed them while they were in his employ, but his foreman, Brewster, would not permit it. The Chilcotin would not accept food as payment, preferring to receive guns and blankets.

In correspondence with Governor Seymour, Chief Inspector of Police, Chartres Brew reported:

> All the time it was known that the Indians were little removed from a state of starvation yet not the slightest effort was made to obtain the goodwill of the Indians or to guard against their enmity. When they worked they complained that Brewster paid them badly and gave them nothing to eat. They ought to have been paid their wages in money... They got orders for powder, balls, clothes or blankets as they pleased. Of course payment in this way was a loss to them. They never took provisions in payment; they thought they had a right to be fed, but they were not.[81]

While these events were enough to foster feelings of enmity between Waddington's men and the Chilcotin, the spread of smallpox provided them with an even longer running grievance with whites in general. Therefore, by the spring of 1864, when William Brewster threatened to reintroduce the smallpox virus, the Chilcotin had ample reason to fear it, and to believe that he was serious. This fear, together with the contempt with which they were treated by Waddington and his party, provided them with all the justification they needed to attack Waddington's men in an attempt to drive the whites off their land.

Just before dawn on 30 April 1864 twenty of Waddington's workmen slept in their camp on the banks of the Homathko River. While they were sleeping, a group of Chilcotin Indians armed with guns and axes quietly approached. The Chilcotin were intent on making what today would be called a 'pre-emptive strike', killing the white men before the white men could destroy their tribe through dispossession and disease. Fourteen white men were killed, shot and hacked to death, including the foreman, Brewster. After shooting him, one of the Chilcotin cut out his heart and, according to the Reverend Lundin-Brown, ate it.[82] Three of Waddington's men escaped.[83]

Twelve days later the *Daily Chronicle* bore the headline 'HORRIBLE MASSACRE'. Sparing its readers no detail, it called for the Government to immediately recruit a party of volunteers to dispense summary justice. It reported:

On the spread of news in this city, the first feeling which showed itself was a strong desire for bloody revenge upon these dangerous races who live around us but whom we can never trust. Had the people of Victoria the power, they would have gladly exterminated the whole tribe to which the murderers belong.[84]

Victoria's *British Colonist* could scarcely believe it. Contrasting the manliness of the whites with the unmanliness of the Chilcotin, its correspondent wrote: 'There is an air of doubt cast over the tragic story, when it is asserted that, seventeen strong, robust, fearless men, even although soundly reposing after a weary day's labor, could be attacked and nearly all murdered by a dozen cowardly savages assisted by a few boys.'[85] On the mainland the *British Columbian* asserted: 'The redskin demons are Chilcotins and plunder is supposed to have been the chief incentive.'[86] Exhibiting more restraint than the *Chronicle*, the *Columbian* a few days after its initial report remembered it was British:

> We are too apt, in the first flush of excited indignation, to cry out for the utter and indiscriminate extermination of the savages, dealing out to them Lynch law instead of British justice. We do not desire to excite sympathy for the Indians concerned in this bloody tragedy; for, as far as is known, they are entitled to none at our hands. But we hope to see the same impartial justice brought into requisition in dealing with the aborigine that we would desire to have meted out by ourselves.[87]

This violent episode, and the further violence to which it led (another party of whites were killed a few days later and eventually five Chilcotin Indians were tried and hanged), is probably the apotheosis of violence on the British Columbia frontier. In terms of attacks by Indigenous people against white intruders its scale and the violent events it precipitated is comparable to the Hornet Bank and Cullin La Ringoe massacres in Queensland in 1857 and 1861, respectively.[88] What is also of interest here are the *preceding* acts of *indirect* violence by whites, of which the Bute Inlet massacre, as it was known, was the culmination. The treatment of the Chilcotin by Waddington's men – Brewster's smallpox threat, the denial of food – and the road construction and Indigenous dispossession, when considered alongside the events described above, illustrate the complementary nature of direct and indirect violence.

At the most fundamental level, the cause of this violence lay in the pursuit of profit and the ideal of progress and its practice in the colonies.

174 *Men and Manliness on the Frontier*

Waddington's road was a symbol of progress. It would bring material wealth and civilisation to Vancouver Island and British Columbia. It was part of a process of turning a fur trade territory into a viable colony, and Victoria into an important centre for business and commerce. The Fraser River gold rush dramatically increased the demand for public works, including roads. During 1860 a corps of Royal Engineers under the command of Colonel Richard Moody built a four-metre-wide wagon road on the Douglas-Lillooet route. In 1862 they began construction on a 600-kilometre Cariboo road from Yale to Barkerville.[89] The gold rush, as well as the increasing demand for infrastructure, shifted the economic balance towards resource-extraction industries dominated by industrial capital, namely, canning (salmon), logging and sawmilling.[90]

The people who came to British Columbia believed in progress, private property and the superiority of British civilisation. Waddington's *The Fraser Mines Vindicated* is a paean to progress and the creation of material wealth, and to British Columbia's unrivalled potential as creators of both:

> Let that population once reach our shores, and measures be taken to encourage them, foreigners or not. Let miners be allowed to make their own bye-laws [sic] and regulations for each bar or district, subject to the approbation of a council of mines; instead of starving them out, let the country be entirely thrown open, so that provisions may be as cheap as possible in the interior, and let the tax on goods be modified, so as to be levied on the superfluities and not the necessities of life. Let everyone be allowed to buy land at American prices and not at five dollars an acre; and instead of throwing obstacles in the way of the colonist, give the poor bona fide settler a right of pre-emption, and a premium of land, taken from the wild waste, to the deserving father of a numerous family. Let us do this and more, if possible, be done, and the progress of this favoured country will be as sure as it will be rapid.[91]

In Waddington's view, society's goals can best be met by aggressive competition and individualism, by self-reliance and self-control. Progress comes from the exercise of power and control over the land and, by implication, uncompetitive Indigenous people. Moreover, that pillar of Victorian society, the patriarchal family, deserves to gain the most from the taming of the wild. Waddington's aggressive prescription for success is a strongly masculinist one which extols many of the virtues associated with manliness. The values of nineteenth-century capitalism were congruent with the manly virtues.

Thus, through the operation of patriarchal capitalism, British Columbia was drawn into the Western sphere and its Indigenous people subdued. This absorption was conditioned by the relationship between patriarchy and capitalism, the dominant position of men within these systems and the congruence of values between capitalism and manliness. The physical violence of the Bute Inlet Massacre and the execution of its perpetrators was the outcome of a policy of dispossession founded on Western capitalist patriarchy.

To state that the origins of frontier violence lay in the prevailing concepts of manliness, civilisation and reason is not to ignore substantive factors such as competition for resources such as land and water, disputes over the sexual services of Aboriginal women or the loss of pastoral stock. Nor is it to deny that some men are prone to violent methods in order to get what they wanted. Rather, it is to say that in instances such as these, the potential for violence within the mid-Victorian ideal of manliness, and its mutually supportive relationship with civilisation, reason and capitalism, came to the surface. It was a potential which many men on both frontiers exercised, in order to assert their superiority over the environment and the people who inhabited it. The manly virtues could be distorted to justify violence; and violence, direct and indirect, was instrumental in the maintenance of white male superiority.

7
A Wild Self-Dependence of Character

> It is men such as these that are flocking to the New Eldorado. Dauntless, fearless and reckless, they will brook no opposition or restraint, but with a wild self dependence of character, plunge wherever gold attracts them, defying everything and surmounting all obstacles.
>
> (Kinahan Cornwallis, *The New Eldorado or British Columbia*)

Cornwallis's description of the men who colonised British Columbia in the mid-nineteenth century is optimistic, seemingly defying contradiction or qualification. His colonists are undoubtedly manly and do not contemplate failure. Fellow travel writer John Emmerson, while believing that 'it is inherent in man's nature to desire the advancement of his condition', recognised that the pursuit of that advancement on the frontier could be problematic:

> The thirst for gold will tempt men to leave their wives, their children, their homes, and everything that is dear to them; encounter the dangers and difficulties of a voyage to the other side of the world, and endure all the hardships, privations, and sufferings that must either more or less attend such an undertaking.[1]

These excerpts evince the problematic nature of masculinity in frontier societies. On the one hand, the frontier was imagined as a place that offered men the opportunity to perform the manly virtues and achieve independence. On the frontiers of Queensland and British Columbia they could practise courage and perseverance, and demonstrate their strength and self-dependence. Many did. Men such as Ernest Henry, Alexander Fortune and Oscar de Satgé become prosperous, independent men, who found that British manliness stood them in good stead, and lived up to their expectations in what it offered them. However, as Robert Harkness, George Carrington and others discovered, on the frontier, the pursuit of manliness could come at a price. The performance of manliness on the frontier was problematic, entailing suffering and hardship, loneliness and deprivation. Not all men attained the manly status they desired.

Analysis of the experiences of men and manliness on the frontier reveals the differing ways in which men responded to a physically harsh environment in which social and cultural norms were in flux, and in which they were remote from the relationships and structures which nurtured them. Focusing on men as gendered actors in various roles as pioneers, explorers, fathers, gentlemen and businessmen offers new perspectives on the history of British Columbia and Queensland.

In the mid-nineteenth century, the 'manliness' constructed in the metropole found diverse expression on the frontier. In mid-nineteenth-century Britain the emergence of a dominant ethos of manliness, although varying across class lines, denoted a particular set of character traits and behaviours – 'configurations of practice' – about which there was a broad consensus. The manly ideal was promulgated in literature, sermons, self-help texts and through the education system and, to varying degrees, pervaded all classes.

British men, imbued with this manly ideal, responded to the opportunities the frontier provided for the performance of manliness in different ways. The frontier was a place where the younger sons of the aristocracy and ambitious middle-class men could carve a place for themselves in the emergent colonial societies. It was anticipated that the frontier would require the exercise of the muscular virtues and many men relished the chance to prove themselves by conquering the wilderness and making the land productive.

Aristocratic and upper-middle-class gentlemen, who supposedly possessed the manly virtues to the fullest, sought to maintain their position at the apex of the social and gender order. On the frontier such men constituted a class-based masculine caste which they protected and maintained through a range of practices including patronage, social monitoring and the exercise of the muscular virtues.

The colonial frontier was a stage on which British men of all classes were able to 'perform' manliness. On the frontier they could exercise the courage, self-reliance and physical prowess there was little opportunity to practise at home. Moreover, in doing so they could achieve the manly independence they desired.

However, the performance of manliness and the masculine domination of the frontier was not a straightforward matter, and nor was frontier manliness a homogenous, monolithic concept. Some men found the going hard. The physical hardships of the frontier, isolation and remoteness tested the manly ideal and led men into despair, damaged their self-esteem and could result in alcoholism – all of which constituted a loss of manly self-control. Not all the virtues extolled by Charles Kingsley at Wimbledon found expression on the frontier. Nevertheless, on the frontier, men could develop a much fuller sense of themselves, their values, limitations and strengths. One feature of frontier life was the absence of the social constraints of home. This could be liberating and many men entered new forms of relationships to overcome the isolating effects of frontier life. To mitigate the effects of loneliness men formed strong homosocial bonds and the sexual norms of the metropole were sometimes violated by relationships that would not be sanctioned at home.

Relationships between Indigenous people and colonisers were partly understood and interpreted through the lens of manliness and perceived differences between white, British manliness and other versions. In depicting non-white, non-British masculinities as inferior and 'uncivilised', British men defended and affirmed the version of masculinity they had absorbed in Britain. The characterisation of Indigenous men and other non-white men as unmanly justified the white British domination of the colonial frontier.

Given the British tolerance for certain types of violence, on the frontier the ideal of manliness, allied with the masculinist ideologies of reason, civilisation and progress, led to violence becoming a routine and normal part of life, particularly against Indigenous peoples. The manly virtues of strength and courage could find distorted expression in 'nigger hunts' and bar-room brawls. Capitalism and manliness extolled common virtues which drove 'progress' and 'development', and which for Indigenous people meant violence and dispossession.

Contemporary narratives of the Queensland and British Columbia frontiers in the form of letters, journals and travel literature emphasised a muscular construction of frontier life. Oscar de Satgé's *Pages from the Journal of a Queensland Squatter*, Milton and Cheadle's *The Northwest Passage by Land* and Ernest Henry's story abound with heroic tales of manly energy and enterprise. These authors would have had their readers believe that they and other frontiersmen were capable of anything and could overcome all obstacles, physical and psychological, to conquer the wilderness and establish a 'New Eldorado' in Britain's colonial outposts.

However, there are exceptions to this imaginative rule. Other personal stories reveal the suffering and hardship attendant upon frontier life. Robert Harkness' letters, George Carrington's *Colonial Adventures* and Charlotte May Wright's memoir reveal that despite being brimful of manly vigour, some men struggled to achieve independence. No matter how conscientiously they exercised the manly virtues, no matter how much they displayed 'character', the fullest expression of manhood eluded them. They either retreated to their family and friends 'at home' or succumbed to the bottle. Either way, their manly self-esteem took a battering.

In what ways does knowing that men responded to the frontier in a variety of ways make any difference to our understanding of masculinities, frontiers and the historical development of Queensland and British Columbia? Firstly, it demonstrates that despite the pervasiveness of a well-defined and articulated ethos of manliness, the actuality was quite different. In practice, there was no absolute standard, no hard and fast line between manliness and unmanliness. Robert Harkness may ultimately have failed in his quest for manly redemption, but along the way he exhibited many of the muscular virtues. Manliness was not absolute. I do not suggest that there were degrees of manliness, but that fulfilment of all the manly virtues was an impossible task. Despite Ernest Henry's manly boasting and derring-do, he did not set up Hughenden station on his own. He may have provided the leadership, but he relied on other, perhaps less assertive, men to do much of the hard work. The ethos of manliness was a driver of frontier life. It set the parameters of what was possible in men's responses to frontier conditions. The ethos enabled certain responses and rendered others less acceptable.

Secondly, it demonstrates that there is not one story of frontier life or of colonial development. The stories of the men who struggled on the frontier challenge the more traditional stories of brave and manly pioneers overcoming all odds to create new societies. In settler societies where the masculine frontier forms a significant part of the national mythology, the knowledge that frontier men were just as likely to fail as to succeed has the potential to weaken the power of the myth.

The settler societies of Queensland and British Columbia were, on the whole, not built by men of exceptional character, endurance, strength or integrity. They were not necessarily sober, pious, pacifist or respectful of women. They *were* men of all classes, possessed of no more and no less of the prescribed manly virtues than any other male. They *were* primarily motivated to attain independence, to become self-made men who, in the words of Australian poet Henry Lawson, 'Call no biped lord or sir/And touch their hat to no man.'

In 1962 Peter Coleman in *Australian Civilization* believed that the 'Australianist legend' was in retreat.[2] Coleman's 'Australianist legend' was essentially Russel Ward's bush legend, the myth of the typical Australian who was a male frontiersman, an egalitarian bush worker. Ward's description of the typical male is well-known. Implicit in Ward's description are the many manly qualities enunciated in this book: courage, stoicism, perseverance, independence, a strong work ethic (though not 'without good cause').[3] In 1962, Coleman thought that not only was the legend in retreat, so was the way of life it 'expressed and encouraged'.[4] In 2007, he may be feeling somewhat discouraged about the continuing prominence of the legend in Australian popular culture.

Until recently, on Queensland's tourist Mecca – the Gold Coast – the bush legend was a major tourist attraction. One could see frontier mythology in action. Tourists could visit the *Australian Outback Spectacular*, an 'extravaganza' that depicted 'the true heart and soul of the Aussie culture'. The show's publicity promised to take the audience on 'a journey to the true heart of this nation from when it all began – right through to everyday life in the outback as it is seen today'. Audiences were promised an 'authentic' show with an 'Australian flavour' and 'stunning images of outback scenes'.[5] The publicity highlights strong men on horseback, wearing the putative garb of Australian frontier men – Driaz-a-bone coats, Akubras and R.M. William's boots – noble pioneers performing the work of nation building and wilderness taming.

The show ran for several years. In 2010 it was replaced by a new show 'The Heroes of the Light Horse' which celebrates the soldiers of Australia's Light Horse Brigade of World War I. It is doubtful whether the script has changed much. The Akubras have no doubt been replaced by slouch hats and ostrich feathers, but the same Aussie masculine values and attributes would transfer easily from the bush to the battlefield.

The promoters of both shows are tapping into what they believe is a profitable vein of public sentiment regarding Australian culture. In the case of the *Outback Spectacular* the frontier is the primary trope. Firmly anchored in the Bush Legend, the promoters were banking on it occupying a prominent place in the Australian psyche. The cast was predominantly male, emphasising the masculinity implicit in the frontier legend. The romantic flavour of the publicity also suggests that what is offered is a very selective portrayal of frontier life. Audiences can watch exhibitions of horse riding, tent pegging and shearing, and enjoy an 'authentic' outback meal of roast beef and damper.

The production did give one nod to modern Australia in the presence of a few women amongst the male performers. Rachel Henning and Charlotte May Wright would probably be surprised to discover that on the frontier women did the same work as men. In all it is an extremely romantic view of the frontier.

This is how Australia's frontier past is represented; this remains the orthodoxy of Australian identity and of Australian history. The Australian Outback Spectacular is not the first or the only major popular cultural production to celebrate frontier mythology. In the 1980s the Stockman's Hall of Fame in Longreach led a revival of what Graeme Turner terms 'rural-nationalist mythologies', reasserting the claim of the frontier as a foundation of Australian national character.[6] Bookshops stock a plethora of 'Australiana' titles; and television advertisements for beer, four-wheel drives and barbeques evoke and make a virtue out of the frontier myth.[7] At the time of writing, one of the stars of the Australian Outback Spectacular, Lee Kernaghan, had a song titled 'Spirit of the Bush' in the country music top thirty.[8]

In Canada, the frontier is a mainstay of national identity. The frontier myth of individualistic, freedom-loving, independent pioneers sustains white identity in twentieth-century rural British Columbia. British Columbian school children are immersed in the mythology of the frontier. Furniss cites one text in particular which enunciates the frontier myth 'in which nature is feared and endured, in which (white) man encounters and eventually conquers the wilderness, in which the territory is unoccupied, "untouched", and thus free for the taking, and in which Indians live a "quiet" life as noble savages'.[9] Daniel Francis identifies seven myths embraced by Canadians as expressing something they want to believe about themselves. These include The Myth of the North, The Myth of Wilderness and the Myth of the Royal Canadian Mounted Police, which evoke strong frontier themes and which have, since the nineteenth century, provided grist for the mills of film-makers, the writers of popular fiction and advertisers. According to Francis, repetition has ensured that these myths 'form the mainstream memory of the culture, our national dreams, the master narrative which explains the culture to itself and seems to express its overriding purpose'.[10] The Calgary Stampede, an annual event of bull riding, chuck wagon races and bucking horses (the largest of its kind in the world), ensures that the ethos of the masculine frontier occupies a prominent place in Canadian popular culture.

It is highly doubtful that the *Australian Outback Spectacular* depicted the rape of Aboriginal women, alcoholic 'broken down swells' or stockmen engaging in homosexual acts, and of course nor do the television advertisements or popular books. To Gold Coast tourists these features of frontier life may be confronting, threatening or unsavoury. Like their nineteenth-century forebears, they like their frontier idealised and sanitised. Just as the travel writers and explorers of the Queensland and British Columbia frontiers in the nineteenth century romanticised frontier life, so do the entrepreneurs of the twenty-first century.

In the nineteenth century popular adventure stories and travel literature presented the reading public with an idealised version of the frontier and of the British men who went there. The adventure stories of C.F. Marryat and R.M. Ballantyne, exploration narratives like that of Sir Thomas Mitchell and the travel narratives of writers such as Kinahan Cornwallis and W.S.S. Tyrwhitt depicted the Queensland and British Columbia frontiers in highly romantic terms, minimising the hardships, and maximising the heroic. The reality proved to be quite different. In the twentieth century popular historical writing replaced adventure literature and travel books, but still evoked a romantic picture of rugged pioneers taming the wilderness. The attractiveness of the frontier has not diminished in the late twentieth and early twenty-first centuries as the promoters of popular culture idealise the frontier and draw on its mythology for profit.

History may provide an antidote to the idealisation of the frontier. Through history we can collectively journey to the frontier, explore its possibilities and limitations and arrive at a better sense of ourselves by questioning what it was like. By challenging conventional narratives, more nuanced accounts of the frontier have the ability to transform traditional/popular historical narratives, offering the possibility of a more mature engagement with the past.

Notes

1 Masculinities and Frontiers

1. Charles Kingsley, *Discipline and Other Sermons* (London: Macmillan, 1890), 5.
2. Kingsley, *Discipline*, 6.
3. Kingsley, *Discipline*, 7, 8.
4. Kinahan Cornwallis, *The New El Dorado or British Columbia* (London: Thomas Cautly Newby, 1858), 234.
5. Cornwallis, *The New El Dorado*, 10.
6. R.W. Connell, *Masculinities* (Sydney, NSW: Allen & Unwin, 1995), 44.
7. Jeff Hearn, "Research in Men and Masculinities: Some Sociological Issues and Possibilities", *Australian and New Zealand Journal of Sociology*, 30, no. 1 (1994), 54.
8. Judith Butler, *Gender Trouble: Feminism and the Subversion of Identity* (New York: Routledge, 1999), 179.
9. Butler, *Gender Trouble*, 178
10. Connell, *Masculinities*, 77.
11. Lynne Segal, *Slow Motion: Changing Masculinities Changing Men* (London: Virago, 1990), 60; Connell, *Masculinities*, ix.
12. John Tosh, "What Should Historians Do with Masculinity? Reflections of Nineteenth-Century Britain", *History Workshop*, 38 (1994), 180.
13. For masculinities in Britain, see Leonore Davidoff and Catherine Hall, *Family Fortunes: Men and Women of the English Middle Class, 1780–1850* (London: University of Chicago Press, 1987); John Tosh, *A Man's Place: Masculinity and the Middle-Class Home in Victorian England* (London: Yale University Press, 1999); Anna Clark, *The Struggle for the Breeches: Gender and the Making of the British Working Class* (Berkeley, CA: University of California Press, 1995). Jessica Meyer, *Men of War: Masculinity and the First World War in Britain* (Basingstoke: Palgrave MacMillan, 2009); Paul R. Deslandes, *Oxbridge Men: British Masculinity and the Undergraduate Experience, 1850–1920* (Bloomington, IN: Indiana University Press, 2005). In Australia prominent works include Marilyn Lake, "The Politics of Respectability: Identifying the Masculinist Context", *Australian Historical Studies*, 22, no. 86 (1986), 116–131; Marilyn Lake, "Frontier Feminism and the Marauding White Man", *Journal of Australian Studies*, 49 (1996), 12–120. Clive Moore and Kay Saunders, *Australian Masculinities: Men and Their Histories*, ed., *Journal of Australian Studies* (Brisbane, QLD: University of Queensland Press, 1998). Martin Crotty, *Making the Australian Male: Middle-Class Masculinity 1870–1920* (Melbourne, VIC: Melbourne University Press, 2001); Canadian literature on masculinities includes Adele Perry, *On the Edge of Empire: Gender, Race, and the Making of British Columbia* (Toronto, ON: University of Toronto Press, 2001); Elizabeth Vibert, *Traders' Tales: Narratives of Cultural Encounters in the Columbia Plateau 1807–1846* (Norman, OK: University of

Oklahoma Press, 1997). The literature from New Zealand includes Jock Phillips, *A Man's Country: The Image of the Pakeha Male* (Auckland: Penguin, 1987); Miles Fairburn, *The Ideal Society and Its Enemies: The Foundations of Modern New Zealand Society, 1850–1900* (Auckland: Auckland University Press, 1989); and Margot Fry, *Tom's Letters: The Private World of Thomas King, Victorian Gentleman* (Wellington: Victoria University Press, 2001). American literature includes Jacqueline M. Moore, *Cow Boys and Cattlemen: Class and Masculinities on the Texas Frontier, 1865–1900* (New York: New York University Press, 2010); and E. Anthony Rotundo, *American Manhood: Transformations in Masculinity from the Revolution to the Modern Era* (New York: Basic Books, 1993).

14. Perry, *On the Edge of Empire*, 198.
15. Frederick Jackson Turner, "The Significance of the Frontier in American History", in *Rereading Frederick Jackson Turner*, ed. John M. Faragher (New Haven, CT: Yale University Press, 1998), 31–60; Ray Allen Billington, *Westward Expansion: A History of the American Frontier* (New York: Macmillan, 1960). For applications of Turner's thesis in Queensland and British Columbia historiography, see A.G.L. Shaw, *The Story of Australia* (London: Faber and Faber, 1955); Sir Raphael Cilento and Clem Lack, *Triumph in the Tropics: An Historical Sketch of Queensland* (Brisbane, QLD: Simon and Paterson, 1959). See also G.C. Bolton, *A Thousand Miles Away: A History of North Queensland to 1920* (Brisbane, QLD: Jacaranda Press, 1963); Margaret Ormsby, *British Columbia: A History* (Vancouver, BC: Macmillan, 1958). For British Columbian histories in a similar vein, see Alexander Begg, *History of British Columbia from Its Earliest Discovery to the Present Time* (Toronto, ON: McGraw-Hill Ryerson, 1972); F.W. Howay, *British Columbia, The Making of a Province* (Toronto, ON: T. Nelson, 1928); E.E. Rich, *The Fur Trade and the Northwest until 1857* (Toronto, ON: McCelland and Stewart, 1967). Doug Owram, *The Promise of Eden: The Canadian Expansionist Movement and the Idea of the West 1856–1900* (Toronto, ON: University of Toronto Press, 1980).
16. Russel Ward, *The Australian Legend* (Melbourne, VIC: Oxford University Press, 1966); John Hirst, "The Pioneer Legend", *Historical Studies*, 18, no. 71 (1978), 316–337.
17. Elizabeth Furniss, *The Burden of History: Colonialism and the Frontier Myth in a Rural Canadian Community* (Vancouver, BC: UBC Press, 1999), 93; Richard Slotkin, *Regeneration Through Violence: The Mythology of the American Frontier* (Middletown, CT: Wesleyan University Press, 1973).
18. Furniss, *The Burden of History*, 87, 205.
19. Furniss, *The Burden of History*, 189.
20. Lynette Russell, ed., *Colonial Frontiers: Indigenous–European Encounters in Settler Societies.* (Manchester: Manchester University Press, 2001), 2; Richard Nile, "Editorial", *Journal of Australian Studies*, 49 (1996), 1.
21. Richard W. Slatta, *Comparing Cowboys and Frontiers* (Norman, OK: Oklahoma University Press, 1997), 23, 32; Mary Louise Pratt, *Imperial Eyes: Travel Writing and Transculturation* (London: Routledge, 1992), 6.
22. Penelope Edmonds, *Urbanizing Frontiers: Indigenous Peoples and Settlers in 19th-Century Pacific Rim Cities* (Vancouver, BC: UBC Press, 2010), 6.

23. Ann Laura Stoler, *Race and the Education of Desire: Foucault's History of Sexuality and the Colonial Order of Things* (Durham, NC: Duke University Press, 1995), 1104.
24. Kirsten McKenzie's *Scandal in the Colonies* (Melbourne, VIC: Melbourne University Press, 2004) offers an excellent account of how colonial societies offered settlers the chance to create new identities, embark on new careers and reinvent themselves in positions far removed from those they occupied in the metropole.
25. Anne McClintock, *Imperial Leather: Race, Gender and Sexuality in the Colonial Contest* (New York: Routledge, 1995), 3–4.
26. Kay Schaffer, *Women and the Bush: Forces of Desire in the Australian Cultural Tradition* (Sydney, NSW: Cambridge University Press, 1988), xiv, 52; Margaret Atwood, *Strange Things: The Malevolent North in Canadian Literature* (Oxford: Clarendon Press, 1995), 3.
27. *British Colonist*, 2 September 1864.
28. *British Colonist*, 2 September 1864.
29. This is not true in all cases. For a number of decades it was believed that whites could not cope well in the tropics. See Warwick Anderson, *The Cultivation of Whiteness: Science, Health and Racial Destiny in Australia* (Melbourne, VIC: Melbourne University Press, 2002).
30. C.P. Harris, *Regional Economic Development in Queensland: 1859 to 1981 With Particular Emphasis on North Queensland* (Canberra, ACT: Australian National University, 1984), 38; Christopher Anderson, "Queensland Aboriginal Peoples Today", in *Queensland: A Geographical Interpretation*, ed. J.H. Holmes (Brisbane, QLD: A Geographical Interpretation, 1986); *Queensland Geographical Journal*, 4th series, 1 (1986), 301.
31. W. Kaye Lamb, ed., "The Census of Vancouver Island, 1855", *British Columbia Historical Quarterly*, 4, no. 1 (1940), 51–58. Additional figures cited in Perry, *On the Edge of Empire*, 13.
32. See Perry's *On the Edge of Empire* regarding immigration programmes to bring women to British Columbia.
33. Nicholas Thomas, *Colonialism's Culture: Anthropology, Travel and Government* (Melbourne, VIC: Melbourne University Press, 1994), 105.
34. Ormsby, *British Columbia*, 118.
35. Davidoff and Hall, *Family Fortune*.
36. Clark, *The Struggle for the Breeches*.
37. Amanda Vickery, "Golden Age to Separate Spheres?: A Review of the Categories and Chronology of English Women's History", *The Historical Journal*, 36, no. 2 (1993), 412.
38. John Tosh, *A Man's Place: Masculinity and the Middle-Class Home in Victorian England* (London: Yale University Press, 2007), 4.
39. Robert Shoemaker, *Gender in English Society 1650–1850: The Emergence of Separate Spheres?* (London: Longman, 1998).
40. Davidoff and Hall, *Family Fortunes*, 149–192.
41. William Secker, *A Wedding Ring, Fit for the Finger, Laid Open in a Sermon, Preached at a Wedding in St Edmond's* (Glasgow: The Chapman's Library, 1877), in *John Cheap the Chapman's Library* (Glasgow, 1877), 11, 20. Cited in Clark, *The Struggle for the Breeches*, 63.

42. Carol Pateman, *The Sexual Contract* (Oxford: Polity Press, 1989).
43. Anna Clark in *The Struggle for the Breeches* cites the example of a group of women in Paisley who defied the decision of the males in the congregation to expel one of their number who disagreed with her husband on a narrow theological point. See pages 102–103.
44. Thomas Laqueur, "Orgasm, Generation, and Politics of Reproductive Biology", in *The Making of the Modern Body: Sexuality and Society in the Nineteenth Century*, eds. Catherine Gallagher and Thomas Laqueur (Berkeley, CA: University of California Press, 1987), 2; Londa Schiebinger, "Skeletons in the Closet: The First Illustrations of the Female Skeleton in Eighteenth Century Anatomy", in *The Making of the Human Body*, eds. Catherine Gallagher and Thomas Laqueur (Berkeley, CA: University of California Press, 1987), 42–43; Carrol Smith-Rosenberg and Charles Rosenberg, "The Female Animal: Medical and Biological Views of Woman and Her Role in Nineteenth Century America", *Journal of American History*, 60, no. 1 (1973), 332–356; Jeffrey Weeks, *Sex, Politics and Society* (London: Longman, 1989), 146; H. Smith, "Gynecology and Ideology", in *Liberating Women's History*, ed. B.A. Carrol (Urbana: University of Chicago Press, 1976), 97–114.
45. Mary Poovey, *Uneven Developments: The Ideological Work of Gender in Mid-Victorian England* (London: Virago Press, 1989), 2.
46. Steffan Collini, *Public Moralists Political Thought and Intellectual Life in Britain 1850–1930* (Oxford: Clarendon Press, 1991), 100.
47. Peter Gay, *The Cultivation of Hatred (The Bourgeois Experience, Victoria to Freud)*, Vol. 3 (New York: Norton, 1986), 502.
48. Samuel Smiles, *Self-Help* (Oxford: Oxford University Press, [1859]2002), 314.
49. Catherine Hall, "Imperial Man: Edward Eyre in Australasia and the West Indies 1833–1866", in *The Expansion of England: Race, Ethnicity and Cultural History*, ed. Bill Schwarz (London: Routledge, 1996), 133.
50. Tosh, *A Man's Place*, and Hall, *White, Male and Middle Class*, 199.
51. William Cobbett, *Advice to Young Men* (London: Ward Lock & Co., [1829]1911), 19.
52. *Letters to Young People Single and Married, Re-Written by an English Author after Timothy Titcomb. Friendly Counsel Series* (London: Ward, Lock, and Tyler, 187*), 25.
53. *Letters to Young People Single and Married*, 12; Samuel Taylor Coleridge, *Aids to Reflection*, 10th ed. (London: Edward Moxon & Co., [1825]1863); Smiles, *Self-Help*; Cobbett, *Advice to Young Men*.
54. *Letters to Young People Single and Married*, 35.
55. Cobbett, *Advice to Young Men*, 27.
56. *Letters to Young People Single and Married*, 36.
57. David Newsome, *Godliness and Good Learning* (London: Murray, 1961), 1.
58. Newsome, *Godliness and Good Learning*, 195.
59. *Edinburgh Review*, January 1858, 177.
60. J.A. Mangan, *Athleticism in the Victorian and Edwardian Public School: The Emergence and Consolidation of an Educational Ideology* (London: Frank Cass, 2000). Mangan has also written on the role of athleticism in Britain's imperial expansion. See J.A. Mangan, *The Games Ethic and Imperialism: Aspects of the Diffusion of the Ideal* (London: Frank Cass, 1998).
61. Thomas Hughes, *The Manliness of Christ* (London: Macmillan, 1879).

62. *Edinburgh Review*, January 1858, 190.
63. *Saturday Review*, 21 February 1857.
64. Terry Eagleton, *Literary Theory: An Introduction* (Oxford: Basil Blackwell, 1983), 33–34.
65. Richard Phillips, *Mapping Men and Empire: A Geography of Adventure* (London: Routledge, 1997), 5, 45; Robert Dixon, *Writing the Colonial Adventure: Race, Gender and Nation in Anglo-Australian Popular Fiction, 1875–1914* (Melbourne, VIC: Cambridge University Press, 1995); Martin Crotty, *Making the Australian Male: Middle-Class Masculinity 1870–1920* (Melbourne, VIC: Melbourne University Press, 2000).
66. Crotty, *Making the Australian Male*, 136.
67. Frederick Cooper and Ann Laura Stoler, "Between Metropole and Colony: Rethinking a Research Agenda", in *Tensions of Empire: Colonial Cultures in a Bourgeois World*, eds. Frederick Cooper and Ann Laura (Berkley, CA: University of California Press, 1997), 232–257.
68. Phillips, *Mapping Men and Empire*, 55.
69. Joseph Bristow, *Empire Boys: Adventures in a Man's World* (London: Harper Collins, 1991), 2.
70. The Reform Act of 1867 extended the vote to most of the working class. The middle class had received these rights in the reforms of 1832.
71. Keith McClelland, "Masculinity and the 'Representative Artisan' in Britain, 1850–1880", in *Manful Assertions: Masculinities in Britain Since 1800*, eds. Michael Roper and John Tosh (London: Routledge, 1991), 82.
72. Clark, *The Struggle for the Breeches*, 220.
73. Smiles, *Self-Help*, 17.
74. Smiles, *Self-Help*, 18.
75. See Michael Banton, *The Idea of Race* (Cambridge: Tavistock, 1977); Kenan Malik, *The Meaning of Race: Race, History and Western Culture* (London: MacMillan, 1996); Gail Bederman, *Manliness and Civilization: A Cultural History of Gender and Race in the United States 1880–1917* (Chicago, IL: University of Chicago Press, 1995); Collette Guillaumin, *Racism, Sexism, Power and Ideology* (London: Routledge, 1995); George M. Frederickson, *Racism: A Short History* (Melbourne, VIC: Scribe Publications, 2002).
76. Mrinalini Sinha, *Colonial Masculinity: The "Manly Englishman" and the "Effeminate Bengali" in the Late Nineteenth Century* (Manchester: Manchester University Press, 1995), 182.
77. Henry Reynolds, ed., *Race Relations in North Queensland*, (Townsville, QLD: James Cook University, 1978), 1–3.
78. Jean Barman, "Taming Aboriginal Sexuality: Gender, Power, and Race in British Columbia, 1850–1900", *BC Studies*, Autumn/Winter 97/98 (1997), 237–266; Wilson Duff, *The Indian History of British Columbia* (Victoria, BC: Royal British Columbia Museum, 1997); Sylvia Van Kirk, *Many Tender Ties* (Norman, OK: University of Oklahoma Press, 1983); Tina Loo, *Making Law Order, and Authority in British Columbia, 1821–1871* (Toronto: University of Toronto Press, 1994).
79. Paul Delany, *British Autobiography in the Seventeenth Century* (London: Routledge and Kegan Paul, 1969), 114.
80. Janet Varner Gunn, *Autobiography: Towards a Poetics of Experience* (Philadelphia, PA: University of Pennsylvania Press, 1982).

81. John Pilling, *Autobiography and Imagination: Studies in Self-Scrutiny* (London: Routledge and Kegan Paul, 1981), 1.
82. Paul de Man, "Autobiography as De-Facement," *Modern Language Notes*, 94 (1979), 920.
83. W.S.S. Tyrwhitt, *A New Chum in the Queensland Bush* (Oxford: Vincent, 1888?); A.W. Stirling, *The Never Never Land: A Ride in North Queensland* (London: Sampson Low, Marston, Searle, and Rivington, 1884); Charles H. Eden, *My Wife and I in Queensland* (London: Longmans, Green & Co, 1872).
84. R.H. Pidcock, *Adventures on Vancouver Island. Being an Account of Six Years Residence, and of Hunting and Fishing Excursions with Some Account of the Indians Inhabiting the Island*. 1862, British Columbia Archives, MS-0728; Dorothy Blakey Smith, "Harry Guillod's Journal of a Trip to Cariboo, 1862," *British Columbia Historical Quarterly*, 19, no. July/October (1955), 187–232; A.G. Doughty and Gustave Lanctot, eds., *Dr Cheadle's Journal of a Trip Across Canada 1862–1863* (Ottawa, ON: Graphic Publishers, 1931).
85. Robert Harkness, Correspondence Outward: personal letters to his wife, 1812–1865, British Columbia Archives, EBH22; Diary of R. Henderson 1862–1863, Fryer Library, University of Queensland, F1517.

2 The Most Manly Class that Exists

1. George Carrington, *Colonial Adventures and Experiences by a University Man* (London: Bell and Daldy, 1871), 5–6.
2. Patrick Leslie to his parents, 27 November 1844.
3. Leonore Davidoff and Catherine Hall, *Family Fortunes: Men and Women of the English Middle Class, 1780–1850* (London: Routledge, 1992), 229.
4. Catherine Hall, "Imperial Man: Edward Eyre in Australasia and the West Indies 1833–1866", in *The Expansion of England: Race, Ethnicity and Cultural History*, ed. Bill Schwarz (London: Routledge, 1996), 130–176.
5. Charles H. Eden, *My Wife and I in Queensland* (London: Longmans, Green, and Co., 1872), 1.
6. John Tosh, *A Man's Place: Masculinity and the Middle-Class Home in Victorian England* (London: Yale University Press, 1999), 11; Peter Gay, *Schnitzler's Century: The Making of Middle-Class Culture 1815–1914* (New York: Norton, 2002); Davidoff and Hall, *Family Fortunes*, 265.
7. Joseph Bristow, *Empire Boys: Adventures in a Man's World* (London: Harper Collins, 199), 67–68.
8. Mark Girouard, *The Return to Camelot: Chivalry and the English Gentleman* (New Haven, CT: Yale University Press, 1981), 260.
9. Rupert Wilkinson, *The Prefects: British Leadership and the Public School Tradition: A Comparative Study in the Making of Rulers* (London: Oxford University Press, 1964), 14–15, cited in, Bristow, *Empire Boys*, 56.
10. Wilkinson, *The Prefects*, 56.
11. See Howard le Couteur, "Gramsci's Concept of Hegemony and Social Formation in Early Colonial Queensland", *Limina*, 6 (2000), 25–39.
12. Martin Green, *Dreams of Adventure Deeds of Empire* (London: Routledge and Keegan Paul, 1980), 15.

13. Russel Ward, *The Australian Legend* (Melbourne, VIC: Oxford University Press, 1966); Geoffrey Dutton, *Squatters: An Illustrated History of Australia's Pastoral Pioneers* (Melbourne, VIC: Viking O'Neil, 1985); Peter Taylor, *Station Life in Australia: Pioneers and Pastoralists* (Sydney, NSW: Allen & Unwin, 1988); Stephen H. Roberts, *The Squatting Age in Australia: 1835–1846* (Melbourne, VIC: Melbourne University Press, 1935); Duncan Waterson, *Squatter, Selector, Storekeeper: A History of the Darling Downs* (Sydney, NSW: University of Sydney Press, 1968); Maurice French, *A Pastoral Romance: The Tribulation and Triumph of Squatterdom* (Toowoomba, QLD: USQ Press, 1990).
14. Roberts, *The Squatting Age in Australia*, 304.
15. Governor George Gipps to Lord Russell, *Historical Records of Australia*, series 1, vol. 21, 130. Cited in Dutton, *Squatters*, 7–8.
16. W. Stamer, *The Gentleman Emigrant: His Daily Life, Sports and Pastimes in Canada, Australia, and the United States* (London: Tinsley Brothers, 1874), 277.
17. Stamer, *The Gentleman Emigrant*, 20.
18. Stamer, *The Gentleman Emigrant*, 15.
19. Stamer, *The Gentleman Emigrant*, 129.
20. Patrick Dunae, *Gentleman Emigrants: From British Public Schools to the Canadian Frontier* (Vancouver, BC: Douglas and McIntyre, 1981), 10.
21. Dunae, *Gentleman Emigrants*, 90.
22. Charles Good, "British Columbia and How I Got There", *Kingston's Magazine for Boys*, 4 (1862), cited in Dunae, *Gentlemen Emigrants*, 31.
23. Rachel Henning to her sister Etta, 18 October 1862, in David Adams, ed., *The Letters of Rachel Henning* (Sydney, NSW: Angus and Robertson, 1963), 109.
24. Rachel Henning to her sister Etta, 18 October 1862, in Adams, *The Letters of Rachel Henning*, 111.
25. W.S.S. Tyrwhitt, *A New Chum in the Queensland Bush* (Oxford: Vincent, 1888?), i.
26. Tyrwhitt, *New Chum*, 78.
27. Tyrwhitt, *New Chum*, 78.
28. Tyrwhitt, *New Chum*, 83.
29. Tyrwhitt, *New Chum*, 81.
30. Peter A. Wright, ed., *Memories of Far Off Days: The Memoirs of Charlotte May Wright 1855–1929* (Armidale, NSW: Peter A. Wright, n.d.).
31. Ann Laura Stoler, *Race and the Education of Desire: Foucault's History of Sexuality and the Colonial Order of Things* (Durham, NC: Duke University Press, 1995), 102.
32. William Leslie to Patrick Leslie, 16 October 1834.
33. William Leslie to Patrick Leslie, 16 October 1834.
34. William Leslie to Patrick Leslie, 16 October 1834.
35. William Leslie to Patrick Leslie, 16 October 1834.
36. William Leslie to Patrick Leslie, 16 October 1834.
37. Patrick Leslie to William Leslie Senior, 4 December 1835.
38. Patrick Leslie to his parents, 27 November 1844, 13 March 1845. Patrick Leslie to his brother William, 1 April 1845; George Leslie to his brother William, 16 November 1841.

190   Notes

39. Walter Leslie to his parents, 6 July 1840; Patrick Leslie to his parents, August 1840.
40. Roberts, *The Squatting Age in Australia*, 112.
41. Patrick Leslie to his parents, 10 May 1835.
42. Patrick Leslie to his parents, 10 May 1835.
43. Patrick Leslie to W.S. Davidson, 14 May 1835.
44. Patrick Leslie to W.S. Davidson, 14 May 1835.
45. Patrick Leslie to his parents, 2 August 1835.
46. Patrick Leslie to his parents, 2 August 1835.
47. Patrick Leslie to his father, 29 November 1839.
48. Patrick Leslie to his parents, 7 January 1845.
49. Patrick Leslie to his parents, 11 September 1840.
50. Eden, *My Wife and I in Queensland*, 3.
51. Dutton, *The Squatters*, 47; Taylor, *Station Life in Australia*, 18.
52. Patrick Leslie to his father, 8 August 1835.
53. Patrick Leslie to his father, 4 December 1835; Patrick Leslie to his parents, 11 September 1840.
54. Bede Nairn, Geoffrey Serle, and Russel Ward, eds., *Australian Dictionary of Biography, Vol. 4, 1851-1890* (Melbourne, VIC: Melbourne University Press, 1966), 61.
55. Oscar De Satge, *Pages from the Journal of a Queensland Squatter* (London: Hurst and Blackett, 1901), 7.
56. De Satgé, *Pages from the Journal of a Queensland Squatter*, 42.
57. De Satgé, *Pages from the Journal of a Queensland Squatter*, 157.
58. De Satgé, *Pages from the Journal of a Queensland Squatter*, 157.
59. De Satgé, *Pages from the Journal of a Queensland Squatter*, 201-202.
60. De Satgé, *Pages from the Journal of a Queensland Squatter*, 202.
61. De Satgé, *Pages from the Journal of a Queensland Squatter*, 218.
62. De Satgé, *Pages from the Journal of a Queensland Squatter*, 140.
63. De Satgé, *Pages from the Journal of a Queensland Squatter*, 160.
64. De Satgé, *Pages from the Journal of a Queensland Squatter*, 166.
65. De Satgé, *Pages from the Journal of a Queensland Squatter*, 172.
66. De Satgé, *Pages from the Journal of a Queensland Squatter*, 177.
67. De Satgé, *Pages from the Journal of a Queensland Squatter*, 45-46.
68. De Satgé, *Pages from the Journal of a Queensland Squatter*, 58.
69. Allan Pritchard, ed., *Vancouver Island Letters of Edmund Hope Verney 1862-1865* (Vancouver, BC: UBC Press, 1996), 3-8.
70. Dorothy Blakey Smith, ed., *The Reminiscences of Doctor John Sebastian Helmcken* (Vancouver, BC: UBC Press, 1975), 115-116.
71. Edmund Hope Verney to his father, 1 June 1862.
72. Edmund Hope Verney to his father, 2 July 1862.
73. Edmund Hope Verney to his father, 20 July 1862.
74. Edmund Hope Verney to his father, 17 July 1862.
75. Edumund Hope Verney to his father, 13 October 1862.
76. Edmund Hope Verney to his father, 8 April 1863.
77. Edmund Hope Verney to his father, 7 December 1864.
78. Edmund Hope Verney to his father, 11 October 1863.
79. Edmund Hope Verney to his father, 11 October 1863; 20 April 1863; 3 August 1863; 10 January 1864; 23 April 1864; 8 September 1864.

80. Edmund Hope Verney to his father, 17 April 1864.
81. Edmund Hope Verney to his father, 6 January 1863; 7 February 1864.
82. Edmund Hope Verney to his father, 20 July 1862.
83. Edmund Hope Verney to his father, 6 January 1863.
84. Edmund Hope Verney to his father, 30 August 1862.
85. Edmund Hope Verney to his father, 29 October 1863.
86. Dorothy Blakey Smith, "The Journal of Arthur Thomas Bushby", *British Columbia Historical Quarterly*, 21 (1957), 83.
87. Smith, "The Journal of Arthur Thomas Bushby", 83.
88. Arthur Thomas Bushby, 20 November 1858, Richard Clement Moody was a colonel in the Royal Engineers and chief commissioner of lands and lieutenant governor of British Columbia. Robert Burnaby was a merchant, spent a time as private secretary to Moody and became a member of the legislative Assembly of Vancouver Island. Elwyn Thomas became a Gold Commissioner and Deputy Provincial Secretary.
89. Smith, "The Journal of Arthur Thomas Bushby", 117.
90. Arthur Bushby, 5 January 1858.
91. Arthur Bushby, 11 February 1859.
92. Arthur Bushby, 29 December 1857.
93. Arthur Bushby, 4 January 1858.
94. Arthur Bushby, 13 January 1858.
95. Arthur Bushby, 29 December 1857.
96. Arthur Bushby, 1 January 1859.
97. Arthur Bushby, 11 February 1859.
98. Arthur Bushby, 11 March 1859.
99. Arthur Bushby, 11 March 1859.
100. Arthur Bushby, 11 February 1859.
101. Arthur Bushby, 26 January 1859.
102. Smith, "The Journal of Arthur Thomas Bushby", 92.
103. Arthur Bushby, 12 March 1859.
104. Arthur Bushby, 18 March 1959.
105. Carrington, *Colonial Adventures and Experiences*, 33–34.
106. Carrington, *Colonial Adventures and Experiences*, 33–34
107. Carrington, *Colonial Adventures and Experiences*, 40.
108. Carrington, *Colonial Adventures and Experiences*, 290.
109. Stamer, *The Gentleman Emigrant*, 269.
110. Charlotte May Wright, *Memories of Far Off Days: The Memoirs of Charlotte May Wright 1855–1929/Edited with Afterword and Additional Family Historical Notes by Peter A. Wright* (Armidale, NSW: P.A. Wright, 1988), 51.
111. Wright, *Memories of Far Off Days*, 50.
112. Wright, *Memories of Far Off Days*, 51.

3 The Sterling Qualities of the Saxon Race

1. Madge Wolfenden, ed., Gilbert Malcolm Sproat, "John Tod: Career of a Scotch Boy", *British Columbia Historical Quarterly*, 18 (1954), 187–188.
2. Edward W. Said, *Culture and Imperialism* (New York: Vintage Books, 1993), 10–12.

3. Said, *Culture and Imperialism*, 52.
4. Sir T.L. Mitchell, *Journal of an Expedition into the Interior of Tropical Australia in Search of a Route from Sydney to the Gulf of Carpentaria* (London: Longman, Brown, Green and Longmans, 1848).
5. Robert A.H. McDonald, *Sons of the Empire: The Frontier and the Boy Scout Movement, 1890–1918* (Toronto, ON: University of Toronto Press, 1993); Richard Slotkin, *The Fatal Environment: The Myth of the Frontier in the Age of Industrialization 1800–1890* (Middleton, CT: Wesleyan University Press, 1985).
6. Richard Phillips, *Mapping Men and Empire: A Geography of Adventure* (London: Routledge, 1997), 5, 45; Robert Dixon, *Writing the Colonial Adventure: Race, Gender and Nation in Anglo-Australian Popular Fiction, 1875–1914* (Melbourne, VIC: Cambridge University Press, 1995); Martin Crotty, *Making the Australian Male: Middle-Class Masculinity 1870–1920* (Melbourne, VIC: Melbourne University Press, 2000).
7. Martin Green, *Dreams of Adventure, Deeds of Empire* (London: Routledge and Kegan Paul, 1980), 3.
8. Kinahan Cornwallis, *The New Eldorado or British Columbia* (London: Thomas Cautley Newby, 1858), 109.
9. Cornwallis, *The New Eldorado*, 193.
10. R.C. Lundin Brown, Rev., *British Columbia: An Essay* (New Westminster, BC: Royal Engineers Press, 1863), 33.
11. Cited in Ian Turner, "The Social Setting", in *The Literature of Australia*, ed. Geoffrey Dutton (Melbourne, VIC: Penguin, 1976), 13–57. For further material on how explorers saw Australia, see Paul Carter, *The Road to Botany Bay: An Essay in Spatial History* (London: Faber and Faber, 1987); Robert Dixon, *The Course of Empire: Neo-Classical Culture in New South Wales 1788–1860* (Melbourne, VIC: Oxford University Press, 1986); Simon Ryan, *The Cartographic Eye: How Explorers Saw Australia* (Melbourne, VIC: Cambridge University Press, 1996).
12. Thomas Campbell, *Lines on the Departure of Emigrants for New South Wales*, in Ian Turner, *The Australian Dream* (Melbourne, VIC: Sun Books, 1968).
13. Cornwallis, *The New Eldorado*, 182.
14. Sproat, "John Tod", 137.
15. *Dictionary of Canadian Biography* (Toronto, ON: University of Toronto Press, 1966), 881. Although this was the year and place of birth admitted to by Tod, Hudson's Bay Company records show that he was born in 1793 in Glasgow. See Sproat, "John Tod", 231.
16. Sproat, "John Tod", 140.
17. Jennifer S.H. Brown, *Strangers in Blood: Fur Trade Company Families in Indian Country* (Norman, OK: University of Oklahoma Press, 1980), 51.
18. Catherine Hall, *White, Male and Middle Class: Explorations in Feminism and History* (Oxford: Polity Press, 1992), 60.
19. Sproat, "John Tod", 189.
20. Sproat, "John Tod", 187.
21. Joanne Leduc, ed., *Overland from Canada to British Columbia by Mr. Thomas McMicking of Queenston, Canada West* (Vancouver, BC: UBC Press, 1981); Thomas McMicking, "An Account of a Journey Overland from Canada to British Columbia During the Summer of 1862", *The British Columbian*,

29 November 1862, 13, 20, 27 December 1862, 10, 17, 24, 28 January 1863; A.L. Fortune, "The Overlanders of 1862", *Kamloops Sentinel*, 27 November 1936, 1, 8, 15, 24 December 1936.
22. Jean Barman, *The West beyond the West: A History of British Columbia* (Toronto, ON: Toronto University Press, 1991), 66. For further accounts of the gold rushes of British Columbia, see also Donald E. Waite, *The Cariboo Gold Rush Story* (Surrey, BC: Hancock House, 1988), and George Woodcock, *British Columbia: A History of the Province* (Vancouver, BC: Douglas and McIntyre, 1990), 92–93, 102–111.
23. Barman, *The West beyond the West*, 64–66.
24. A.L. Fortune, "The Overlanders of 1862", *Kamloops Sentinel*, 27 November 1936.
25. A.L. Fortune Miscellanea, University of British Columbia Rare Books and Special Collections, VF-48.
26. Robert McMicking Personal and Business Records 1862–1910, British Columbia Archives, MS-117; J.B. Kerr, *Biographical Dictionary of Well Known British Columbians with a Historical Sketch* (Vancouver, BC: Kerr and Begg, 1890), 253–261.
27. Leduc, ed., *Overland from Canada to British Columbia*, xx.
28. A.L. Fortune, 'The Overlanders', *Kamloops Sentinel*, 27 November 1926.
29. Catherine Hall, "Imperial Man: Edward Eyre in Australasia and the West Indies 1833–1866", in *The Expansion of England: Race, Ethnicity and Cultural History*, ed. Bill Schwarz (London: Routledge, 1996), 139.
30. A.L. Fortune, "The Overlanders", *Kamloops Sentinel*, 4 December 1936.
31. R.M. Ballantyne, *The Coral Island* (Barcelona: Fabbri Publishing Ltd, 1991), 21.
32. Thomas McMicking, "An Account of a Journey Overland", *The British Columbian*, 28 January 1863.
33. Thomas McMicking, "An Account of a Journey Overland", *The British Columbian*, 28 January 1863.
34. A.L. Fortune, "The Overlanders", *Kamloops Sentinel*, 4 December 1936.
35. Kay Schaffer, *Women and the Bush: Forces of Desire in the Australian Cultural Tradition* (Sydney, NSW: Cambridge University Press, 1988), 59–61.
36. A.L. Fortune, "The Overlanders", *Kamloops Sentinel*, 11 December 1936.
37. A.L. Fortune, "The Overlanders", *Kamloops Sentinel*, 11 December 1936.
38. A.L. Fortune, "The Overlanders", *Kamloops Sentinel*, 11 December 1936.
39. Thomas McMicking, "An Account of a Journey Overland", *The British Columbian*, 13 December 1862.
40. Thomas McMicking, "An Account of a Journey Overland", *The British Columbian*, 16 January 1862.
41. Thomas McMicking, "An Account of a Journey Overland", *The British Columbian*, 16 January 1862.
42. Thomas McMicking, "An Account of a Journey Overland", *The British Columbian*, 20 December 1862.
43. Leonore Davidoff and Catherine Hall, *Family Fortunes: Men and Women of the English Middle Class* (London: Routledge, 1992).
44. G.D. Brown, "Introduction to 'The Overlanders of 1862'", *Kamloops Sentinel*, 27 November, 1936; Leduc, ed., *Overland from Canada to British Columbia*, xix–xx.

194 Notes

45. Thomas McMicking, "An Account of a Journey Overland", *The British Columbian*, 24 January 1863.
46. Thomas McMicking, "An Account of a Journey Overland", *The British Columbian*, 24 January 1863.
47. These themes were to be reproduced in the adventure fiction of the mid- to late-nineteenth century, the quintessential example being Rider Haggard's *King Solomon's Mines*. The role of such fiction in gendering the frontier and expressing the desire of men to conquer and possess it has been explored by a number of scholars including Anne McClintock, Kay Schaffer and Rebecca Stott. See Anne McClintock, *Imperial Leather: Race, Gender and Sexuality in the Colonial Contest* (New York: Routledge, 1995), particularly Chapter 6 titled "The White Family of Man: Colonial Discourse and the Reinvention of Patriarchy", 232–257; Schaffer, *Women and the Bush*, and Rebecca Stott, "The Dark Continent: Africa as Female Body in Haggard's Adventure Fiction", *Feminist Review*, 32 (1989), 69–89. For an investigation of these themes in nineteenth-century Australian adventure stories, see Crotty, *Making the Australian Male*, 133–167.
48. Leduc, ed., *Overland from Canada to British Columbia*, xxvii–xxviii.
49. A.L. Fortune Miscellanea.
50. Particulars of Ernest Henry's Family, Supplied by his Daughter Miss Ernestine Henry and an Account Given by his Brother Arthur Henry, Fryer Library, mss 2/1239–1244, np.
51. *An Account by Ernest Henry of an Exploring Trip Resulting in the Taking Up of Hughenden Station*. FL, mss 2/1239–1244, 2.
52. *An Account by Ernest Henry*, 2–3.
53. *An Account by Ernest Henry*, 3.
54. David Spurr, *The Rhetoric of Empire: Colonial Discourse in Journalism, Travel Writing, and Imperial Administration* (London: Duke University Press, 1993), 28, 46.
55. Dixon, *The Course of Empire*, 83; Mary Louise Pratt, *Imperial Eyes: Travel Writing and Transculturation* (London: Routledge, 1992), 51.
56. McClintock, *Imperial Leather*, 30.
57. McClintock, *Imperial Leather*, 30.
58. *An Account by Ernest Henry*, 10.
59. *An Account by Ernest Henry*, 8.
60. *An Account by Ernest Henry*, 10.
61. *An Account by Ernest Henry*, 14.
62. *An Account by Ernest Henry*, 15.
63. *An Account by Ernest Henry*, 15–16.
64. *An Account by Ernest Henry*, 11.
65. Viscount Milton and W.B. Cheadle, *The North-West Passage by Land* (London: Cassel, Petter and Galpin, 1865).
66. V.G. Hopgood in *Canadian Dictionary of Biography* (Toronto, ON: University of Toronto Press, 1966), 699.
67. A.G. Doughty and Gustave Lanctot, eds., *Dr Cheadle's Journal of a Trip across Canada 1862–1863* (Ottawa, ON: Graphic Publishers, 1931).
68. Viscount Milton and W.B. Cheadle, *The North-West Passage by Land*, xvi.
69. Walter Cheadle, *Journal*, 11 July 1863, 173.
70. Walter Cheadle, *Journal*, 7 and 8 June 1863, 149–150.

71. Walter Cheadle, *Journal*, 24 June 1863, 158.
72. Walter Cheadle, *Journal*, 10 July 1863, 172. A muskeg is a swamp or bog.
73. Walter Cheadle, *Journal*, 22 June 1863, 157.
74. Walter Cheadle, *Journal*, 14 July 1863, 176.
75. Walter Cheadle, *Journal*, 22 June 1863, 155.
76. Walter Cheadle, *Journal*, 8 June 1863, 148.
77. Walter Cheadle, *Journal*, 3 July 1863, 166.
78. Harry Guillod, 2 August 1862 in Dorothy Blakey Smith, "Harry Guillod's Journal of a Trip to Cariboo, 1862", *British Columbia Historical Quarterly*, 19, no. July/October (1955), 209.
79. Harry Guillod, *Journal*, 14 July 1862, 211.
80. Harry Guillod, *Journal*, 28 August 1862, 218.
81. Harry Guillod, *Journal*, 19 October 1862, 196.
82. Harry Guillod, *Journal*, 19 October 1862, 195.
83. Arthur Neame, *A Few Reminiscences of North Queensland by One of the Early Pioneers*, manuscript, John Oxley Library, OM65-09 (n.d.), 2.
84. Neame, *A Few Reminiscences of North Queensland*, 2. The verse is from John Greenleaf Whittier's "On Receiving an Eagle's Quill from Lake Superior".
85. Neame, *A Few Reminiscences of North Queensland*, 6.
86. Neame, *A Few Reminiscences of North Queensland*, 10.
87. Neame, *A Few Reminiscences of North Queensland*, 6–7.
88. Neame, *A Few Reminiscences of North Queensland*, 9.
89. Neame, *A Few Reminiscences of North Queensland*, 9.
90. Neame, *A Few Reminiscences of North Queensland*, 34.
91. John M. MacKenzie, "The Imperial Pioneer and Hunter and the British Masculine Stereotype in Late Victorian and Edwardian Times", in *Manliness and Morality: Middle Class Masculinity in Britain and America 1800–1940*, eds. J.A. Mangan and James Walvin (Manchester: Manchester University Press, 1987).

4 Men without (White) Women

1. Miles Fairburn, *The Ideal Society and Its Enemies: The Foundations of Modern New Zealand Society 1850–1900* (Auckland: Auckland University Press, 1984), 191.
2. Fairburn, *The Ideal Society and Its Enemies*, 192.
3. This applied to the goldfields of Queensland as well as British Columbia. For a description of how men worked together on a Queensland frontier goldfield, see Chas. H. Allen, *A Visit to Queensland and Her Goldfields* (London: Chapman and Allen, 1870), 134–137.
4. Arthur Neame, *A Few Reminiscences of North Queensland by One of the Early Pioneers*, John Oxley Library, OM65-09 (1922), 16.
5. George Carrington, *Colonial Adventures and Experiences by a University Man* (London: Bell and Daldy, 1871), 63–64.
6. Carrington, *Colonial Adventures and Experiences*, 69.
7. Carrington, *Colonial Adventures and Experiences*, 69.
8. Anne Digby, "Women's Biological Straitjacket", in *Sexuality and Subordination: Interdisciplinary Studies of Gender in the Nineteenth Century*, eds. Susan Mendus and Jane Rendall (London: Routledge, 1989), 193. See also Mary

Poovey, "'Scenes of an Indelicate Character': The Medical 'Treatment' of Victorian Women", in *The Making of the Modern Body: Sexuality and Society in the Nineteenth Century*, eds. Catherine Gallagher and Thomas Laqueur (Berkeley, CA: University of California Press, 1987), 144–146, and Thomas Laqueur, *Making Sex: Body and Gender from the Greeks to Freud* (Cambridge, MA: Harvard University Press, 1990), 207–227.
9. Diary of R. Henderson 1862–1863, Fryer Library, University of Queensland, F1517, n.p.
10. Diary of R. Henderson 1862–1863, n.p.
11. Thomas McMicking, "An Account of a Journey Overland from Canada to British Columbia During the Summer of 1862". *The British Columbian* 1862; A.L. Fortune, "The Overlanders", *Kamloops Sentinel*, 1936; Joanne Leduc, ed., *Overland from Canada to British Columbia by Mr. Thomas McMicking of Queenston, Canada West* (Vancouver, BC: UBC Press, 1981).
12. Robert Harkness to Sabrina Harkness, 1 July 1862. British Columbia Archives, EB H22A.
13. Robert Harkness to Sabrina Harkness, c1862.
14. Robert Harkness to Sabrina Harkness, 1 April 1864.
15. Robert Harkness to Sabrina Harkness, 22 April 1862.
16. Robert Harkness to Sabrina Harkness, 9 May 1862.
17. John Tosh, *A Man's Place: Masculinity and the Middle-Class Home in Victorian England* (London: Yale University Press, 1999); Wally Seccombe, "Patriarchy Stabilized: The Construction of the Male Breadwinner Wage Norm in Nineteenth-Century Britain", *Social History*, 11, no. 1 (1986), 53–76; Leonore Davidoff and Catherine Hall, *Family Fortunes: Men and Women of the English Middle Class, 1780–1850* (London: Routledge, 1987); Anna Clark, *The Struggle for the Breeches: Gender and the Making of the British Working Class* (Berkeley, CA: University of California Press, 1997).
18. Mary Dell Harkness to Isabel Kathleen Race Eddy, circa 1952.
19. Robert Harkness to Sabrina Harkness, 28 June 1864.
20. Adele Perry, *On the Edge of Empire: Gender, Race, and the Making of British Columbia* (Toronto, ON: University of Toronto Press, 2001), 48.
21. Robert Harkness to Sabrina Harkness, 28 June 1864.
22. Robert Harkness to Sabrina Harkness, 23 July 1862.
23. Robert Harkness to Sabrina Harkness, n.d. c. 1862.
24. Robert Harkness to Sabrina Harkness, 3 April 1864.
25. Christopher Lane, *The Burdens of Intimacy: Psychoanalysis and Victorian Masculinity* (Chicago, IL: University of Chicago Press, 1999), 1.
26. Robert Harkness to Sabrina Harkness, 3 April 1864.
27. Robert Harkness to Sabrina Harkness, 31 May 1864.
28. Robert Harkness to Sabrina Harkness, 5 March 1865.
29. Robert Harkness to Sabrina Harkness, 5 March 1865.
30. Robert Harkness to Sabrina Harkness, 28 April 1865.
31. Robert Harkness to Sabrina Harkness, 15 June 1862.
32. Robert Harkness to Sabrina Harkness, 9 May 1862.
33. Robert Harkness to Sabrina Harkness, 15 June 1862.
34. Robert Harkness to Sabrina Harkness, 28 April 1865.
35. Robert Harkness to Sabrina Harkness, 3 April 1864.
36. Tosh, *A Man's Place*, 2–3.

37. Robert Harkness to Sabrina Harkness, 28 June 1864.
38. Perry, *On the Edge of Empire*, 28–29.
39. Robert Harkness to Sabrina Harkness, 28 April 1865.
40. Richard Arthur Preston, ed., *For Friends at Home: A Scottish Immigrant's Letters from Canada, California and the Cariboo* (Montreal, QC: McGill-Queens University Press, 1974), 6–7.
41. Preston, *For Friends at Home*, 1.
42. James Thomson diary 14 May 1862, 7 June 1862, 14 June 1862, in *For Friends at Home*, 287.
43. James Thomson diary 27 May 1862, 288; 8 June 1862, 289; 14 June 1862.
44. Robert Harkness to Sabrina Harkness, 23 July 1862.
45. James Thomson, diary 14 June 1862.
46. James Thomson, diary 24–28 June 1862.
47. James Thomson, diary 29 June 1862.
48. Williams Creek and Williams Lake are different localities.
49. James Thomson to Mary Thomson 27 July 1862.
50. James Thomson to Mary Thomson 27 July 1862.
51. James Thomson to Mary Thomson 27 July 1862. Micah IV:ii reads, "Come, let us go up to the mountain of the Lord, and to the house of the God of Jacob; and he will teach us of his ways, and we shall walk in his paths."
52. James Thomson to Mary Thomson 27 July 1862.
53. James Thomson to Mary Thomson 27 July 1862.
54. Diary of Charles Hayward, 7 May 1862. British Columbia Archives Microfilm Reel No. A00714.
55. Diary of Charles Hayward, 12 May 1862.
56. Diary of Charles Hayward, 12 September 1862.
57. Diary of Charles Hayward, 23 October 1862, and 27 October 1862.
58. Diary of Charles Hayward, 26 August 1862.
59. Diary of Charles Hayward, 6 September 1862.
60. Diary of Charles Hayward, 5 October 1862.
61. Hayward Family Business, Personal and Political Papers, 1862–1963, British Columbia Archives, Mss-0503
62. Tosh, *A Man's Place*, 2.
63. Jennifer S.H. Brown, *Strangers in Blood: Fur Trade Company Families in Indian Country* (Norman, OK: University of Oklahoma Press, 1996); Sylvia Van Kirk, *Many Tender Ties: Women in Fur Trade Society, 1670–1870* (Norman, OK: University of Oklahoma Press, 1983).
64. Leonore Davidoff and Catherine Hall, *Family Fortunes: Men and Women of the English Middle Class 1780–1850* (Chicago, IL: University of Chicago Press, 1987), 401–403.
65. Anna Clark, *The Struggle for the Breeches: Gender and the Making of the British Working Class* (London: University of California Press, 1995), 58, 61.
66. Robert Shoemaker, *Gender in English Society, 1650–1850: The Emergence of Separate Spheres* (London: Longman, 1998), 64–65; Lesley A. Hall, "Forbidden by God, Despised by Men: Masturbation, Medical Warnings, Moral Panic, and Manhood in Great Britain, 1850–1950", in *Forbidden History: The State, Society, and the Regulation of Sexuality in Modern Europe*, ed. John C. Fout (Chicago, IL: University of Chicago Press, 1992), 294; Steven Marcus, *The Other Victorians: A Study of Sexuality and Pornography*

in Mid-Nineteenth Century England (London: Weidenfeld and Nicholson, 1966).
67. Perry, *On the Edge of Empire*, 48–78.
68. Perry, *On the Edge of Empire*, 59–61.
69. Perry, *On the Edge of Empire*, 62–65.
70. Diary of George Blair, 17 February 1862–29 December 1863, entry undated, 20, British Columbia Archives Add Mss 186.
71. Dorothy Blakey Smith, ed., *The Reminiscences of Doctor John Sebastian Helmcken* (Vancouver, BC: University of British Columbia Press, 1975), 81.
72. C.E. Barrett-Lennard, *Travels in British Columbia with the Narrative of a Yacht Voyage Round Vancouver's Island* (London: Hurst and Brackett, 1862), 47.
73. Raymond Evans, Kay Saunders, and Katherine Cronin, *Exclusion, Exploitation, Extermination: Race Relations in Colonial Queensland* (Sydney, NSW; Australian and New Zealand Book Co., 1975), 88. See also Richard Broome, *Aboriginal Australians; Black Responses to White Dominance 1788–1994*, 2nd ed. (Sydney, NSW; Allen and Unwin, 1994), 55–56; and Henry Reynolds, *The Other Side of the Frontier: Aboriginal Resistance to the European Invasion of Australia* (Melbourne, VIC: Penguin, 1982), 70–72.
74. Rachel Henning to her sister Etta, 29 September 1862, *The Letters of Rachel Henning*, David Adams ed. (Harmondsworth Middx. 1969)
75. Reverend Henry Stobart to his mother, 9 July 1853, Fryer Library, University of Queensland, Mic7368.
76. Charles Eden, *My Wife and I in Queensland* (London: Longmans, Green and Co., 1872), 211.
77. Raymond Evans, *A History of Queensland* (Melbourne, VIC: Cambridge University Press, 2007), 58.
78. William Telfer, *The Wallabahdah Manuscript: Recollections of the Early Days: The Early History of the Northern Districts of New South Wales.* Roger Milliss ed. (Sydney, NSW: University of New South Wales Press, 1980), 87.
79. Frederick Richmond, *Queensland in the Seventies: Reminiscences of the Early Days of a Young Clergyman* (Singapore: C.A. Ribeiro, 1928), 88.
80. Eden, *My Wife and I in Queensland*, 211–212.
81. Richmond, *Queensland in the Seventies*, 87.
82. Anne McClintock, *Imperial Leather: Race, Gender and Sexuality in the Colonial Conquest* (New York: Routledge, 1995).
83. Fairburn, *The Ideal Society and Its Enemies*, 203.
84. Clive Moore, "Colonial Manhood and Masculinities", *Journal of Australian Studies*, no. 56 (1998), 45.
85. Carrington, *Colonial Adventures and Experiences*, 48.
86. Carrington, *Colonial Adventures and Experiences*, 72.
87. Neame, A Few Reminiscences of North Queensland by One of the Early Pioneers, 51.
88. Perry, *On the Edge of Empire*, 39.
89. George Woodcock, *British Columbia: A History of the Province* (Vancouver, BC: Douglas and McIntyre, 1990), 101.
90. W.K. Lamb, "The Diary of Robert Melrose Part 2", *British Columbia Historical Quarterly*, 7 (1943), 199.
91. Lamb, "The Diary of Robert Melrose", 205.
92. Arthur Thomas Bushby, *Journal*, 140.

93. Arthur Thomas Bushby, *Journal*, 123.
94. Douglas cited in Perry, *On the Edge of Empire*, 40.
95. Smith, ed., *The Reminiscences of Doctor John Sebastian Helmcken*, 111–112.
96. Diary of Charles Haywood 1862, 13 October 1862. The Haywood family went on to own the St. James Hotel in Johnson St., Victoria.
97. Catherine Murdoch, *Domesticating Drink: Women, Men and Alcohol in America, 1800–1933* (Baltimore, MD: John Hopkins University Press, 1998), 15.
98. Denis Altman, "The Myth of Mateship", *Meanjin*, 46, no. 2 (1987), 163–172; David Buchbinder, "Mateship, Gallipoli and the Eternal Masculine", in *Representation, Discourse and Desire: Contemporary Australian Culture & Critical Theory*, ed. Patrick Fuery (Melbourne, VIC: Longman Cheshire, 1994), 115–137; C.M.H. Clark, *A History of Australia III: The Beginning of an Australian Civilisation 1824–1851* (Melbourne, VIC: Melbourne University Press, 1962), W.K. Hancock, *Australia* (Brisbane, QLD: Jacaranda, 1963), Max Harris, "Morals and Manners", in *Australian Civilisation*, ed. Peter Coleman (Melbourne, VIC: F.W. Cheshire, 1962), John Rickard, *Australia: A Cultural History* (London: Longman, 1996).
99. Russel Ward, *The Australian Legend* (Melbourne, VIC: Oxford University Press, 1966), 99.
100. Ward, *The Australian Legend*, 100. Other authors have reflected on the ambiguity of the term 'mate' and the association of mateship and homosexuality. See Robert Hughes, *The Fatal Shore: A History of the Transportation of Convicts to Australia, 1787–1868* (London: Collins Harvill, 1987), 320; Miriam Dixson, *The Real Matilda: Women and Identity in Australia – 1788 to the Present* (Sydney, NSW: University of NSW Press, 1999), 81.
101. Anne O'Brien, "Missionary Masculinities, the Homoerotic Gaze and the Politics of Race: Gilbert White in Northern Australia, 1885–1915", *Gender & History*, 20, no. 1 (April 2008), 73.
102. J.C. Byrne, 1848, cited in Ward, *The Australian Legend*, 97.
103. Perry, *On the Edge of Empire*, 21–28.
104. Perry, *On the Edge of Empire*, 25.
105. Aldrich, *Colonialism and Homosexuality*, 57.
106. R.H. Pidcock, *Adventures on Vancouver Island, Being an Account of Six Years Residence, and of Hunting and Fishing Excursions with Some Account of the Indians Inhabiting the Island*. 1862, British Columbia Archives, Add Mss728, Vol. 4a, n.p.
107. For a discussion on the role of hunting in constructing British masculinity in the nineteenth and early-twentieth centuries, see John M. MacKenzie, "The Imperial Pioneer and Hunter and the British masculine stereotype in late Victorian and Edwardian Times", in *Middle Class Masculinity in Britain and America 1800–1940*, eds. J.A. Mangan and James Walvin (Manchester: Manchester University Press, 1987), 176–198.
108. Pidcock, *Adventures on Vancouver Island*, n.p.
109. Pidcock, *Adventures on Vancouver Island*, n.p.
110. Pidcock, *Adventures on Vancouver Island*, n.p.
111. Pidcock, *Adventures on Vancouver Island*, n.p.
112. Pidcock, *Adventures on Vancouver Island*, n.p.
113. Pidcock, *Adventures on Vancouver Island*, n.p.

114. John Beynon, *Masculinities and Culture* (Buckingham: Open University Press, 2002), 31.
115. Neil Miller, *Out of the Past: Gay and Lesbian History from 1869 to the Present* (New York: Vintage Books, 1995), 40–41.
116. Perry, *On the Edge of Empire*, 32–36.
117. David F. Greenberg, *The Construction of Homosexuality* (Chicago, IL: The University of Chicago Press, 1984), 347–396, 397–433.
118. Sean Brady, *Masculinity and Male Homosexuality in Britain, 1861–1913* (Basingstoke: Palgrave Macmillan, 2005), 23–24.
119. Jeffrey Weeks, *Against Nature: Essays on History, Sexuality and Identity* (London: Oram Press, 1991), 17.
120. H.G. Cocks, *Nameless Offences: Homosexual Desire in the 19th Century* (London: I.B. Taurus, 2003), 22.
121. Cocks, *Nameless Offences*, 17.
122. Walter J. Fogarty, " 'Certain Habits': The Development of a Concept of the Male Homosexual in New South Wales Law, 1788–1900", in *Gay Perspectives: Essays in Australian Gay Culture*, eds. Gary Wotherspoon and Robert Aldrich (Sydney, NSW: Department of Economic History, University of Sydney, 1992), 61.
123. Jeffrey Weeks, *Coming Out: Homosexual Politics in Britain from the Nineteenth Century to the Present* (London: Quartet Books, 1990), 13.
124. Graham Robb, *Strangers: Homosexual Love in the Nineteenth Century* (New York: W.W. Norton & Company, 2004), 24.
125. Greenberg, *The Construction of Homosexuality*, 35.
126. Clive Moore, " 'Feloniously Wicked and against the Order of Nature': A Research Agenda for Gay Studies in Queensland", *Hecate*, 20, no. 1 (1994), 139–150.
127. Government of British Columbia Act, 1858 (UK), 21 & 22 Vict., c99.
128. Perry, *On the Edge of Empire*, 32.
129. O'Brien, "Missionary Masculinities, the Homoerotic Gaze and the Politics of Race".
130. Aldrich, *Colonialism and Homosexuality*, 4.
131. Bob Hay, "A Charge of Something Unnatural: A Brief History from the Records of Australia's Earliest Known 'Homosexual' Convict", in *Gay Perspectives II: More Essays in Australian Gay Culture*, ed. Robert Aldrich (Sydney, NSW: Department of Economic History with The Australian Centre for Gay and Lesbian Research University of Sydney, 1994), 63.
132. Hay, "A Charge of Something Unnatural", 63–65.
133. Libby Connors, "Two Opposed Traditions: Male Popular Culture and the Criminal Justice System in Queensland", in *Gay Perspectives II: More Essays in Australian Gay Culture*, ed. Robert Aldrich (Sydney, NSW: Department of Economic History with The Australian Centre for Gay and Lesbian Research University of Sydney, 1994), 91.

5 Blacks, Chinks and a Pig-Headed German

1. R.W. Connell, *Masculinities* (Sydney, NSW: Allen & Unwin, 1995), 77–81; Leonore Davidoff, Keith McClelland, and Eleni Varikas, "Introduction",

in *Gender and History: Retrospect and Prospect*, eds. Leonore Davidoff, Keith McClelland, and Eleni Varikas (Oxford: Blackwell, 1999), ix.
2. Mrinalini Sinha, "Giving Masculinity a History: Some Contributions from the Historiography of India", in *Gender and History: Retrospect and Prospect*, eds. Leonore Davidoff, Keith McClelland, and Eleni Varikas (Oxford: Blackwell, 1999), 35.
3. Henry Mort to his mother and sister, 28 January 1844. Here Mort is recording the views of his friends John and David McConnel of Cressbrook Station, west of Brisbane. McConnel Family Papers, Fryer Library, UQFL89.
4. Bain Attwood and John Arnold, *Power, Knowledge and Aborigines, Journal of Australian Studies* (Melbourne, VIC: La Trobe University Press, 1992), 1.
5. Benjamin Disraeli, *Tancred*, cited in Michael Banton, *The Idea of Race* (Cambridge: Tavistock, 1977), 25.
6. Robert Knox, *The Races of Man*, cited in Michael D. Biddis, *Images of Race* (New York: Holmes & Meiers, 1979), 12.
7. Kenan Makik, *The Meaning of Race: Race, History, and Culture in Western Society* (London: Macmillan, 1996), 42–49.
8. Malik, *The Meaning of Race*, 70.
9. Malik, *The Meaning of Race*, 75.
10. Robert Bernasconi, "Who Invented the Concept of Race? Kant's Role in the Enlightenment Construction of Race", in *Race*, ed. Robert Bernasconi (Oxford: Blackwell, 2001), 17.
11. David R. Roediger, *The Wages of Whiteness: Race and the Making of the American Working Class* (New York: Verso, 1999), 21; Warwick Anderson, *The Cultivation of Whiteness: Science, Health and Racial Destiny in Australia* (Melbourne, VIC: Melbourne University Press, 2002), 2.
12. Nancy Stepan, *The Idea of Race in Science: Great Britain 1800–1960* (London: Macmillan, 1982), ix–xii.
13. Stepan, *The Idea of Race in Science*, 23–27.
14. George M. Frederickson, *Racism: A Short History* (Melbourne, VIC: Scribe Publications, 2002), 60.
15. Warren Montag, "The Universalization of Whiteness: Racism and Enlightenment", in *Whiteness a Critical Reader*, ed. Mike Hill (New York: New York University Press), 285.
16. Montag, "The Universalization of Whiteness", 292.
17. Ruth Frankenburg, "Whiteness and Americanness: Examining Constructions of Race, Culture and Nation in White Women's Life Narratives", in *Race*, eds. Steven Gregory and Roger Sanjek (New Brunswick, NJ: Rutgers University Press, 1994), 63.
18. Roy Harvey Pearce, *The Savages of America: A Study of the Indians and the Idea of Civilisation* (Baltimore, MD: John Hopkins Press, 1965), 85–86, 103–104.
19. Pearce, *The Savages of America*, 82.
20. Gail Bederman, *Manliness and Civilisation: A Cultural History of Gender and Race in the United States 1880–1917* (Chicago, IL: University of Chicago Press, 1995), 25.
21. Bederman, *Manliness and Civilisation*, 25.
22. George W. Stocking, *Victorian Anthropology* (New York: The Free Press, 1987), 106.
23. Bederman, *Manliness and Civilisation*, 29.

24. Alfred Russel Wallace, "The Origin of Human Races and the Antiquity of Man Deduced from the Theory of 'Natural Selection'", in *Images of Race*, ed. Michael D. Biddis (New York: Holmes & Meier, 1979), 47.
25. John William Jackson, "Race in Legislation and Political Economy", in *Images of Race*, ed. Michael D. Biddis (New York: Holmes and Meier, 1976), 122.
26. Cited in Banton, *The Idea of Race*, 70.
27. L. Figuier, *The Human Race*, newly edited and revised by Robert Wilson, London, Cassell n.d. (c1880), 63–64, cited in Raymond Evans, Kay Saunders, and Kathryn Cronin, *Exclusion, Exploitation and Extermination: Race Relations in Colonial Queensland* (Sydney, NSW: ANZ, 1975), 19–20.
28. Ruth Frankenburg, "Whiteness and Americanness: Examining Constructions of Race, Culture and Nation in White Women's Life Narratives", in *Race*, eds. Steven Gregory and Roger Sanjek (New Brunswick, NJ: Rutgers University Press, 1994), 63.
29. Cited in George Woodcock, *British Columbia: A History of the Province* (Vancouver, BC: Douglas McIntyre, 1990).
30. Cited in Robin Fisher and J.M. Bumstead, eds., *An Account of a Voyage to the Northwest Coast of America in 1785 and 1786 by Alexander Walker* (Vancouver, BC/Seattle, WA: Douglas and McIntyre/University of Washington Press, 1982), 37.
31. Charles Alford Bayley, "Early Life on Vancouver Island", *British Columbia Archives*, EB B34.2 (n.d.), 4.
32. Dorothy Blakey Smith, "Harry Guillod's Journal of a Trip to Cariboo, 1862", *British Columbia Historical Quarterly*, 19, no. July/October (1955), 200.
33. R.C. Lundin Brown, Rev., *Klatsassan* (London: Society for Promoting Christian Knowledge, 1873), 54.
34. Anthony Trollope, *Australia*, eds. P.D. Edwards and R.B. Joyce (Brisbane, QLD: University of Queensland Press, [1873]1967), 100.
35. *An Account by Ernest Henry of an Exploration Trip Resulting in the Taking up of Hughenden Station*, 1. Fryer Library, mss 2/1239–1244.
36. *An Account by Ernest Henry*, 4.
37. Charles H. Eden, *Australia's Heroes* (London: Society for Promoting Christian Knowledge, 1882), 258.
38. Eden, *Australia's Heroes*, 259.
39. A.W. Stirling, *The Never Never Land: A Ride in North Queensland* (London: Sampson Low, Marston, Searle, and Rivington, 1884), 80.
40. Stirling, *The Never Never Land*, 80–92.
41. Chas H. Allen, *A Visit to Queensland and Her Goldfields* (London: Chapman and Hall, 1870), 179, 180–182.
42. Ross Gibson, *The Diminishing Paradise* (Sydney, NSW: Sirius, 1984), 158.
43. Frederick Richmond, *Queensland in the Seventies* (Singapore: C.A. Ribeiro, 1928), 109.
44. Nehemiah Bartley, *Australian Pioneers and Reminiscences: Together with Portraits of Some of the Founders of Australia* (Brisbane, QLD: Gordon and Gotch, 1896), 170, 202, 218.
45. Bartley, *Australian Pioneers and Reminiscences*, 167.
46. Arthur John McConnel, "Blacks", McConnel Family Papers, Fryer Library, mss 89/206.

47. Kinahan Cornwallis, *The New Eldorado or British Columbia* (London: Thomas Cautley Newby, 1858), 109.
48. Cornwallis, *The New Eldorado*, 241.
49. Robin Fisher, *Contact and Conflict* (Vancouver, BC: UBC Press, 1992), 76. For the history and anthropology of Indigenous Canadians, see James S. Frideres, *Native People in Canada: Contemporary Conflicts* (Scarborough, ON: Prentice-Hall Canada, 1983); John W. Friesen, *Rediscovering the First Nations of Canada* (Calgary, AB: Detselig Enterprises, 1997); Allan D. McMillan, *Native Peoples and Cultures of Canada* (Vancouver, BC: Douglas &McIntyre, 1995).
50. Pearce, *The Savages of America*, 4–6.
51. Legislative Assembly Queensland, *Minutes of Evidence on The Native Police Force and the Condition of Aborigines Generally*, 1861, 1.
52. For more detailed histories of the NMP, see Jonathan Richards, *The Secret War: A True History of Queensland's Native Police* (Brisbane, QLD: University of Queensland Press, 2008); and B.F. Skinner, *Police of the Pastoral Frontier* (Brisbane, QLD: University of Queensland Press, 1975).
53. Micahel Taussig, "Culture of Terror – Space of Death. Roger Casement's Putumayo Report and the Explanation of Torture", *Comparative Studies in Society and History*, 26 (1984), 494.
54. *Minutes of Evidence*, 2.
55. *Minutes of Evidence*, 55.
56. *Minutes of Evidence*, 19, 37, 55, 112.
57. *Minutes of Evidence*, 8.
58. *Minutes of Evidence*, 10. The credibility of the evidence of Lieutenant Wheeler must also be in question as at the time the coroner investigating the murder of two Aborigines at Fassifern, Dr Challinor, who also gave evidence to the Committee, wrote to the Attorney-General stating that 'the shooting of the said blacks is now distinctly and unequivocally traced to Lieutenant Wheeler and the detachment of Native Police under his command...' Henry Challinor to Attorney-General Ratcliffe Pring, 29 January 1861, Col/A12 61/359. Lieutenant Wheeler therefore had every reason to denigrate Aborigines.
59. "Native Police Force Report", 4.
60. *Minutes of Evidence*, 63.
61. Dr Challinor at pages 9, 14 and 15; Captain John Coley at p21; R.B. Sheridan at p25; A.W. Compigne at p37; J. Davies at p57 are some of the witnesses questioned on this issue.
62. *Minutes of Evidence*, 54.
63. Richard C. Trexler, *Sex and Conquest: Gendered Violence, Political Order, and the European Conquest of the Americas* (Ithaca, NY: Cornell University Press, 1995), 1.
64. Connell, *Masculinities*, 42, 74; Arthur Brittain, *Masculinity and Power* (Oxford: Basil Blackwell, 1989), 110; Jane Flax, "Postmodernism and Gender Relations in Feminist Theory", in *Feminism/Postmodernism*, ed. L. Nicholson (New York: Routledge, 1990), 51; Lynne Segal, *Slow Motion: Changing Masculinities, Changing Men* (London: Virago, 1990), 252, 254.
65. *Minutes of Evidence*, 5.
66. *Minutes of Evidence*, 26.

67. *Minutes of Evidence*, 60.
68. *Brisbane Courier*, 24 July 1861.
69. *The Guardian*, 27 July 1861
70. *Maryborough Chronicle*, 1 August 1861.
71. John Emmerson, *British Columbia and Vancouver Island: Voyages Travels and Adventures* (Durham, NC: W. Ainsley, 1865), 51–52.
72. Emmerson, *British Columbia and Vancouver Island*, 51.
73. Emmerson, British Columbia and Vancouver Island, 49.
74. William Carew Hazlitt, *British Columbia and Vancouver Island, Comprising an Historical Sketch of the British Settlements in the North-West Coast of America and a Survey of the Physical Character, Capabilities, Climate, Topography, Natural History, Geology and Ethnology of that Region, with a Map* (London: Routledge & Co., 1858), 69–70.
75. Hazlitt, *British Columbia and Vancouver Island*, 71.
76. Hazlitt, *British Columbia and Vancouver Island*, 79.
77. Hazlitt, *British Columbia and Vancouver Island*, 98.
78. Hazlitt, *British Columbia and Vancouver Island*, 190–191.
79. Hazlitt, *British Columbia and Vancouver Island*, 192.
80. Gilbert Sproat, *Scenes and Studies of a Savage Life* (London: Smith, Elder and Co., 1868), 30.
81. Sproat, *Scenes and Studies of a Savage Life*, 30.
82. Sproat, *Scenes and Studies of a Savage Life*, 120.
83. Sproat, *Scenes and Studies of a Savage Life*, 120.
84. Sproat, *Scenes and Studies of a Savage Life*, 160.
85. Sproat, *Scenes and Studies of a Savage Life*, 150–166.
86. Sproat, *Scenes and Studies of a Savage Life*, 150.
87. Sproat, *Scenes and Studies of a Savage Life*, 32.
88. Sproat, *Scenes and Studies of a Savage Life*, 62.
89. Ann Curthoys, " 'Men of all Nations, Except Chinamen': Europeans and Chinese on the Goldfields of New South Wales", in *Gold: Forgotten Histories and Lost Objects in Australia*, eds. Iain McCalman, Alexander Cook, and Andrew Reeves (Cambridge: Cambridge University Press, 2001), 104.
90. Raymond Evans, Kay Saunders, and Kathryn Cronin, *Race Relations in Colonial Queensland* (Brisbane, QLD: University of Queensland Press, 1988), 237–238.
91. E.M. Andrews, *Australia and China: The Ambiguous Relationship* (Melbourne, VIC: Melbourne University Press, 1985), 20–21; Henry Reynolds, *North of Capricorn: The Untold Story of Australia's North* (Sydney, NSW: Allen & Unwin, 2003), x; Evans et al., *Race Relations in Colonial Queensland*, 255.
92. Kay J. Anderson, *Vancouver's Chinatown: Racial Discourse in Canada, 1875–1980* (Montreal, QC: McGill-Queens University Press, 1991), 34.
93. Jin Tan and Patricia E. Roy, *The Chinese in Canada* (Saint John, NB: Canadian Historical Association, 1985), 6; Smith, "Harry Guillod's Journal of a Trip to Cariboo, 1862", 213.
94. Anderson, *Vancouver's Chinatown*, 35.
95. George Woodcock, "Cariboo and Klondike: The Gold Mines in Western Canada", *History Today*, 5 (1955), 43.
96. Anthony B. Chan, *Gold Mountain: The Chinese in the New World* (Vancouver, BC: New Star Books, 1983), 73.
97. Chan, *Gold Mountain*, 49.

98. Chan, *Gold Mountain*, 50.
99. Tan and Roy, *The Chinese in Canada*, 7.
100. Raymond Evans, *Fighting Words: Writing About Race* (St. Lucia, QLD: University of Queensland Press, 1999), 85.
101. Brisbane Courier, 17 November 1870.
102. Charles Eden, *My Wife and I in Queensland* (London: Longmans, Green & Co., 1872), 266.
103. Eden, *My Wife and I in Queensland*, 266.
104. Northern Miner, 26 May 1877, cited in Evans et al., *Race Relations in Colonial Queensland*, 249.
105. Cited in Evans, *Fighting Words: Writing About Race*, 81.
106. W.R.O. Hill, *Forty-Five Years Experiences in North Queensland* (Brisbane, QLD: Poole and Co, 1907), 48, 68; Stirling, *The Never Never Land: A Ride in North Queensland*, 66.
107. Smith, "Harry Guillod's Journal of a Trip to Cariboo, 1862", 215.
108. *The Handbook of British Columbia and Emigrant's Guide to the Gold Fields* (London: W. Oliver, 1862), 62; *Colonist*, 17 August 1865.
109. *Colonist*, 10 May 1860.
110. Government of Canada, *Report of the Royal Commission on Chinese Immigration* (1885), 164–166.
111. W. Peter Ward, *White Canada Forever: Popular Attitudes and Public Policy Towards Orientals in British Columbia* (Montreal, QC: McGill-Queens University Press, 2002), 10.
112. C.E. Barret-Lennard, *Travels in British Columbia with the Narrative of a Yacht Voyage around Vancouver's Island* (London: Hurst and Brackett, 1862), 147–148.
113. Edmund Hope Verney to his father, 14 July 1863.
114. Newton H. Chittenden, *Settlers, Prospectors, and Tourists Guide or, Travels Through British Columbia* (Victoria, TX: Newton H. Chittenden, 1882).
115. O'Bierne is the spelling used by the *Canadian Dictionary of Biography*.
116. Viscount Milton and W.B. Cheadle, *The North-West Passage by Land* (London: Cassel, Petter and Galpin, 1865), 192–193.
117. Milton and Cheadle, *The North-West Passage*, 205.
118. Milton and Cheadle, *The North-West Passage*, 210.
119. Milton and Cheadle, *The North-West Passage*, 221. Pemmican is dried and pounded buffalo meat mixed with melted fat. While life sustaining it is apparently not appealing.
120. Walter Cheadle, *Journal*, 5 June 1863 in A.G. Doughty and Gustave Lanctot, eds. *Dr Cheadle's Journal of a Trip across Canada 1862–63* (Ottawa, ON: Graphic Publishers, 1931).
121. Milton and Cheadle, *The North-West Passage*, 223.
122. Milton and Cheadle, *The North-West Passage*, 230.
123. Eden, *My Wife and I in Queensland*, 199.

6 A Hand Prepared to be Red

1. Pieter Spierenburg, ed., *Men and Violence: Gender, Honor and Rituals in Modern Europe and America* (Columbus, OH: Ohio State University Press, 1998), 1.
2. John Archer, ed., *Male Violence* (London: Routledge, 1994), 24.

3. Elizabeth Stanko, *Everyday Violence: How Women and Men Experience Sexual and Physical Danger* (London: Pandora, 1990), 5–7.
4. Brian Moon, "Theorising Violence in the Discourse of Masculinities", *Southern Review*, 24 (1992), 195.
5. Moon, "Theorising Violence in the Discourse of Masculinities", 197.
6. John E. Archer, " 'Men Behaving Badly'?: Masculinity and the Uses of Violence, 1850–1900", in *Everyday Violence in Britain, 1850–1950*, ed. Shani D'Cruze (London: Longman, 2000), 41–42.
7. V.A.C. Gatrell, "Crime, Authority and the Policeman State", in *The Cambridge Social History of Britain 1750–1950, Vol. 3*, ed. F.M.L. Thompson (Cambridge: Cambridge University Press, 1990).
8. Gatrell, "Crime, Authority and the Policeman State", 296–297.
9. Henry Mayhew, *London Labour and the London Poor* (London: Griffen, Bohn & Company, 1861), especially Volume 4 which is devoted to "vice" and crime; Charles Booth, *Life and Labour of the People of London, Vol. 1* (London: Macmillan, 1902), 6, 37.
10. Judith Rowbotham, "Only When Drunk: The Stereotyping of Violence in England, C. 1850–1900", in *Everyday Violence in Britain, 1850–1950*, ed. Shani D'Cruze (London: Longman, 2000), 159.
11. Shani D'Cruze, ed., *Everyday Violence in Britain, 1850–1950* (London: Longman, 2000), 3; J.A. Mangan, "Social Darwinism and Upper-Class Education in Late Victorian and Edwardian England", in *Manliness and Morality: Middle Class Masculinity in Britain and America*, eds. J.A. Mangan and James Walvin (Manchester: Manchester University Press, 1987); Edward Royle, *Modern Britain: A Social History 1750–1997* (London: Arnold, 1997), 364.
12. Thomas Hughes, *Tom Brown's Schooldays* (London: Cassell and Company, 1907), 227.
13. Rowbotham, "Only when Drunk", 159.
14. D'Cruze, *Everyday Violence in Britain*, 15.
15. Raymond Evans, "A Gun in the Oven: Masculinism and Gendered Violence", in *Gender Relations in Australia: Domination and Negotiation*, eds. Kay Saunders and Raymond Evans (Sydney, NSW: Harcourt, 1994), 203.
16. *Brisbane Courier*, 26 December 1867.
17. Marilyn Lake, "Frontier Feminism and the Marauding White Man", *Journal of Australian Studies*, 49 (1996), 12–20.
18. Kay Saunders, "The Study of Domestic Violence in Queensland: Sources and Problems", *Historical Studies*, 21, no. 82 (1984), 78.
19. Nicola Henningham, " 'Perhaps If There Had Been More Women in the North, the Story Would Have Been Different': Gender and the History of White Settlement in North Queensland, 1840–1930", PhD Thesis (Department of History, Melbourne University, Melbourne, VIC, 1999), 159.
20. David Adams, ed., *The Letters of Rachel Henning* (Sydney, NSW: Angus and Robertson, 1963), 154.
21. Cited in Katie Spearritt, "The Market for Marriage in Colonial Queensland", *Hecate*, 16, no. 1 (1990), 34.
22. Cited in Katie Spearritt, "The Poverty of Protection: Women and Marriage in Colonial Queensland", Honours Thesis (Department of History, University of Queensland, Brisbane, QLD, 1988), 31.

23. George Carrington, *Colonial Adventures and Experiences by a University Man* (London: Bell and Daldy, 1871), 256.
24. Richard Symes Alford, "Memoirs of Years Gone By and Other Items", 1908, 23, FL DU272.A54.A3.
25. Alford, "Memoirs", 11.
26. Alford, "Memoirs", 14–16.
27. Carrington, *Colonial Adventures and Experiences*, 80.
28. C.D. Rowley, *The Destruction of Aboriginal Society* (Canberra, ACT: ANU Press, 1970), 157.
29. Patrick Collins, *Goodbye Bussamarai: The Mandandanji Land War, Southern Queensland 1842–1852* (St. Lucia, QLD: University of Queensland Press, 2002); Tony Roberts, *Frontier Justice: A History of the Gulf Country to 1900* (Brisbane, QLD: University of Queensland Press, 2005).
30. Henry Reynolds, "The Unrecorded Battlefields of Queensland", in *Race Relations in North Queensland*, ed. Henry Reynolds (Townsville, QLD: James Cook University, 1978), 23, 28.
31. Raymond Evans, Kay Saunders, and Kathryn Cronin, *Exclusion, Exploitation and Extermination: Race Relations in Colonial Queensland* (Sydney, NSW: ANZ, 1975), 29.
32. George Leslie to William Leslie, 1 January 1844. John Oxley Library, OM71-43/2.
33. Edmund Morey to Colonial Secretary, 12 September 1862, QSA Col/A32, 62/2239.
34. Commissioner for Crown Lands Stephen Simpson to Colonial Secretary, 13 July 1842, in Peter K. Lauer, ed., *The Simpson Letterbook, Cultural and Historical Records of Queensland* (Brisbane, QLD: Queensland University Printery, 1979).
35. Edward Palmer, *Early Days in North Queensland* (Sydney, NSW: Angus & Robertson, 1903), 213–214.
36. Oscar De Satgé, *Pages from the Journal of a Queensland Squatter* (London: Hurst and Blackett, 1901), 160.
37. De Satgé, *Pages from the Journal of a Queensland Squatter*, 160.
38. Allan McPherson, *Maranoa 70 Years Ago and How I Lost Mt. Abundance*, 1879, Fryer Library, University of Queensland, F1500, n.p.
39. McPherson, *Maranoa 70 Years Ago and How I Lost Mt. Abundance*, n.p.
40. Anthony Trollope, *Australia*. P.D. Joyce and R.B. Edwards eds. (Brisbane, QLD: University of Queensland Press, 1967[1873]), 103.
41. Anthony Trollope, *Australia*, 107.
42. George Cain to Elizabeth Miles, 7 May 1866 in B.J Dalton ed. *News from Nulla: Correspondence of Rebecca and George Cain, 1866–71* (Townsville, QLD: Department of History and Politics, James Cook University, 1991), 3.
43. George Leslie to his parents, 24 June 1841. John Oxley Library, OM71-43/2.
44. Adele Perry, *On the Edge of Empire: Gender, Race, and the Making of British Columbia* (Toronto, ON: University of Toronto Press, 2001), 44.
45. Perry, *On the Edge of Empire*, 44.
46. Cole Harris, *The Resettlement of British Columbia: Essays on Colonialism and Geographical Change* (Vancouver, BC: UBC Press, 1997), 46.
47. George Woodcock, *British Columbia: A History of the Province* (Vancouver, BC: Douglas and McIntyre, 1990), 56. See also Barry M. Gough, *Gunboat*

Frontier: British Maritime Authority and Northwest Coast Indians, 1846–1890 (Vancouver, BC: UBC Press, 1984), 32–72.
48. Woodcock, *British Columbia*, 57.
49. Malcolm McLeod, ed., *Peace River. A Canoe Voyage from Hudson's Bay to Pacific, by the Late Sir George Simpson (Governor, Hon. Hudson's Bay Company) in 1828 Journal of the late Chief Factor, Archibald MacDonald (Hon. Hudson's Bay Company) who Accompanied Him*, cited in Cole Harris, *The Resettlement of British Columbia*, 30.
50. Malcolm McLeod cited in Harris, 31.
51. Matthew Begbie to James Douglas, 3 February 1859, British Columbia, Colonial Correspondence (Inward Correspondence to the Colonial Government), BCA, file 142a.
52. Fisher, *Contact and Conflict*, 98.
53. James Douglas to Captain Frederick Montressor, 24 August 1858, Vancouver Island, Governor, Correspondence Outward, cited in Fisher, 99.
54. Kinahan Corwallis, *The New Eldorado or British Columbia* (London: Thomas Cautley Newby, 1858), 223.
55. Wilson Duff, *The Indian History of British Columbia* (Victoria, BC: Royal British Columbia Museum, 1997), 59; Woodcock, *British Columbia*, 115.
56. Henry Spencer Palmer, *Report of a Journey of Survey from Victoria to Fort Alexandria via Bentinck Arm* (New Westminster, BC: UBCL Microforms, 1863), 12.
57. Mel Rothenberger, *The Chilcotin War* (Langley, BC: Mr. Paperback, 1978), 41.
58. John Gascoigne, *The Enlightenment and the Origins of European Australia* (Melbourne, VIC: Cambridge University Press, 2002), xi, 3.
59. Genevieve Lloyd, *The Man of Reason: "Male" and "Female" in Western Philosophy* (London: Methuen, 1984), x.
60. Connell, *Masculinities*, 90.
61. V.J. Seidler, *Rediscovering Masculinity: Reason, Language and Sexuality* (London: Routledge, 1989), 5.
62. Seidler, *Rediscovering Masculinity*, 4.
63. George Pearce Sercold, *Memoirs* (Unpublished, Canberra: Australian National Library, 1908). Cited in Gordon Reid, *A Nest of Hornets: The Massacre of the Fraser Family at Hornet Bank Station, Central Queensland, 1957, and Related Events* (Melbourne, VIC: Oxford University Press, 1982), 161.
64. Henry Stuart Russell, *The Genesis of Queensland* (Toowoomba, QLD: Vintage Books, 1989), 211.
65. J.T.S. Bird, *The Early History of Rockhampton: Dealing with Events Chiefly Up Till 1870* (Rockhampton, QLD: The Morning Bulletin, 1904), 5.
66. Russell, *The Genesis of Queensland*, 211.
67. Reid, *A Nest of Hornets*, 161.
68. *Rockhampton Bulletin*, 7 September 1871.
69. W.H. Wiseman, Rannes, to Commissioner for Crown Lands, Sydney, 28 August 1855, Q.S.A. Class No. CCL7/G1.
70. W.H. Wiseman, Rannes, to C.C.L., Sydney, 5 January 1856, Q.S.A. Class No. CCL7/G1.
71. W.H. Wiseman, Rannes, to C.C.L., Sydney, 5 January 1856, Q.S.A. Class No. CCL7/G1.
72. W.H. Wiseman to C.C.L., Sydney, 5 January 1856.

73. W.H. Wiseman, Rannes, to C.C.L., Sydney, 5 January 1856, QSA Class No. CCL7/G1.
74. W.H. Wiseman to C.C.L., Sydney, 5 January 1856.
75. John Beynon, *Masculinities and Culture* (Buckingham: Open University Press, 2002), 33.
76. Zillah Eisenstein, "Developing a Theory of Capitalist Patriarchy and Socialist Feminism", in *Capitalist Patriarchy and the Case for Socialist Feminism*, ed. Zillah R. Esienstein (New York: Monthly Review Press, 1979), 5.
77. Jean Lipman-Bluman, *Gender Roles and Power* (New Jersey: Prentice-Hall, 1984), cited in Arthur Brittan, *Masculinity and Power* (Oxford: Basil Blackwell, 1989), 7; Leonore Davidoff and Catherine Hall, *Family Fortunes: Men and Women of the English Middle Class* (London: Routledge, 1992), 229.
78. *Canadian Dictionary of Biography* (Toronto, ON: University of Toronto Press, 1966), 696; W.K. Lamb, "Introduction", in *The Fraser Mines Vindicated*, ed. Alfred Penderill Waddington (Fairfield, WA: Ye Galleon Press, [1858]2000), 11.
79. Alfred Waddington, letter to the editor *British Colonist*, 1 August 1862.
80. George Woodcock, *British Columbia: A History of the Province* (Vancouver, BC: Douglas McIntyre, 1990), 115.
81. Chartres Brew to Governor Seymour, 23 May 1864, British Columbia Colonial Correspondence BCA, GR1372.
82. R.C. Lundin Brown, Rev., *Klatsassan* (London: Society for Promoting Christian Knowledge, 1873), 15–16.
83. *British Colonist*, 10 May 1864.
84. *Daily Chronicle*, 12 May 1864.
85. *British Colonist*, 13 May 1864.
86. *British Columbian*, 14 May 1864.
87. *British Columbian*, 18 May 1864.
88. Henry Reynolds, *Frontier* (Sydney, NSW; Allen and Unwin, 1987), 47–48. A full account of the Hornet Bank massacre and its aftermath is given in Reid, *A Nest of Hornets*.
89. J.I. Little, "The Foundations of Government", in *The Pacific Province: A History of British Columbia*, ed. Hugh J.M. Johnston (Vancouver, BC: Douglas & McIntyre, 1996), 76.
90. Harris, *The Resettlement of British Columbia*, 81.
91. Waddington, *The Fraser Mines Vindicated*, 56.

7 A Wild Self-Dependence of Character

1. John Emmerson, *British Columbia and Vancouver Island: Voyages Travels and Adventures* (Durham, NC: W.M. Ainsley, 1865), 1.
2. Peter Coleman, "Introduction: The New Australia", in *Australian Civilization*, ed. Peter Coleman (Sydney, NSW: F.W. Cheshire, 1962), 1.
3. Russel Ward, *The Australian Legend* (Melbourne, VIC: Oxford University Press, 1958), 2.
4. Coleman, "The New Australia", 2.
5. http://www.outbackspectacular.com.au [accessed 30 June 2007].
6. Graeme Turner, *Making It National: Nationalism and Australian Popular Culture* (Sydney, NSW: Allen & Unwin, 1994), 9.

7. Richard Nile, *The Australian Legend and Its Discontents* (Brisbane, QLD: University of Queensland Press, 2000), 3.
8. Lee Kernaghan, "The Spirit of the Bush", WM Australia, 2007.
9. Elizabeth Furniss, *The Burden of History: Colonialism and the Frontier Myth in a Rural Canadian Community* (Vancouver, BC: UBC Press, 1999), 58.
10. Daniel Francis, *National Dreams: Myth Memory and Canadian History* (Vancouver, BC: Arsenal Pump Press, 1997), 10.

Bibliography

Primary Sources

Manuscripts

Alford, Richard Symes. "Memoirs of years Gone By and Other Items". (1908). FL DU272.A54.A3.

A.L. Fortune Miscellenea, University of British Columbia Rare Book as and Special Collections, VF-48.

An Account by Ernest Henry of an Exploring Trip Resulting in the Taking Up of Hughenden Station. FL, mss 2/1239-1244.

Bayley, Charles Alford. "Early Life on Vancouver Island". (n.d.). BCA, Add Mss E/B/B34.2.

Blair, George. Diary 17 February 1862-29 December 1863. BCA Add mss186.

British Columbia, Colonial Correspondence (Inward Correspondence to the Colonial Government), BCA, GR-1372, file 142a.

Government of Canada, *Report of the Royal Commission on Chinese Immigration* (1885), UBCL Microforms, CIHM14563.

Harkness, Robert. Correspondence Outward: Personal Letters to His Wife, 1812-1865, BCA, EB H22A.

Hayward, Charles. Diary 1862. BCA A00714.

Hayward Family Business, Personal and Political Papers, 1862-1963, BCA, Mss-0503

Henderson, R. Diary 1862-1863. FL, Mss, F1517.

Historical Records of Australia. Sydney, NSW: Library Committee of the Commonwealth Parliament, 1914-1925. FL, DU80.H49.

Hogg, J.J., *An Early Day Rush: Reminiscences,* 1873. FL, Mss F357.

Leslie Family Papers, JOL, OM71-43.

McConnel Family Papers, FL, Mss, F89/5.

McMicking, Robert Personal and Business Records 1862-1910, BCA, MS-117.

McPherson, Allan. *Maranoa 70 Years Ago and How I Lost Mt. Abundance.* 1879, FL, mss, F1500.

Neame, Arthur. *A Few Reminiscences of North Queensland by One of the Early Pioneers.* JOL, OM65-09.

Palmer, Henry Spencer. *Report of a Journey of Survey from Victoria to Fort Alexandria via Bentinck Arm.* New Westminster, BC: UBCL Microforms. CIHM52681, 1863.

Papers of Reverend Henry Stobart, FL Mic 7368.

Particulars of Ernest Henry's Family, Supplied by his Daughter Miss Ernestine Henry and an Account Given by His Brother Arthur Henry. FL, mss2/1239-1244.

Pidcock, R.H. *Adventures on Vancouver Island. Being an account of six years residence, and of hunting and fishing excursions with some account of the Indians inhabiting the island.* 1862. BCA, Ddd Mss728, Vol. 4a.

Queensland, Colonial Correspondence, Inward Correspondence to the Colonial Secretary, QSA, A/322.
Sercold, George Pearce. *Memoirs*. Unpublished. Canberra, ACT: Australian National Library, 1908.
Whish, Claudius Buchanan. Diaries 1862–1906, JOL, OM65-33.
Wiseman Letter Book, QSA, CCL7/G1

Newspapers

British Columbian
British Colonist
Edinburgh Review
Kamloops Sentinel
Rockhampton Bulletin
Saturday Review
Victoria Chronicle
Brisbane Courier
Guardian
Maryborough Chronicle
Northern Miner

Published Primary Works

Adams, David, ed. *The Letters of Rachel Henning*. Sydney, NSW: Angus and Robertson, 1963.
Allen, Chas H. *A Visit to Queensland and Her Goldfields*. London: Chapman and Hall, 1870.
Arnold, Thomas. *Introductory Lectures on Modern History*. London: Fellowes, 1849.
Barret-Lennard, C.E. *Travels in British Columbia with the Narrative of a Yacht Voyage around Vancouver's Island*. London: Hurst and Brackett, 1862.
Bartley, Nehemiah. *Australian Pioneers and Reminiscences: Together with Portraits of Some of the Founders of Australia*. Brisbane, QLD: Gordon and Gotch, 1896.
Bennett, M.M. *Christison of Lammermoor*. London: Alston Rivers Ltd, 1927.
Berens, Edward. *Advice to Young Men, Particularly Those in Country Villages*. Oxford: W. Baxter, 1831.
Bird, J.T.S. *The Early History of Rockhampton: Dealing with Events Chiefly Up Till 1870*. Rockhampton, QLD: The Morning Bulletin, 1904.
Booth, Charles. *Life and Labour of the People of London*, Vol. 1. London: Macmillan, 1902.
Carrington, George. *Colonial Adventures and Experiences by a University Man*. London: Bell and Daldy, 1871.
Chittenden, Newton H. *Settlers, Prospectors, and Tourists Guide or, Travels through British Columbia*. Victoria, TX: Newton H. Chittenden, 1882.
Cobbett, William. *Advice to Young Men*. London: Ward Lock & Co, [1829]1911.
Coleridge, Samuel Taylor. *Aids to Reflection*, 10th ed. London: Edward Moxon & Co., [1825]1863.
Cornwallis, Kinahan. *The New Eldorado or British Columbia*. London: Thomas Cautley Newby, 1858.

Dalton, B.J., ed. *News from the Nulla: Correspondence of Rebecca and George Cain, 1866–71*. Townsville, QLD: James Cook University Department of History and Politics, 1991.

Demarr, James. *Adventures in Australia Fifty Years Ago*. London: Swan Sonnenschein & Co, 1893.

Doughty, A.G., and Gustave Lanctot, eds. *Dr Cheadle's Journal of a Trip across Canada 1862–63*. Ottawa, ON: Graphic Publishers, 1931.

Eden, Charles H. *My Wife and I in Queensland*. London: Longmans, Green & Co, 1872.

Eden, Charles H. *Australia's Heroes*. London: Society for Promoting Christian Knowledge, 1882.

Emmerson, John. *British Columbia and Vancouver Island: Voyages Travels and Adventures*. Durham, NC: W. Ainsley, 1865.

Fisher, Robin, and J.M. Bumstead, eds. *An Account of a Voyage to the Northwest Coast of America in 1785 and 1786 by Alexander Walker*. Vancouver/Seattle: Douglas and McIntyre/University of Washington Press, 1982.

Fortune, A.L. "The Overlanders of 1862". *Kamloops Sentinel*, 27 November–24 December, 1936.

Grainger, M. Allerdale. *Woodsman of the West*. London: Edward Arnold, 1908.

Handbook of British Columbia and Emigrant's Guide to the Gold Fields. London: W. Oliver, 1862.

Hazlitt, William Carew. *British Columbia and Vancouver Island, Comprising an Historical Sketch of the British Settlements in the North-West Coast of America and a Survey of the Physical Character, Capabilities, Climate, Topography, Natural History, Geology and Ethnology of That Region, with a Map*. London: Routledge & Co, 1858.

Hill, W.R.O. *Forty-Five Years Experiences in North Queensland*. Brisbane, OLD: Poole and Co, 1907.

Hughes, Thomas. *Tom Brown's Schooldays/by an Old Boy*. London: Cassell and Company, 1907.

Hughes, Thomas. *The Manliness of Christ*. London: Macmillan, 1879.

Kerr, J.B. *Biographical Dictionary of Well Known British Columbians with a Historical Sketch*. Vancouver, BC: Kerr and Begg, 1890.

Kingsley, Charles. *Discipline and Other Sermons*. London: Macmillan, 1890.

Lamb, W.K., ed. "The Diary of Robert Melrose Part 1". *British Columbia Historical Quarterly* 7, no. 2 (1943): 119–34.

Lamb, W.K., ed. "The Diary of Robert Melrose Part 2". *British Columbia Historical Quarterly* 7, no. 3 (1943): 199–218.

Lamb, W.K., ed. "The Diary of Robert Melrose Part 3". *British Columbia Historical Quarterly* 7, no. 4 (1943): 283–95.

Lauer, Peter K., ed. *The Simpson Letterbook*. Transcribed by Gerry Langevad, Cultural and Historical Records of Queensland. Brisbane, QLD: Queensland University Printery, 1979.

Leduc, Joanne, ed. *Overland from Canada to British Columbia by Mr. Thomas McMicking of Queenston, Canada West*. Vancouver, BC: UBC Press, 1981.

Letters to Young People Single and Married Re-Written by an English Author after Timothy Titcomb. Friendly Counsel Series. London: Ward, Lock, and Tyler, 187*.

Lundin-Brown, R.C., Rev. *Klatsassan*. London: Society for Promoting Christian Knowledge, 1873.

Lundin-Brown, R.C., Rev. *British Columbia: An Essay*. New Westminster: Royal Engineers Press, 1863.
Mayhew, Henry. *London Labour and the London Poor*. London: Griffen, Bohn & Company, 1861.
McLeod, Malcolm, ed. *A Canoe Voyage from Hudson's Bay to Pacific, by the late Sir George Simpson; (Governor, Hon. Hudson's Bay Company) in 1828 Journal of the late Chief Factor, Archibald MacDonald (Hon. Hudson's Bay Company) who Accompanied Him*.
McMicking, Thomas. "An Account of a Journey Overland from Canada to British Columbia during the Summer of 1862". *The British Columbian*, November 1862–January 1863.
Milton, Viscount, and W.B. Cheadle. *The North-West Passage by Land*. London: Cassel, Petter and Galpin, 1865.
Mitchell, Lt. Col. Sir. T.L. *Journal of an Expedition into the Interior of Tropical Australia in Search of a Route from Sydney to the Gulf of Carpentaria*. London: Longman, Brown, Green and Longmans, 1848.
Official Year Book of the Commonwealth of Australia, no. 23, 1930.
Palmer, Edward. *Early Days in North Queensland*. Sydney, NSW: Angus & Robertson, 1903.
Palmer, Henry Spencer. *Report of a Journey of Survey from Victoria to Fort Alexandria via Bentinck Arm*. New Westminster, BC: Royal Engineers Press, 1863.
Preston, Richard Arthur, ed. *For Friends at Home: A Scottish Immigrants Letters from Canada, California and the Cariboo 1844–1864*. Montreal, QC: McGill-Queens University Press, 1974.
Pritchard, Allan, ed. *Vancouver Island Letters of Edmund Hope Verney 1862–65*. Vancouver, BC: UBC Press, 1996.
Queensland Legislative Assembly, "Native Police Report and Minutes of Evidence", 1861 QV&P. FL, MIC4620.
Richmond, Frederick. *Queensland in the Seventies*. Singapore: C.A. Ribeiro, 1928.
Russell, Henry Stuart. *The Genesis of Queensland*. Toowoomba, QLD: Vintage Books, 1989.
Secker, William. *A Wedding Ring, Fit for the Finger, Laid Open in a Sermon, Preached at a Wedding in St. Edmond's*. Glasgow: The Chapman's Library, 1877.
Smiles, Samuel. *Self-Help*. Oxford: Oxford University Press, 1859/2002.
Smith, Dorothy Blakey, ed. "Harry Guillod's Journal of a Trip to Cariboo, 1862". *British Columbia Historical Quarterly* 19 (1955): 187–232.
Smith, Dorothy Blakey, ed. "The Journal of Arthur Thomas Bushby". *British Columbia Historical Quarterly* 21 (1957): 83–159.
Smith, Dorothy Blakey, ed. *The Reminiscences of Doctor John Sebastian Helmcken*. Vancouver, BC: UBC Press, 1975.
Sproat, Gilbert Malcolm. *Scenes and Studies of Savage Life*. London: Smith, Elder and Co, 1868.
Stamer, W. *The Gentleman Emigrant: His Daily Life, Sports and Pastimes in Canada, Australia, and the United States*. London: Tinsley Brothers, 1874.
Stirling, A.W. *The Never Never Land: A Ride in North Queensland*. London: Sampson Low, Marston, Searle, and Rivington, 1884.
Trollope, Anthony. *Australia*. Edited by P.D. Edwards and R.B. Joyce. Brisbane, QLD: University of Queensland Press, 1967 [1873].
Tyrwhitt, W.S.S. *A New Chum in the Queensland Bush*. Oxford: Vincent, 1888?

Waddington, Alfred Pendrill. *The Fraser Mines Vindicated*. Fairfield, CA: Ye Galleon Press, 2000. First published 1858.
William, Telfer. *The Wallabahdah Manuscript: Recollections of the Early Days: The Early History of the Northern Districts of New South Wales*. Edited by Roger Milliss. Sydney, NSW: University of New South Wales Press, 1980.
Wolfenden, Madge. "Career of a Scotch Boy Who Became Hon. John Tod: An Unfashionable True Story, by Gilbert Malcolm Sproat". *British Columbia Historical Quarterly* 18 (1954): 133–238.
Wright, Charlotte May. *Memories of Far Off Days: The Memoirs of Charlotte May Wright 1855–1929/Edited with Afterword and Additional Family Historical Notes by Peter A. Wright*. Armidale, NSW: P.A. Wright, 1988.

Secondary Sources

Adams, James Eli. *Dandies and Desert Saints*. Ithaca, NY: Cornell University Press, 1995.
Aldrich, Robert, ed. *Gay Perspectives II: More Essays in Australian Gay Culture*. Sydney, NSW: Department of Economic History with the Australian Centre for Gay and Lesbian Research University of Sydney, 1994.
Aldrich, Robert. *Colonialism and Homosexuality*. London: Routledge, 2003.
Alexander, Fred. *Moving Frontiers: An American Theme and Its Application to Australian History*. Port Washington, NY: Kennikat Press, 1969.
Allen, H.C. *Bush and Backwoods: A Comparison of the Frontier in Australia and the United States*. Sydney, NSW: Angus and Robertson, 1959.
Allingham, Anne. *Taming the Wilderness*. Studies in North Queensland History No.1. Townsville, QLD: Department of History, James Cook University, 1978.
Altman, Denis. "The Myth of Mateship". *Meanjin* 46, no. 2 (1987): 163–72.
Anderson, Kay J. *Vancouver's Chinatown: Racial Discourse in Canada, 1875–1980*. Montreal, QC: McGill-Queens University Press, 1991.
Anderson, Warwick. *The Cultivation of Whiteness: Science, Health and Racial Destiny in Australia*. Melbourne, VIC: Melbourne University Press, 2002.
Andrews, E.M. *Australia and China: The Ambiguous Relationship*. Melbourne, VIC: Melbourne University Press, 1985.
Archer, John, ed. *Male Violence*. London: Routledge, 1994.
Atwood, Margaret. *Strange Things: The Malevolent North in Canadian Literature*. Oxford: Clarendon Press, 1995.
Attwood, Bain, and John Arnold. *Power, Knowledge and Aborigines, Journal of Australian Studies*. Melbourne, VIC: La Trobe University Press, 1992.
Attwood, Bain, and S.G. Foster, eds. *Frontier Conflict: The Australian Experience*. Canberra, ACT: National Museum of Australia, 2003.
Banton, Michael. *The Idea of Race*. Cambridge: Tavistock, 1977.
Barman, Jean. "Taming Aboriginal Sexuality: Gender, Power, and Race in British Columbia, 1850–1900". *BC Studies* Autumn/Winter 97/98 (1997): 237–66.
Barman, Jean. *The West Beyond the West: A History of British Columbia*. Toronto, ON: University of Toronto Press, 1991.
Barrett, Lindsay. "The Self-Made Man: Narrative and National Character in Post-War Australia". *Southern Review* 25, no. 1 (1992): 78–105.

Bederman, Gail. *Manliness and Civilization: A Cultural History of Gender and Race in the United States 1880–1917*. Chicago, IL: University of Chicago Press, 1995.

Begg, Alexander. *History of British Columbia from Its Earliest Discovery to the Present Time*. Toronto, ON: McGraw-Hill Ryerson, 1972.

Berger, Mark T. "Imperialism and Sexual Exploitation: A Response to Ronald Hyam's 'Empire and Sexual Opportunity' ". *Journal of Imperial and Commonwealth History* 17, no. 1 (1988): 83–89.

Bernasconi, Robert, ed. *Race*. Oxford: Blackwell, 2001.

Beynon, John. *Masculinities and Culture*. Buckingham: Open University Press, 2002.

Biber, Katherine, Tom Sear, and Dave Trudinger. *Playing the Man: New Approaches to Masculinity*. Sydney, NSW: Pluto Press, 1999.

Biddis, Michael D. *Images of Race*. New York: Holmes & Meiers, 1979.

Billington, Ray Allen. *Westward Expansion: A History of the American Frontier*. New York: Macmillan, 1960.

Blainey, Geoffrey. *The Tyranny of Distance*. Melbourne, VIC: Sun Books, 1966.

Bolton, G.C. *A Thousand Miles Away: A History of North Queensland to 1920*. Brisbane, QLD: Jacaranda Press, 1963.

Bradley, Ian. *The Call to Seriousness: The Evangelical Impact on the Victorians*. London: Johnathon Cape, 1976.

Breward, Christopher. *The Culture of Fashion*. Manchester: Manchester University Press, 1995.

Briggs, Asa. *The Age of Improvement: 1783–1867*. Harlow: Longman, 1959.

Bristow, Joseph. *Empire Boys: Adventures in a Man's World*. London: Harper Collins, 1991.

Brittan, Arthur. *Masculinity and Power*. Oxford: Basil Blackwell, 1989.

Broome, Richard. *Aboriginal Australians*. Sydney, NSW: Allen and Unwin, 1994.

Brown, Jennifer S.H. *Strangers in Blood: Fur Trade Company Families in Indian Country*. Norman, OK: University of Oklahoma Press, 1996.

Bullough, Vern L. *Homosexuality: A History*. New York: Meridian, 1979.

Canadian Dictionary of Biography. Toronto, ON: University of Toronto Press, 1966.

Cannadine, David. *Ornamentalism: How the British Saw Their Empire*. London: Penguin, 2002.

Carnes, Mark C., and Clyde Griffen, eds. *Meanings for Manhood: Constructions of Masculinity in Victorian America*. Chicago, IL: University of Chicago Press, 1990.

Carter, Paul. *The Road to Botany Bay: An Essay in Spatial History*. London: Faber and Faber, 1987.

Chan, Anthony B. *Gold Mountain: The Chinese in the New World*. Vancouver, BC: New Star Books, 1983.

Charters Towers Centenary. Charters Towers, QLD: Charters Towers City Council, 1972.

Cilento, Sir Raphael, and Clem Lack. *Triumph in the Tropics: An Historical Sketch of Queensland*. Brisbane, QLD: Simon and Paterson, 1959.

Clark, C.M.H. *A History of Australia V.II: The Beginning of an Australian Civilisation 1824–1851*. Melbourne, VIC: Melbourne University Press, 1962.

Clarke, Anna. *The Struggle for the Breeches: Gender and the Making of the British Working Class*. Berkeley, CA: University of California Press, 1995.

Clayton, Daniel W. *Islands of Truth: The Imperial Fashioning of Vancouver Island*. Vancouver, BC: UBC Press, 2000.

Critchett, Jan. *A 'Distant Field of Murder': Western District Frontiers 1834–1848*. Melbourne, VIC: Melbourne University Press, 1990.
Coleman, Peter, ed. *Australian Civilisation*. Melbourne, VIC: F.W. Cheshire, 1962.
Collier, James. *The Pastoral Age in Australia*. London: Whitcombe & Tombs Limited, 1911.
Collini, Stefan. *Public Moralists: Political Thought and Intellectual Life in Britain 1850–1930*. Oxford: Clarendon Press, 1991.
Collins, Patrick. *Goodbye Bussamarai: The Mandandanji Land War, Southern Queensland 1842–1852*. St. Lucia: University of Queensland Press, 2002.
Connell, R.W. *Masculinities*. Sydney, NSW: Allen & Unwin, 1995.
Cooper, Frederick, and Ann Laura Stoler eds. *Tensions of Empire: Colonial Cultures in a Bourgeois World*. Berkley, CA: University of California Press, 1997.
Crosby, E.B.V., and J.C. Hodge. *The Aborigines of Queensland*, Rev. Ed. Brisbane, QLD: Queensland Museum, 1968.
Crotty, Martin. *Making the Australian Male: Middle-Class Masculinity 1870–1920*. Melbourne, VIC: Melbourne University Press, 2000.
Davidoff, Leonore, and Catherine Hall. *Family Fortunes: Men and Women of the English Middle Class*. London: Routledge, 1992.
Davidoff, Leonore, McCleland Keith, and Eleni Varikas. *Gender and History: Retrospect and Prospect*. Oxford: Blackwell, 1999.
D'Cruze, Shani, ed. *Everyday Violence in Britain, 1850–1950*. London: Longman, 2000.
de Man, Paul. "Autobiography as De-Facement". *Modern Language Notes* 94 (1979): 919–30.
Delany, Paul. *British Autobiography in the Seventeenth Century*. London: Routledge and Kegan Paul, 1969.
Deslandes, Paul R. *Oxbridge Men: British Masculinity and the Undergraduate Experience, 1850–1920*. Bloomington, IN: Indiana University Press, 2005.
Disraeli, Benjamin. *Tancred*. London: R. Brimley Johnson, 1904.
Dixon, Robert. *The Course of Empire: Neo-Classical Culture in New South Wales 1788–1860*. Melbourne, VIC: Oxford University Press, 1986.
Dixon, Robert. *Writing the Colonial Adventure: Race, Gender and Nation in Anglo-Australian Popular Fiction, 1875–1914*. Melbourne, VIC: Cambridge University Press, 1995.
Dixson, Miriam. *The Real Matilda: Women and Identity in Australia – 1788 to the Present*. Sydney, NSW: University of NSW Press, 1999.
Duberman, Martin, Martha Vicinus, and George Chauncey Jr., eds. *Hidden from History: Reclaiming the Gay & Lesbian Past*. New York: Meridian, 1990.
Duff, Wilson. *The Indian History of British Columbia*. Victoria, BC: Royal British Columbia Museum, 1997.
Dunae, Patrick A. *Gentleman Emigrants: From the British Public Schools to the Canadian Frontier*. Vancouver, BC: Douglas and McIntyre, 1981.
Dutton, Geoffrey, ed. *The Literature of Australia*. Melbourne, VIC: Penguin, 1976.
Dutton, Geoffrey. *The Squatters: An Illustrated History of Australia's Pastoral Pioneers*. Melbourne: Viking O'Neil, 1985.
Dyer, Richard. *White*. London: Routledge, 1997.
Eagleton, Terry. *Literary Theory: An Introduction*. Oxford: Basil Blackwell, 1983.
Edmonds, Penelope. *Urbanizing Frontiers: Indigenous Peoples and Settlers in 19th-Century Pacific Rim Cities*. Vancouver, BC: UBC Press, 2010.

Eisenstein, Zillah R., ed. *Capitalist Patriarchy and the Case for Socialist Feminism.* New York: Monthly Review Press, 1979.

Elder, Bruce. *Blood on the Wattle: Massacres and Maltreatment of Aboriginal Australians since 1788.* Sydney, NSW: New Holland, 1988.

Entwistle, Joanne. *The Fashioned Body: Fashion, Dress and Modern Social Theory.* Cambridge: Polity Press, 2000.

Evans, Ray, and Bill Thorpe. "Indigenocide and the Massacre of Aboriginal History". *Overland* 163 (2001): 21–29.

Evans, Raymond. "The Owl and the Eagle: The Significance of Race in Colonial Queensland". *Social Alternatives* 5, no. 4 (1986): 16–22.

Evans, Raymond. *Fighting Words: Writing about Race.* St. Lucia, QLD: University of Queensland Press, 1999.

Evans, Raymond. *A History of Queensland.* Melbourne, VIC: Cambridge University Press, 2007.

Evans, Raymond, and Bill Thorpe. "Commanding Men: Masculinities and the Convict System". *Journal of Australian Studies* 22, no. 56 (1998): 17–34.

Evans, Raymond, Kay Saunders, and Kathryn Cronin. *Exclusion, Exploitation and Extermination: Race Relations in Colonial Queensland.* Sydney, NSW: ANZ, 1975.

Faragher, John M., ed. *Rereading Frederick Jackson Turner.* New Haven: Yale University Press, 1998.

Fairburn, Miles. *The Ideal Society and Its Enemies: The Foundations of Modern New Zealand Society 1850–1900.* Auckland: Auckland University Press, 1984.

Figuier, L. *The Human Race.* Edited and Revised by Robert Wilson. London: Cassell c, 1880.

Fisher, Robin. "Joseph Trutch and Indian Land Policy". *BC Studies* Winter 71/72, no. 12 (1971): 3–33.

Fisher, Robin. *Contact and Conflict.* Vancouver, BC: UBC Press, 1992.

Fitzgerald, Ross. *From the Dreaming to 1915: A History of Queensland.* Brisbane, QLD: UQP, 1982.

Forrestall, Nancy M., Kathryn M. McPherson, and Cecilia Morgan. *Gendered Pasts: Historical Essays in Femininity and Masculinity.* Don Mills, ON: Oxford University Press, 1999.

Fout, John C., ed. *Forbidden History: The State, Society and the Regulation of Sexuality in Modern Europe.* Chicago, IL: Chicago University Press, 1992.

Francis, Daniel. *National Dreams: Myth Memory and Canadian History.* Vancouver, BC: Arsenal Pump Press, 1997.

Frankenberg, Ruth. *White Women, Race Matters: The Social Construction of Whiteness.* London: Routledge, 1993.

Frederickson, George M. *Racism: A Short History.* Melbourne, VIC: Scribe Publications, 2002.

French, Maurice. *A Pastoral Romance: The Tribulation and Triumph of Squatterdom.* Toowoomba, QLD: USQ Press, 1990.

Frideres, James S. *Native People in Canada: Contemporary Conflicts.* Scarborough, ON: Prentice-Hall Canada, 1983.

Friesen, Gerald. *Citizens and Nation: An Essay on History, Communication, and Canada.* Toronto, ON: University of Toronto Press, 2000.

Friesen, John W. *Rediscovering the First Nations of Canada.* Calgary, AB: Detselig Enterprises, 1997.

Fry, Margot. *Tom's Letters: The Private World of Thomas King, Victorian Gentleman.* Wellington: Victoria University Press, 2001.

Furniss, Elizabeth. *The Burden of History: Colonialism and the Frontier Myth in a Rural Canadian Community.* Vancouver, BC: UBC Press, 1999.

Galbraith, John S. *The Hudson's Bay Company as an Imperial Factor 1821–1869.* Berkeley, CA: University of California Press, 1957.

Gallagher, Catherine, and Thomas Laqueur, eds. *The Making of the Modern Body: Sexuality and Society in the Nineteenth Century.* Berkeley, CA: University of California Press, 1987.

Gardiner, John. *The Victorians: An Age in Retrospect.* London: Hambeldon and London, 2002.

Gascoigne, John. *The Enlightenment and the Origins of European Australia.* Melbourne, VIC: Oxford University Press, 2002.

Gay, Peter. *Education of the Senses. The Bourgeois Experience: Victoria to Freud,* Vol. 1. New York: Norton, 1984.

Gay, Peter. *The Cultivation of Hatred: The Bourgeois Experience, Victoria to Freud,* Vol. 3. New York: Norton, 1986.

Gay, Peter. *Schnitzler's Century: The Making of Middle Class Culture 1815–1914.* New York: W.W. Norton, 2002.

Gibson, Ross. *The Diminishing Paradise.* Sydney, NSW: Sirius, 1984.

Girouard, Mark. *The Return to Camelot: Chivalry and the English Gentleman.* New Haven, CT: Yale University Press, 1981.

Godden, Judith. "A New Look at the Pioneer Woman". *Hecate* 5, no. 2 (1979): 7–21.

Gough, Barry M. *Gunboat Frontier: British Maritime Authority and Northwest Coast Indians, 1846–90.* Vancouver, BC: UBC Press, 1984.

Green, Martin. *Dreams of Adventure, Deeds of Empire.* London: Routledge and Kegan Paul, 1980.

Greenberg, David F. *The Construction of Homosexuality.* Chicago, IL: The University of Chicago Press, 1988.

Guillaumin, Collette. *Racism, Sexism, Power and Ideology.* London: Routledge, 1995.

Gunn, Janet Varner. *Autobiography: Towards a Poetics of Experience.* Philadelphia, PA: University of Pennsylvania Press, 1982.

Hall, Catherine. *White, Male and Middle Class.* Cambridge: Polity Press, 1992.

Hamilton, Susan. *Criminals, Idiots, Women and Minors: Victorian Writing by Women on Women.* Peterborough, ON: Broadview, 2004.

Hancock, W.K. *Australia.* Brisbane, QLD: Jacaranda, 1963.

Harris, Cole. *The Resettlement of British Columbia: Essays on Colonialism and Geographical Change.* Vancouver, BC: UBC Press, 1997.

Harris, Cole. "Social Power and Cultural Change in Pre-colonial British Columbia". *BC Studies* Autumn/Winter 97/98 (1997): 45–82.

Harris, C.P. *Regional Economic Development in Queensland: 1859 to 1981 with Particular Emphasis on North Queensland.* Canberra, ACT: Australian National University, 1984.

Hartz, Louis. *The Founding of New Societies: Studies in the History of the United States, Latin America, South Africa, Canada and Australia.* New York: Harcourt, Brace and World, 1964.

Hearn, Jeff. "Research in Men and Masculinities: Some Sociological Issues and Possibilities". *Australian and New Zealand Journal of Sociology* 30, no. 1 (1994): 47–67.
Hilton, Boyd. *The Age of Atonement*. Oxford: Clarendon Press, 1988.
Hirst, John. "The Pioneer Legend". *Historical Studies* 18, no. 71 (1978): 316–37.
Holmes, J.H., ed. *Queensland: A Geographical Interpretation Queensland Geographical Journal*, 4th series, 1. Brisbane, QLD, 1986.
Howay, F.W. *British Columbia, the Making of a Province*. Toronto, ON: T Nelson, 1928.
Hughes, Robert. *The Fatal Shore: A History of the Transportation of Convicts to Australia, 1787–1868*. London: Collins Harvill, 1987.
Hunt, Susan. *Spinifex and Hessian: Women in North West Australia*. Perth, WA: UWA Press, 1986.
Hutchins, Brett, and Jannine Mikosza. "Australian Rugby League and Violence 1970 to 1995: A Case Study in the Maintenance of Masculine Hegemony". *Journal of Sociology* 34, no. 3 (1998): 247–63.
Hyam, Ronald. *Empire and Sexuality: The British Experience*. Manchester: Manchester University Press, 1992.
Jay, Elisabeth, ed. *The Evangelical and Oxford Movements*. Cambridge: Cambridge University Press, 1983.
Johnston, Hugh J.M., ed. *The Pacific Province: A History of British Columbia*. Vancouver, BC: Douglas & McIntyre, 1996.
Johnston, W. Ross. *The Call of the Land: A History of Queensland to the Present Day*. Brisbane, QLD: Jacaranda Press, 1982.
Katie, Spearritt. "The Market for Marriage in Colonial Queensland". *Hecate* 16, no. 1 (1990): 23–42.
Kernaghan, Lee. "The Spirit of the Bush". WM Australia, 2007.
Kidd, Allan, and Nicholls, David, eds. *Gender, Civic Culture and Consumerism: Middle Class Identity in Britain*. Manchester: Manchester University Press, 1997.
Kimmel, Michael S., ed. *Changing Men: New Directions in Research on Men and Masculinity*. Newbury Park: Sage, 1987.
Kimmel, Michael S. *The Gendered Society*, 2nd ed. New York: Oxford University Press, 2004.
Kingston, Beverly. *My Wife, My Daughter, and Poor Mary Ann: Women and Work in Australia*. Melbourne, VIC: Nelson, 1975.
Lake, Marilyn. "Building Themselves up with Aspros: Pioneer Women Reassessed". *Hecate* 7, no. 2 (1981): 7–19.
Lake, Marilyn. "The Politics of Respectability: Identifying the Masculinist Context". *Historical Studies* 22, no. 86 (1986): 116–31.
Lake, Marilyn. "Frontier Feminism and the Marauding White Man". *Journal of Australian Studies* 49 (1996): 12–20.
Lamar, Howard, and Leonard Thompson, eds. *The Frontier in History: North America and Southern Africa Compared*. New Haven: Yale University Press, 1981.
Lamb, Kaye W., ed. "The Census of Vancouver Island, 1855". *British Columbia Historical Quarterly* 4, no. 1 (1940): 51–58.
Lane, Christopher. *The Burdens of Intimacy: Psychoanalysis and Victorian Masculinity*. Chicago, IL: University of Chicago Press, 1999.
Laqueur, Thomas. *Making Sex: Body and Gender from the Greeks to Freud*. Cambridge, MA: Harvard University Press, 1990.

le Couteur, Howard. "Gramsci's Concept of Hegemony and Social Formation in Early Colonial Queensland". *Limina* 6 (2000): 25–39.
Lipman-Bluman, Jean. *Gender Roles and Power*. New Jersey: Prentice-Hall, 1984.
Lloyd, Genevieve. *The Man of Reason: "Male" and "Female" in Western Philosophy*. London: Methuen, 1984.
Loo, Tina. *Making Law Order, and Authority in British Columbia, 1821–1871*. Toronto, ON: University of Toronto Press, 1994.
Loos, Noel. *Invasion and Resistance: Aboriginal–European Relations on the North Queensland Frontier*. Canberra, ACT: ANU Press, 1982.
Mac an Ghaill, Mairtin. *Understanding Masculinities: Social Relations and Cultural Arenas*. Buckingham: Open University Press, 1996.
Mackay, Douglas. *The Honourable Company: A History of the Hudson's Bay Company*. London: Cassell and Company Limited, 1937.
Mackie, Richard. *Trading beyond the Mountains: The British Fur Trade on the Pacific 1793–1843*. Vancouver, BC: UBC Press, 1997.
Malik, Kenan. *The Meaning of Race: Race, History and Western Culture*. London: MacMillan, 1996.
Mangan, J.A. *The Games Ethic and Imperialism: Aspects of the Diffusion of the Ideal*. London: Frank Cass, 1998.
Mangan, J.A. *Athleticism in the Victorian and Edwardian Public School: The Emergence and Consolidation of an Educational Ideology*. London: Frank Cass, 2000.
Mangan, J.A., and James Walvin, eds. *Manliness and Morality: Middle Class Masculinity in Britain and America 1800–1940*. Manchester: Manchester University Press, 1987.
Marcus, Steven. *The Other Victorians: A Study of Sexuality and Pornography in Mid-Nineteenth Century England*. London: Weidenfeld and Nicholson, 1966.
Markus, Andrew. *Australian Race Relations: 1788–1993*. Sydney, NSW: Allen & Unwin, 1994.
Mason, Michael. *The Making of Victorian Sexuality*. Oxford: Oxford University Press, 1994.
Matthew, H.C.G., and Brian Harrison, eds. *Oxford Dictionary of National Biography*. Oxford: Oxford University Press, 2004.
McClintock, Anne. *Imperial Leather: Race, Gender and Sexuality in the Colonial Contest*. New York: Routledge, 1995.
McDonald, Robert A.H. *Sons of the Empire: The Frontier and the Boy Scout Movement, 1890–1918*. Toronto, ON: University of Toronto Press, 1993.
McKelvie, B.A. *Pageant of BC: Glimpses into the Romantic Development of Canada's Western Province*. Toronto, ON: T. Nelson, 1955.
McKenzie, Kirsten. *Scandal in the Colonies*. Melbourne, VIC: Melbourne University Press, 2004.
McMillan, Allan D. *Native Peoples and Cultures of Canada*. Vancouver, BC: Douglas &McIntyre, 1995.
Mendus, Susan, and Rendall Jane, eds. *Sexuality and Subordination: Interdisciplinary Studies of Gender in the Nineteenth Century*. London: Routledge, 1989.
Meyer, Jessica. *Men of War: Masculinity and the First World War in Britain*. Basingstoke: Palgrave Macmillan, 2009.
Midgley, Clare. *Gender and Imperialism*. Manchester: Manchester University Press, 1998.

Miller, Neil. *Out of the Past: Gay and Lesbian History from 1869 to the Present*. New York: Vintage Books, 1995.
Milton, Viscount, and W.B. Cheadle. *The North-West Passage by Land*. London: Cassel, Petter and Galpin, 1865.
Mitchell, Sally. *Daily Life in Victorian England*. Westport, CT: Greenwood Press, 1996.
Moon, Brian. "Theorising Violence in the Discourse of Masculinities". *Southern Review* 24 (1992): 168–184.
Moore, Clive. *Sunshine and Rainbows*. Brisbane, QLD: University of Queensland of Press, 2001.
Moore, Clive, Jacqueline Leckie, and Doug Munro, eds. *Labour in the South Pacific*. Townsville, QLD: James Cook University, 1990.
Moore, Clive, and Kay Saunders. "Colonial Manhood and Masculinities". *Journal of Australian Studies* 56 (1998): 35–50.
Moore, Lisa. "Something More Tender Still Than Friendship". *Feminist Studies* 18, no. 3 (1992): 499–520.
Murdoch, Catherine. *Domesticating Drink: Women, Men and Alcohol in America, 1800–1933*. Baltimore, MD: John Hopkins University Press, 1998.
Nairn, Bede, Geoffrey Serle, and Russel Ward, eds. *Australian Dictionary of Biography*, Vol. 4. Melbourne, VIC: Melbourne University Press, 1966.
Newlyn, Lucy, ed. *The Cambridge Companion to Coleridge*. Cambridge: Cambridge University Press, 2002.
Newsome, David. *Godliness and Good Learning*. London: John Murray, 1961.
Nicholson, L., ed. *Feminism/Postmodernism*. New York: Routledge, 1990.
Nile, Richard. "Editorial". *Journal of Australian Studies* 49 (1996): 1–3.
Nile, Richard. *The Australian Legend and Its Discontents*. Brisbane, QLD: University of Queensland Press, 2000.
Ormsby, Margaret. *British Columbia: A History*. Vancouver, BC: McMillan, 1958.
Owram, Doug. *The Promise of Eden: The Canadian Expansionist Movement and the Idea of the West 1856–1900*. Toronto, ON: Toronto University Press, 1980.
Parr, Joy, and Mark Rosenfeld. *Gender and History in Canada*. Mississauga, ON: Copp Clark, 1996.
Pateman, Carol. *The Sexual Contract*. Oxford: Polity, 1989.
Pearce, Roy Harvey. *The Savages of America: A Study of the Indian and the Idea of Civilisation*. Baltimore, MD: John Hopkins Press, 1965.
Pearsall, Ronald. *The Worm in the Bud: The World of Victorian Sexuality*. Harmondsworth: Penguin, 1971.
Perry, Adele. "'Oh I'm Just Sick of the Faces of Men': Gender Imbalance, Race, Sexuality, and Sociability in Nineteenth-Century British Columbia". *BC Studies* Spring/Summer 1995, no. 105–06 (1995): 27–43.
Perry, Adele. *On the Edge of Empire: Gender, Race, and the Making of British Columbia*. Toronto, ON: University of Toronto Press, 2001.
Phillips, Jock. *A Man's Country: The Image of the Pakeha Male*. Auckland: Penguin, 1987.
Phillips, Richard. *Mapping Men and Empire: A Geography of Adventure*. London: Routledge, 1997.
Pilling, John. *Autobiography and Imagination: Studies in Self-Scrutiny*. London: Routledge and Kegan Paul, 1981.

Plummer, Kenneth, ed. *The Making of the Modern Homosexual*. Totowa, NJ: Barnes and Noble, 1981.
Poovey, Mary. *Uneven Developments: The Ideological Work of Gender in Mid Victorian England*. London: Virago Press, 1989.
Pratt, Mary Louise. *Imperial Eyes: Travel Writing and Transculturation*. London: Routledge, 1992.
Prentice, Alison. *Canadian Women: A History*. Toronto, ON: Harcourt Brace, 1996.
Pringle, Helen. "The Making of an Australian Civic Identity: The Bodies of Men and the Memory of War". In *The Politics of Identity in Australia*, Geoffrey Stokes, ed., 92–104. Melbourne, VIC: Cambridge University Press, 1997.
Putnis, Peter. "The Construction of Queensland: Historical and Contemporary Perspectives". *Journal of Australian Studies* no. 25 (1989): 34–42.
Radcliffe-Brown, A.R. "Former Numbers and Distribution of the Australian Aborigines". *Official Year Book of the Commonwealth of Australia* no. 23 (1930).
Ray, Arthur J. *The Canadian Fur Trade in the Industrial Age*. Toronto, ON: University of Toronto Press, 1990.
Reid, Gordon. *A Nest of Hornets: The Massacre of the Fraser Family at Hornet Bank Station, Central Queensland 1857, and Related Events*. Melbourne, VIC: Oxford University Press, 1982.
Reynolds, Henry, ed. *Race Relations in North Queensland*. Townsville, QLD: James Cook University, 1978.
Reynolds, Henry. *The Other Side of the Frontier*. Melbourne, VIC: Penguin, 1982.
Reynolds, Henry. *Frontier*. Sydney, NSW: Allen & Unwin, 1987.
Reynolds, Henry. *With the White People*. Melbourne, VIC: Penguin, 1990.
Reynolds, Henry. *North of Capricorn: The Untold Story of Australia's North*. Sydney, NSW: Allen & Unwin, 2003.
Rich, E.E. *The History of the Hudson's Bay Company, 1670–1870. Vol. 2: 1763–1870*. London: Hudson's Bay Record Society, 1959.
Rich, E.E. *The Fur Trade and the Northwest until 1857*. Toronto, ON: McCelland and Stewart, 1967.
Richards, Jeffrey, ed. *Imperialism and Juvenile Literature*. Manchester: Manchester University Press, 1989.
Rickard, John. *Australia: A Cultural History*. London: Longman, 1996.
Robb, Graham. *Strangers: Homosexual Love in the Nineteenth Century*. New York: W.W. Norton & Company, 2004.
Roberts, M.J.D. "Making Victorian Morals? The Society for the Suppression of Vice and Its Critics, 1802–1886". *Historical Studies* 21 (1984): 157–63.
Roberts, Stephen H. *The Squatting Age in Australia: 1835–1846*. Melbourne, VIC: Melbourne University Press, 1935.
Roberts, Tony. *Frontier Justice: A History of the Gulf Country to 1900*. Brisbane, QLD: University of Queensland Press, 2005.
Robinson, J. Lewis, ed. *Studies in Canadian Geography: British Columbia*. Toronto, ON: University of Toronto Press, 1972.
Roediger, David R. *The Wages of Whiteness: Race and the Making of the American Working Class*. New York: Verso, 1999.
Roper, Michael, and John Tosh, eds. *Manful Assertions: Masculinities in Britain since 1800*. London: Routledge, 1991.
Rothenberger, Mel. *The Chilcotin War*. Langley, BC: Mr. Paperback, 1978.

Rotundo, E. Anthony. *American Manhood: Transformations in Masculinity from the Revolution to the Modern Era.* New York: Basic Books, 1993.
Rowley, C.D. *The Destruction of Aboriginal Society.* Canberra, ACT: ANU Press, 1970.
Roy, Patricia E. *A History of British Columbia: Selected Readings.* Toronto, ON: Copp Clark Pittman, 1989.
Rule, John. *The Labouring Classes in Early Industrial England, 1750–1850.* London: Longman, 1986.
Russell, Lynette, ed. *Colonial Frontiers: Indigenous-European Encounters in Settler Societies.* Manchester: Manchester University Press, 2001.
Rutherdale, Myra. "Revisiting Colonisation through Gender: Anglican Missionary Women in the Pacific Northwest and Arctic, 1860–1945". *BC Studies* Winter, no. 104 (1994): 3–23.
Ryan, Simon. *The Cartographic Eye: How Explorers Saw Australia.* Melbourne, VIC: Cambridge University Press, 1996.
Said, Edward W. *Culture and Imperialism.* New York: Vintage Books, 1993.
Sargent, Lydia. *The Unhappy Marriage of Marxism and Feminism: A Debate on Class and Patriarchy.* London: Pluto Press, 1981.
Saunders, Kay. *Workers in Bondage.* St. Lucia, QLD: University of Queensland Press, 1982.
Saunders, Kay. "The Study of Domestic Violence in Queensland: Sources and Problems". *Historical Studies* 21, no. 82 (1984): 68–84.
Saunders, Kay. *Breaking the Cake of Custom.* Russel Ward Memorial Lecture, University of New England, 1998.
Saunders, Kay. "'Specimens of Superb Manhood': The Life Saver as National Icon". *Journal of Australian Studies* 22, no. 56 (1998): 96–105.
Saunders, Kay, and Raymond Evans, eds. *Gender Relations in Australia: Domination and Negotiation.* Sydney, NSW: Harcourt, 1994.
Schaffer, Kay. *Women and the Bush: Forces of Desire in the Australian Cultural Tradition.* Sydney, NSW: Cambridge University Press, 1988.
Schwarz, Bill, ed. *The Expansion of England: Race, Ethnicity and Cultural History.* London: Routledge, 1996.
Scott, Joan Wallach. *Gender and the Politics of History.* New York: Columbia University Press, 1988.
Sear, Tom, Katherine Biber, and Dave Trudinger, eds. *Playing the Man: New Approaches to Masculinity.* Sydney, NSW: Pluto Press, 1999.
Seccombe, Wally. "Patriarch Stabilized: The Construction of the Male Breadwinner Wage Norm in Nineteenth-Century Britain". *Social History* 11, no. 1 (1986): 53–76.
Sedgewick, Eve Kosofsky. *Between Men: English Literature and Male Homosocial Desire.* New York: Columbia University Press, 1985.
Segal, Lynne. *Slow Motion: Changing Masculinities Changing Men.* London: Virago, 1990.
Seidler, V.J. *Rediscovering Masculinity: Reason, Language and Sexuality.* London: Routledge, 1989.
Sennett, Richard. *The Fall of Public Man.* Cambridge: Cambridge University Press, 1977.
Shaw, A.G.L. *The Story of Australia.* London: Faber and Faber, 1955.

Shoemaker, Robert. *Gender in English Society, 1650–1850: The Emergence of Separate Spheres*. London: Longman, 1998.

Shoemaker, Robert, and Mary Vincent, eds. *Gender and History in Western Europe*. London: Arnold, 1998.

Sinha, Mrinalini. *Colonial Masculinity: The 'Manly Englishman' and the 'Effeminate Bengali' in the Late Nineteenth Century*. Manchester: Manchester University Press, 1995.

Skinner, B.F. *Police of the Pastoral Frontier*. Brisbane, QLD: University of Queensland Press, 1975.

Slatta, Richard W. *Comparing Cowboys and Frontiers*. Norman, OK: Oklahoma University Press, 1997.

Slotkin, Richard. *Regeneration through Violence: The Mythology of the American Frontier, 1600–1860*. Middletown, CT: Wesleyan University Press, 1973.

Slotkin, Richard. *The Fatal Environment: The Myth of the Frontier in the Age of Industrialization 1800–1890*. Middletown, CT: Wesleyan University Press, 1985.

Smith-Rosenberg, Carrol, and Charles Rosenberg. "The Female Animal: Medical and Biological Views of Woman and Her Role in Nineteenth Century America". *Journal of American History* 60, no. 1 (1973): 332–56.

Spirenburg, Pieter, ed. *Men and Violence: Gender, Honor and Rituals in Modern Europe and America*. Columbus, OH: Ohio State University Press, 1998.

Spurr, David. *The Rhetoric of Empire: Colonial Discourse in Journalism, Travel Writing, and Imperial Administration*. London: Duke University Press, 1993.

Stanko, Elizabeth. *Everyday Violence: How Women and Men Experience Sexual and Physical Danger*. London: Pandora, 1990.

Stanner, W.H. *After the Dreaming: The 1968 Boyer Lectures*. Sydney, NSW: ABC, 1969.

Stanton, Domna C. *Discourses of Sexuality: From Aristotle to Aids*. Ann Arbour, MI: University of Michigan Press, 1992.

Stocking, George W. *Victorian Anthropology*. New York: The Free Press, 1987.

Stokes, Geoffrey, ed. *The Politics of Identity in Australia*. Melbourne, VIC: Cambridge University Press, 1997.

Stoler, Ann Laura. *Race and the Education of Desire: Foucault's History of Sexuality and the Colonial Order of Things*. Durham, NC: Duke University Press, 1995.

Stone, Lawrence. *The Family, Sex and Marriage in England 1500–1800*. London: Weidenfeld & Nicholson, 1977.

Stott, Rebecca "The Dark Continent: Africa as Female Body in Haggard's Adventure Fiction". *Feminist Review* 32 (1989): 69–89.

Strong-Boag, Veronica, Mona Gleeson, and Adele Perry. *Rethinking Canada: The Promise of Women's History*. Toronto, ON: Oxford University Press, 2002.

Sussman, Herbert. *Victorian Masculinities: Manhood and Masculine Poetics in Early Victorian Literature and Art*. Cambridge: Cambridge University Press, 1995.

Tan, Jin, and Patricia E. Roy. *The Chinese in Canada*. Saint John, NB: Canadian Historical Association, 1985.

Taussig, Michael. "Culture of Terror – Space of Death. Roger Casement's Putumayo Report and the Explanation of Torture". *Comparative Studies in Society and History* 26 (1984): 467–97.

Taylor, Peter. *Station Life in Australia: Pioneers and Pastoralist*. Sydney, NSW: Allen & Unwin, 1988.

Trexler, Richard C. *Sex and Conquest: Gendered Violence, Political Order and the European Conquest of the Americas*. Ithaca, NY: Cornell University Press, 1995.

Thomas, Nicholas. *Colonialism's Culture: Anthropology, Travel and Government*. Cambridge: Polity Press, 1994.

Thompson, F.M.L. *The Rise of Respectable Society: A Social History of Victorian Britain 1830–1900*. Cambridge, MA: Harvard University Press, 1988.

Thompson, F.M.L., ed. *The Cambridge Social History of Britain 1750–1950*, Vol. 3. Cambridge: Cambridge University Press, 1990.

Thorpe, Bill. *Colonial Queensland: Perspectives on a Frontier Society*. Brisbane, QLD: UQP, 1996.

Tosh, John. "What Should Historians Do with Masculinity? Reflections of Nineteenth-Century Britain". *History Workshop*, no. 38 (1994): 179–202.

Tosh, John. *A Man's Place: Masculinity and the Middle-Class Home in Victorian England*. London: Yale University Press, 1999.

Trudgill, Eric. *Madonnas and Magdalens: The Origins and Development of Victorian Sexual Attitudes*. London: Heinemann, 1976.

Truss, Alex J. "Divergent and Conflicting Voices: Victorian Images of the Male". *Journal of Men's Studies*. 4, no. 1 (1995): 43–57.

Turner, Graeme. *Making it National: Nationalism and Australian Popular Culture*. Sydney, NSW: Allen & Unwin, 1994.

Turner, Ian. *The Australian Dream*. Melbourne, VIC: Sun Books, 1968.

Vance, Norman. *Sinews of the Spirit: The Idea of Christian Manliness in Victorian Literature and Religious Thought*. Cambridge: Cambridge University Press, 1985.

Van Kirk, Sylvia. *Many Tender Ties: Women in Fur-Trade Society. 1670–1870*. Norman, OK: University of Oklahoma Press, 1983.

Van Kirk, Sylvia. "Tracing the Fortunes of Five Founding Families of Victoria". *BC Studies* Autumn/Winter 97/98: 149–79.

Vibert, Elizabeth. "Real Men Hunt Buffalo: Masculinity Race, and Class in British Fur Traders Narratives". Paper presented at B.C. Studies Conference '94, Okanagan University College, Kelowna, BC, 7–10 October 1994.

Vibert, Elizabeth. *Traders' Tales: Narratives of Cultural Encounters in the Columbia Plateau 1807–1846*. Norman, OK: University of Oklahoma Press, 1997.

Waite, Donald E. *The Cariboo Gold Rush Story*. Surrey, BC: Hancock House, 1988.

Walvin, James. *Victorian Values*. Athens, GA: The University of Georgia Press, 1988.

Ward, Russell. *The Australian Legend*. Melbourne, VIC: Oxford University Press, 1966.

Ward, W. Peter. *White Canada Forever: Popular Attitudes and Public Policy towards Orientals in British Columbia*. Montreal, QC: McGill-Queens University Press, 2002.

Ware, Vron. *Beyond the Pale: White Women, Racism and History*. London: Verso, 1992.

Waterson, D.B. *Squatter, Selector, and Storekeeper: A History of the Darling Downs*. Sydney, NSW: Sydney University Press, 1968.

Wedgwood, Nikki. "'Spewin', Mate!' – A Day at the Cricket". *Social Alternatives* 16, no. 3 (1997): 26–30.

Weeks, Jeffrey. *Sex, Politics and Society: The Regulation of Sexuality since 1800*. London: Longman, 1989.

Weeks, Jeffrey. *Coming Out: Homosexual Politics in Britain from the Nineteenth Century to the Present*. London: Quartet Books, 1990.
Weeks, Jeffrey. *Against Nature: Essays on History, Sexuality and Identity*. London: Rivers Oram Press, 1991.
Wiener, Martin J. *English Culture and the Decline of the Industrial Spirit 1850–1980*. New York: Cambridge University Press, 1981.
Wilkinson, Rupert. *The Prefects: British Leadership and the Public School Tradition: A Comparative Study in the Making of Rulers*. London: Oxford University Press, 1964.
Woodcock, George. "Cariboo and Klondike: The Gold Mines in Western Canada". *History Today* 5 (1955): 33–42.
Woodcock, George. *British Columbia: A History of the Province*. Vancouver, BC: Douglas and McIntyre, 1990.
Wotherspoon, Gary, and Robert Aldrich, eds. *Gay Perspectives: Essays in Australian Gay Culture*. Sydney, NSW: Department of Economic History University of Sydney, 1992.

Unpublished Theses

Henningham, Nicola. " 'Perhaps If There Had Been More Women in the North, the Story Would Have Been Different': Gender and the History of White Settlement in North Queensland, 1840–1930". Phd, University of Melbourne, Parkville, VIC, 1999.
Spearritt, Katie. "The Poverty of Protection: Women and Marriage in Colonial Queensland". Honours thesis, Department of History, University of Queensland, Brisbane, QLD, 1988.

Index

aboriginalism, 122, 133, 141
adventure, 2, 4, 19, 21, 23, 25, 28, 29, 49, 58, 60, 63, 68, 69, 73, 75, 77, 83, 92, 113, 115, 131, 132
   literature, 17, 56
alcohol, 19, 22, 32, 52, 85, 87, 104, 106, 109, 110–12, 119, 178, 182
Allen, Charles H., 131
aristocracy, 19, 23, 29, 77, 106, 177
   see also upper class
Australian Aborigines, 9, 19, 21, 82, 108, 122, 124, 130, 131, 132–42, 155, 157–61, 165–9, 173
   see also Indigenous peoples
Australian Outback Spectacular, 180–2
autobiography, 19–20, 31, 91

Ballantyne, R.M., 17, 56
Barrett-Lennard, C.E., 107
Bartley, Nehemiah, 132
Bayley, Charles, 129, 130
Begbie, James, 46, 47, 49
Bird, J.T.S., 165
Blair, George, 107
breadwinner role, 12
Brew, Chartres, 172
Brewster, William, 163, 172, 173
Brisbane, 7–8, 36, 39, 52, 81–2, 86, 89, 108, 138, 146, 158, 165
Brisbane Courier, 140, 145, 155
Britain, 2–12, 17, 19, 23–4, 26, 29, 30–1, 41, 45, 51, 54–5, 57, 59, 63, 66–7, 77, 116, 118, 153–4, 169, 177
British Colonist, 147, 173
British Columbia, 2–4, 6–9, 19–28, 40, 45–9, 52, 54, 56–7, 60–2, 68, 72–3, 78–80, 86, 90–1, 93–6, 98–9, 105–7, 109, 112–13, 116, 118, 121–2, 128–9, 131–3, 141–5, 147–9, 152, 161–3, 165, 170, 173–9, 181–2
   population, 9
British Columbian, 60, 173
British Empire, 6, 9, 17–18, 33, 55, 77, 116, 143, 154
Burnaby, Robert, 46–8
Bushby, Arthur Thomas, 30, 31, 45, 46–9
bush legend, 112, 180
Bute Inlet, 163, 170–1, 173, 175

Cain, George, 160
Calgary Stampede, 181
Cambridge University, 1, 16, 28, 73, 109, 149
Campbell, Thomas, 58
Capitalism, 11–12, 25, 54, 125–6, 170
   and patriarchy, 169, 175
Cariboo, 7, 9, 21, 60–2, 73, 78–9, 90–4, 96–7, 99–100, 104, 113, 145, 147, 149, 171, 174
Carrington, George, 24, 49, 50, 52, 53, 88, 89, 109, 110, 121, 122, 156, 177, 179
caste, 25–7, 30, 34–40, 42–3, 45, 47, 48–9, 52
character, 2–3, 6, 13, 16, 20, 25–7, 31–2, 40–2, 65, 123, 126–9, 141, 143, 150, 153, 161, 167, 176, 179, 181
Chartism, 18
Cheadle, W.B., 72–8
Chinese, 9, 144–9
Chittenden, Newton H., 148–9
Christianity, 1–2, 4, 16, 31, 33, 65–7, 94, 106, 113, 116, 125–6, 135, 139–40, 168
   Church of England, 11, 26
   dissenting churches, 11–12
   evangelical, 10–11

Index

church, 5, 15, 26, 66–8, 104–5, 109, 119, 155
civilisation, 45, 58, 65, 80, 152–3, 162, 164–9, 174–5, 178
Clarendon Commission, 25
class, 2–4, 6, 19, 26, 27, 30, 35, 39, 49, 50, 52, 54–5, 58, 77, 110, 121–2, 153–4, 169, 177, 179
  see also middle class; working class; upper class
Cobbett, William, 14, 15
Coleridge, Samuel Taylor, 14
Configuration of practice, 4–5, 27
Cook, James, 8, 64
Cooper, James Fenimore, 56
Cornwallis, Kinahan, 2, 3, 54, 56–8, 132, 176, 182
Cowper, William, 11
Crease, Henry Pellew, 46–48
Cridge, Reverend Henry, 47

Dalrymple, Ernest, 35, 36
Darling Downs, 34, 37, 38, 81, 108, 157, 165
Davidson, Walter, 33
de Cosmos, Amor, 147
De Satgé, Oscar, 30, 31, 37, 38–40, 44, 45, 52, 53, 158, 159, 176, 178
Disraeli, Benjamin, 122
domesticity, 10–12, 18, 29, 54, 59, 63, 86, 90, 94, 96, 98, 102–3, 105, 112, 114–16, 119, 155, 170
Douglas, Agnes, 47
Douglas, Cecilia, 107
Douglas, Sir James, 41, 45, 47, 61, 107, 111, 162, 171

Eden, Charles, 20, 25, 37, 108, 110, 130, 146, 150
Ellis, Sarah Stickney, 11
Emerson, John, 141–3, 176
Enlightenment, 123, 125, 164
  Scottish, 125
Esquimalt, 42, 46, 100

family, 4, 10–11, 18, 22–3, 27–8, 33–4, 37, 41, 47, 53–5, 58–9, 80, 86–96, 99, 102–3, 105, 109, 112, 116–20, 131, 146, 165, 174, 179

Fortune, A.L., 60–8, 176
Fraser River, 9, 61, 100, 144, 163, 170–1, 174
frontier, 2–5, 7, 17, 19–22
  as contact zone, 7
  and gender, 8
  mythology, 3–4, 6, 20, 28, 56, 69, 84, 87, 92, 112, 179–81
  Turnerian thesis, 5
  urban, 7
fur trade, 25, 27, 58–60, 106, 128–9, 161–2, 174
  and women, 59, 106

gentlemen, 14, 17–18, 23, 25–35, 38–40, 42–3, 45, 49–53, 107, 108, 146, 149, 155, 165–6, 177
  and dress, 30
  and speech, 30
  'geography of adventure,' 17
  'godliness and good learning,' 15
gold mining, 4, 7–9, 20, 23, 50, 54, 60–2, 73, 75, 78–9, 90, 93, 95–102, 104, 113, 144–9, 162, 170–1, 174, 176
Gordon Downs, 38
Grainger, M. Allerdale, 85, 90–1, 103
Gregory, Henry, 39, 158–9
Guillod, Henry, 21, 78–80

Haggard, Rider, 17, 56, 116
Harkness, Robert, 21, 90–104, 177, 179
Harkness, Sabrina, 90–6
Hayward, Charles, 103–5, 112
Hayward, Sarah, 104–5
Hazlitt, William Carew, 141–2
hegemonic masculinity, 2, 5, 10, 24, 27, 56, 121, 149–50, 164
Helmcken, Dr. John, 40, 107, 111
Henderson, R., 89–90
Henning, Biddulph, 29, 155
Henning Rachel, 29
Henry, Ernest, 68–72
heterosexuality, 4, 87, 116, 118–19
Hill, Bishop George, 41
homosexuality, 4, 87, 112–13, 116–19, 182
  'Abominable Vice of Buggery,' 117

230 Index

homosociality, 87, 111–13, 116, 119, 178
Hudson Bay Company, 9, 25, 40–1, 58–61, 104, 106, 111, 118, 147, 162
Hughenden, 68–70, 72
Hughes, Thomas, 16, 154

imperialism, 8–9, 13, 17, 21, 55–6, 62, 81, 118, 131, 160, 164
independence, 2, 14, 17–18, 22, 24–5, 28, 33, 45, 55, 57–8, 60, 62, 68, 77, 81–2, 84, 88, 91, 103–5, 120, 176–7, 179–80
indigenous peoples, 7, 9, 19–21, 88, 94, 113–14, 121–2, 124, 128–33, 141–4, 151–2, 158, 160–4, 170, 173–5, 178
  Aht, 142–3. *see also* Australian Aborigines
  Chilcotin, 163, 171–3
  Euclawtaw, 171
  gin busting, 107
  Homathko, 171
  Klayoosh, 171
  Talkellies, 142
  Talkotin, 142
  women, 105–9, 126
industrialisation, 10–12, 25, 54, 116, 125–6, 169, 174
isolation, 85–91, 98–9, 103, 109, 113, 115, 119–20, 125, 155, 164, 178

Jackey-Jackey, 130
Jackson, John William, 127

Kamloops, 72–3
Kamloops Sentinel, 60
Kant, Immanuel, 123
Kendrick, Captain, 161–2
King, Lieutenant James, 128
Kingsley, Charles, 1–3, 16, 127, 178
Knox, Robert, 122

Lane, William, 146
Leslie, George, 31, 33–4, 157
Leslie, Patrick, 31–7, 39, 42, 45, 49, 52–3
Leslie, Walter, 31, 33–4, 157

Leslie, William Senior, Laird of Warthill, 31–3
Lundin-Brown, Rev. R. C

Macarthur family, 33, 37
Mackenzie, Robert Ramsey, 133
manhood, manliness, manly, 2–6, 9–18, 20, 22, 24–6, 28–30, 39, 42, 44–5, 51–2, 55, 57, 60, 63–4, 67–8, 75–7, 80, 82–91, 103–5, 110–12, 117, 119, 122, 126, 128–9, 132–3, 140–4, 147, 149, 151–2, 154, 158, 164, 169–70, 175, 180
marriage, 10–12, 41, 59, 90, 93–4, 105
  a la facon du pay, 58
Marryat, C.F., 17, 56
Maryborough Chronicle, 140
masculinity, 4–5, 10, 13, 17–20, 29, 62, 65, 84, 87–8, 92, 96, 98, 110, 112, 117, 121–2, 133, 140, 152–3, 155, 164, 169, 176, 178
  see also hegemonic masculinity
mateship, 86, 99, 112, 118–19
McConnel, Arthur, 132
McMicking, Thomas, 60–7
McPherson, Alan, 159
Melrose, Robert, 111
middle class, 3, 6, 10–14, 17–18, 20, 23–5, 54, 58–60, 66–7, 83–4, 105–6, 126, 154, 177
Milton, William Wentworth-Fitzwilliam, Viscount, 72–8, 178
Mitchell, Sir Thomas, 56–7
Moody, Colonel Richard, 46–7
More, Hannah, 11
Morey, Edmund, 163
myth, 6, 20, 28, 34, 56, 69, 84, 87, 92, 112, 179–81

Native Mounted Police, 133–4
  Enquiry of Select Committee of Legislative Assembly, 133–41
  Testimony of
    Challinor, Dr Henry, 138
    Collins, Carden, 136
    Compigne, A.W., 135
    Davies, J., 135
    Fraser, John, 135

Index

Frazer, C.M., 135
Lowe, Jacob, 136
Petrie, Thomas, 136
Rode, Augustus, 140
Wheeler, Lieutenant Frederick, 136
Neame, Arthur, 80–4, 87, 89, 110
New Westminster, 9, 48, 67, 78, 97, 99, 171
Northern Miner, 146
North Queensland, 82, 86–7, 112, 118, 144, 155, 157
North West Company, 106

O'Bierne, Eugene Francis, 149–50
Overlanders, 60–7, 91
Oxford University, 15, 24, 28, 49, 109, 165–6

pastoralism, 4, 8, 20, 24, 28, 33–4, 38–9, 51, 57, 69–70, 108, 113, 144, 166, 175
patriarchy, 5, 11, 63
Peel, Robert, 117
Pidcock, Reginald Heber, 113–18
private sphere, 10, 98, 105
'property in skill,' 18
public schools, 1, 14, 16, 23, 25–6, 30
public sphere, 10–11, 17–18, 98, 105, 170

Queensland, 3–9, 19–29, 36–40, 45, 50–2, 54, 68, 80, 82, 86–8, 105–7, 109–10, 112, 117–18, 121–2, 128, 130–4, 141–6, 152, 154–7, 160–2, 165–6, 173, 176–82
population, 9

race, 1, 4, 6, 19, 21, 59, 79, 94, 105–9, 121–49, 154, 160, 162, 167–9, 173
monogenism, 123
phrenology, 124
polygenism, 123
reason, 152, 164–5, 169, 175
Richmond, Reverend Frederick, 108, 131, 152
Rockhampton Bulletin, 166
Royal Navy, 28, 40, 46, 51, 154

Russell, Henry Stuart, 165
Russell, Lord John, 117

Saturday Review, 17
Secker, Reverend William, 11
Self-governance, 15, 18, 26, 53
separate spheres, 10–11, 17–18, 54, 98, 115, 126
see also private sphere; public sphere
sexuality, 4, 8, 11–12, 15, 19, 22, 87, 94, 98, 105–9, 112–19
see also homosexuality; heterosexuality
shepherding, 20, 50, 52, 87–9, 109, 144, 150, 159, 161
Simpson, George Sir, 162
Simpson, Steven, 158, 165
Smallpox, 163, 172–3
Smiles, Samuel, 13–14, 18
sobriety, 11, 15, 32, 104, 110, 179
see also alcohol
Sodomy. see homosexuality
Sproat, Glibert Malcolm, 58, 142–3, 147
squatters, 23, 27–30, 36–40, 51, 88, 108, 132–6, 160, 165–6, 178
Stamer, William, 28, 51
Stirling, A.W., 20, 131
Stobart, Reverend Henry, 108

Telfer, Henry, 108
Thomson, James, 90–1, 99–105
Thomson, Mary, 101–2
Thring, Edward, 16
Tod, John, 55, 58–60
Tom Brown's Schooldays. see Hughes, Thomas
Trollope, Anthony, 23, 130, 160
Tyrwhitt, W.S.S., 20, 29, 182

upper class, 6, 10, 24–5, 51, 54, 154, 166, 177

Vancouver Island, 7–9, 40, 43–6, 61, 100, 103, 111, 113, 118, 128, 141–3, 145, 174
Verney, Edmund Hope, 30–1, 40–5, 52–3

Victoria, Vancouver Island, 7–9, 41, 46–9, 86, 100–5, 111–13, 118, 145, 163, 171–3
violence, 152–70, 173, 175, 178
　against indigenous women, 107–8
　of nature, 156–7
　against white women, 155–6

Waddington, Alfred Pendrill, 170–4
Walker, Alexander, 129
Wallace, Alfred Russell, 126
Ward, Russel, 112
Weise, Ammelie, 156
Wiseman, William, 165–9

Wolfgang Station, 38
women, 5, 9–12, 17–18, 20, 26, 45, 63, 87, 94, 105–12, 126, 145–6
　and biology, 12
　and fur trade, 59, 106
　indigenous, 105–9
　and sexuality, 12, 106
　work, 12–16, 19, 24, 26, 28, 30, 33, 37, 39, 44, 47, 50–1, 54–6, 63, 72, 77, 79, 80–3, 86–9, 97–104, 112, 115, 139, 141–7, 156, 172, 179–81
working class, 3, 10–12, 17–20, 49, 51–2, 106, 110, 153–4
Wright, Charlotte May, 51–3, 179